GREEN LIGHT

CW00818954

GREEN LIGHT ON EUROPE

EDITED BY

SARA PARKIN

First published 1991 by Heretic Books Ltd,
        P O Box 247, London N17 9QR
Individual essays World Copyright © 1991 The Authors
Collection World Copyright © 1991 Heretic Books Ltd

Distributed in North America by Inbook,
        P O Box 120470, East Haven, CT 06512, USA

British Library CIP Data:

Green light on Europe
I.. Parkin, Sara
304.2094

ISBN 0-946097-29-1

Printed and bound in the EC on environment-friendly paper
by Nørhaven A/S, Viborg, Denmark

Contents

Publisher's Note

Like most anthologies, this has had an awkward birth; its 30 contributors hail from some 16 countries, several of which are in the throes of turbulent change. The original plan when Sara and I devised the book was to group the essays under a number of main headings: Europe in the Biosphere, Change in the East, Addressing Common Problems (physical environment, economic aspects, conflict resolution, social and cultural), and The Institutional Dimension. These themes are certainly reflected in the finished product, and in the order in which we've placed the essays. But as key thinkers and activists of the Green movement, contributors necessarily had their own priorities, which within limits we were happy to accommodate. To impose a rigid division by subject-matter would have been artificial, and readers will easily find from the Contents what particularly interests them.

David Fernbach
Heretic Books

Introduction

> The finest plans have always been spoiled by the
> littleness of those supposed to carry them out.
> Even emperors can't do it all by themselves.
> — Bertolt Brecht, *Mother Courage*

One thing Europe is not short of is plans for its future. What it
is short of, though, is a coherent plan, one that recognizes that
the foundation on which past plans were based has crumbled.
Not only have relationships inside Europe undergone revolutionary changes, but the assumptions on which both east and
west built their empires are being rapidly demolished by global
environmental and economic trends.[Harrison]*

Because they don't acknowledge this new reality, east and
west European plans appear vague, contradictory or both. The
only real difference between them is that western Europe still
sees central roles for cold war institutions in the future of
Europe, while the east is abandoning them as fast as it can.

Discussions in the European Community over political and
economic union, for example, are as unimaginative as the fried
egg on a plate which (schematically speaking) this resembles.
Having a yolk of the current member countries committed to
full-scale union, surrounded by a European Economic Space for
sceptics and (rich) serious suitors like the EFTA countries, all
sitting on a plate of (poor) Associate Members from east Europe,
doesn't hide enormous vagueness about objectives and practical
arrangements.[Gahrton] And designing a three-caste Europe
does not resolve the contradictions that are already beleaguer-
ing the current 1992 project for a Single Market.[Robins, Blau]

Even the confident presentation of NATO's proposals for a

Rapid Reaction Corps cannot hide vagueness about what it is supposed to rapidly react to, or the contradiction that several European powers, including a nuclear one — France — would prefer Europe's defence to be assured through the European Community rather than NATO.

Perestroika, by contrast, quickly dumped its economic and security organizations (COMECON and the Warsaw Pact) and east Europeans have been strong supporters of the institution-alization of the Conference for Security and Cooperation in Europe which eventually took place in November 1990. Al-though current demands by Czechoslovakia and Hungary, for example, to join NATO and the EC are held up as evidence that these institutions have a major future role, it is likely that requests for membership from the east will only highlight the impossibility of creating a larger Europe through the expansion of western institutions.

With west Germany, Britain and France being the only net contributors to the EC (all other countries being net recipients) who, for example, is going to pay for the incorporation of weaker economies into the EC?

In fact the original intention of perestroika was not to create a USSR in the mirror image of the west. From the beginning Mr Gorbachev saw the new Soviet Union and the independent east European countries developing their economies and taking part in world trade as a world region which was economically healthy in its own right. This was the original plan for which he solicited western backing.[1] Since then, however, plans from the Soviet Union and the other east European countries for a so-called 'Third Way' have remained vague and confused. Crushed be-tween 'west-knows-best' advice from western government agen-cies, and acute domestic difficulties in meeting the basic needs of their citizens, there has been little opportunity for careful discussion and a clear rethink about the long-term future — a situation which helps rather than hinders the remaining conser-vative forces in east Europe. As the build-up to the fortunately futile coup attempt in the Soviet Union demonstrated, they tend to thrive in a climate of uncertainty. Particularly inappropriate and unhelpful was the ideological triumphalism with which the west met the collapse of east Europe's institutions:

> America has nothing much to do just now because it
> has been a spectacular success. Its economy and
> society run along roughly the right lines, and the
> western order it put together after 1945 has, both in
> Europe and in Asia, done pretty much everything that
> could have been expected of it.[2]

Within months, these words from the *Economist*'s review of
The World in 1990 had developed a hollow ring. Looming world
recession, famine in Africa, tough negotiations over trade,
global warming and the Gulf War were all too soon bringing calls
for a new world order from several quarters — including the US
president.

In retrospect, the failure of *all* world leaders to recognize in
the collapse of east Europe signs of a more widespread malaise
may well be seen as a dangerously missed opportunity. Mr Gorbachev's pitch for multi-billion dollar support for an imploding
USSR economy may be crafted according to the rules of western
economic thinking, but it is addressed to western economies
beset with difficulties, not least of which is the new fragility of the
Deutschmark since German unification.

> Simply breathing is a great hazard.
> — Maria Guminska

Innumerable reports from all over the world confirm that,
regardless of household income or the ideological persuasion of
national governments, environmental degradation is increasingly threatening human health and security. As the Berlin Wall
came down, revealing horrendous environmental degradation,
[Guminska, Beres, Vavrousek] so the Dutch government fell
over the implementation of a National Environment Plan.[Wams]
This had been prompted by a worrying survey of the environment in the densely populated and heavily polluted Netherlands. A recent report on *The State of the Environment* of the

world's richest countries concluded that: 'the key challenge for the 1990s is to bring about cost-effective solutions to environmental problems through the structural adjustment of OECD economies.'[3]

Concern about the dislocation between human economic activities (development) and the well-being of both the environment and people is now so great that the United Nations will hold a Conference on Environment and Development in Brazil in June 1992 to negotiate critical conventions on greenhouse gases, deforestation and biodiversty. For the first time in human history, representatives from every country of the world will come together to discuss 'our common future'.[Leggett] The Bruntland Report, which inspired the conference, confirmed that we have now entered what World Bank economist Herman Daly calls an era of 'uneconomic growth', one which impoverishes rather than enriches.[4] Yet Europe's plans for 1992 remain oblivious to calls for *ecological* perestroika and the imperatives which will be imposed by any meaningful conventions negotiated in Brazil.

> By seeming to fight the economic battles of today,
> Europe could lose tomorrow's ecological war.
> The Community is in fact pulling the ecological
> rug from under its own feet.
> – Nick Robins

In the west governments are mesmerized by the fundamental contradictions between the the twin goals enshrined in the 1987 Single European Act. Far too late in the day they have discovered that the sort of policies which will create an internal market with reasonably fair access for all members are the opposite of those which will render the EC a serious competitor to Japan and the USA on the world market. Furthermore, both goals turn out to be incompatible with the sort of policies which will be needed to put into practice the energy- and raw-material-conserving activities implicit in any attempt to halt global warming.

In eastern Europe, governments seem set to learn the hard way that to survive in the unforgiving world marketplace, you must be strong before you start. Relative power may not be factored into the economist's calculations, but it has as much (if not more) to do with setting prices as has supply and demand. [Goldsmith, Beres]

> The rich, textured cultures and long-established
> communities of the east should not be thrown out
> with the bathwater of communism — nor be laundered
> in the detergents of capitalism.
> — Karen Christensen

But is there such a thing as a *coherent* plan for Europe — one that marries human economic and social needs with environment imperatives? Is there a 'third way' to a new world order? Greens would answer with a clear and confident yes. Unlike all other political formations, which rely simply on a social analysis, Greens have made an *ecological* analysis of the predicament of humankind. They recognize that all human activities are intimately connected to the environment in which we live, and those connections can be infinitely complicated both in time and in space.[Grinevald, Galtung, Prime]

Many years before Mrs Bruntland's commission sat down to wonder about the sustainability of current patterns of human development, Green parties were using this ecological analysis to put together practical programmes for ecologically sustainable futures. In 1972, for example, the UK Green Party, the first in Europe, was inspired by what *A Blueprint for Survival* offered as:

> the principal conditions of a stable society — one that
> to all intents and purposes can be sustained indefi-
> nitely while giving optimum satisfaction to its mem-
> bers...
>
> 1. Minimum disruption of ecological processes,
> 2. Maximum conservation of materials and energy,

3. A population in which recruitment equals loss,
4. A social system in which individuals can enjoy, rather than feel restricted by the first three conditions.[5]

Twenty years later, in preparation for the Brazil conference, the European Greens, an organization which brings together 24 Green parties from west and east Europe and which has links with Greens on other continents, will be using the same principles to prepare what they see as their minimum conditions for a *Green* new world order.

At the top of their list is the need to negotiate a historic compromise between rich and poor, an agreement which stops all development in rich countries (with development defined tightly as consumption of energy and raw materials) in exchange for an admission from poor countries that they cannot follow the same development path (as defined above) as the rich. The compromise would be sealed with a commitment by the rich 'to pay back some of what they owe', so as to help the poor deal with immediate crises and move to ecologically sustainable development paths. No treaty on greenhouse gases, no international legal regime for the environment, will be worth the paper it is written on unless it can be underpinned by a 'compromise' which gives *all* countries a vested interest in turning the treaty into action.[Cheyne] Furthermore, past experience confirms that while governments and international institutions may be necessary for setting standards and targets, the practical details of transferring cash, technology and know-how are best decided by local communities.[Dauncey]

The end of the cold war has left one of the most expensive security organizations in the world short on credibility and short on vision. NATO was caught on the hop by the collapse of the Warsaw Pact, and its current proposals for reorganizing are still more concerned with past perceptions of *military* threats to Europe's security than with the reality that the state of the environment poses more threats to human security than any army.[Guminska, Robertson, Blau] Around 20 million people worldwide have died in armed conflict since the Second World

War, yet today around 20 million people are thought to die *annually* from starvation. The World Bank classifies around 1 billion people (one-fifth of humanity) as *food insecure*, and about half the world's people may be considered *water insecure* in that they either have inadequate access to safe drinking water and sanitary facilities or have to rely on a shared river system for their supplies. Disputes about water simmer in most parts of the world and nowhere more acutely than in the Middle East.[6]

When their environment can no longer provide for their basic needs, people, of course, move. And the concern of many in Europe is that breakdown in the east will lead to growing numbers of people 'swarming' towards the west's fragile and expensive social security systems. Will NATO's Rapid Reaction Force then be deployed not against enemy armies but against European citizens? Greens are arguing that the time has come to measure security, not in terms of battalions and bombs but in numbers of people able to meet their needs near to where they live.[Pohla, Irvine]

In Europe, east and west, this would mean focusing cash, know-how and resources more on diversifying and strengthening *local* economies than on pulling national economies into the very tough regime of the world market.[Goldsmith] Taking even a small chunk of today's military budgets and transferring it into supporting appropriate land reform,[Harrison] or introducing a Basic Income Scheme to liberate the immense amount of work that needs to be done from the constraints imposed by current systems of employment,[Parijs] would revolutionize Europe's economies in a truly sustainable way. Any 'Marshall Plan' of aid to east Europe should also be used to prime local banks and develop local enterprise boards, differentiating monetary policy to keep money active where it is most needed — in the community.[Dauncey, Robins] Securing environmental and human well-being and making people happy to stay at home in this way is a much more realistic plan than the current unsustainable projects of either the European Community's Jacques Delors or his Soviet counterpart.

> If [western financial institutions] 'open up' the markets
> and prescribe a financial regime in east Europe in the
> same way as they have done in the rest of the world,
> then it may not be too long before the Second World
> joins the Third World in subsidizing the First World.
> — Edward Goldsmith

Over 300 climate scientists, most of them in government posts, strongly recommended to the International Panel on Climate Change that large and immediate cuts in greenhouse gases will be needed if global warming is to be avoided. The principal gas is carbon dioxide. Not only does it make up around 50 per cent of all global warming gases, it also is the result of what are largely 'luxury' activities. Methane, by contrast, comes from essentially survival activities, while CFCs, although molecule for molecule much more damaging than CO_2, are entirely artificial and simple to ban — as they should be.

In response to the warnings of the climate scientists, the restructuring economies of east Europe have a golden opportunity to abandon hugely polluting energy intensive industries, and adopt energy efficiency in a big way as they transfer to dependence on solar technologies. The environmental case for doing so is compelling. The technologies are there and the economic logic (whether market-led or green) is overwhelming in favour of effiency.[Lovins] In both east and west Europe there are no reasons why an energy-efficient economic plan should not be adopted immediately.[Vavrousek, Wams] The only problem seems to be what Amory Lovins calls 'corporate socialism', where governments 'protect' their favourite industries even when the market, as in the case of nuclear energy, has declared them dead. It is lack of western government support for industries promoting energy efficiency and solar technologies which prevents them from mounting effective programmes in east Europe.[Beres, Leggett]

It would behove west Europe to invest in the energy
economy of east Europe... [this] is one of the litmus
tests for whether or not humankind has the collective
will to escape the global warming threat.

Jeremy Legett

All over Europe, the notion of honouring nature for its own
sake has been overwhelmed by the idea that the environment
and other species exist simply to be used by us.[Galtung,
Harrison] Our pursuit of happiness through material growth
has forgotten that real progress is measured not in bank bal-
ances or golden palaces but in the depth of our personal and
spiritual lives.[Prime] We do have a very practical need for
nature, of course, as a provider of food, medicines and climatic
stability for example. But we also need an ethical framework to
our lives; even if we are hell-bent on the extinction of our own
species, what right do we have to deprive other species of their
right to evolutionary satisfaction?[Tudge]

For most Greens, reconnecting ourselves with all life is a
prerequisite to living our own lives in a way which conserves the
environment rather than consumes it; in order to live our own
lives ecologically, we can learn a lot from nature's vast experience with ecological balance.[McGlade, Knabe]

The bottom line, of course, is that nature is not known for her
compassion to species which find themselves, ecologically speaking, out of line. Therefore the sooner we get our own ecology in
harmony with the world's natural ecology the better. The Green
project is not about managing the environment, but about
managing human ecology. [Christensen] And it is urgent to start
with our absolute numbers.[Irvine] West Europe is one of the
most densely populated regions of the world. If it had not been
able to import most of its raw materials and export much of its
waste, it would have become a desert a long time ago. In all
societies, reducing the number of children born depends on
women. Giving them confidence that the children they do have
will survive,[Robertson] plus the information and practical

support they need to control their own fertility and obtain more power (in the family and in the community), will be essential.[Kelly, Beres] More responsible teaching from the main European religons is also urgently needed. For example, the Roman Catholic Church must give a broader meaning to being pro-life than simply being pro-more-and-more babies, and although the Koran places a 'divine responsibility' on parents to provide for their children, the high infant and maternal mortality rates of some Moslem countries suggest this responsibility is not divine enough to improve the status of women.

Getting the present international hotchpotch of principles and rules concerning the environment into some sort of coherent and integrated legal regime must be a top priority for the future. At the moment, however, our legal systems and institutions serve particular political and social boundaries which environmental issues ignore.[Cheyne] There is a strong case for reviewing the current political boundaries we have adopted in Europe, so that in future they fit, not only the problems, but also the boundaries in which the solutions would best be enacted.[Gahrton, Galtung] The notion of the nation state is, after all, a relatively modern one (dating back to around 1789), and organizations like the UN and NATO are not yet 50 years old. The European Economic Community is under 35. The extent of the economic and environmental problems facing Europe and the world make a rethink of the way human beings organize themselves very worthwhile.

Two general rules guide Green thinking about institutional arrangements. One is that moving ethics away from the individual and into society encourages a higher intellectual content. The other is that the more decisions are made by those who pay for the decision *and* live the consequences of it, the better the decision is likely to be for people and for the environment. These general rules are crystallized into the concept of subsidiarity.[Robins]

For Greens, therefore, global institutions like the United Nations and world regions like the Europe covered by the newly institutionalized Conference for Security and Cooperation (CSCE) are the fora in which binding standards for environmental quality and justice should be set and promoted, and ethical frameworks for trade, diplomacy, etc. established. [Gahrton] Nations, sub-national regions and communities are the fora in which more *practical* details should be decided and carried out. For Greens, it is getting a commonly agreed framework of ethics and principles right and in place which is critical, details are always negotiable.

> All measures aimed at improving the quality
> of the environment must be founded
> on broad international cooperation.
> — Josef Vavrousek

In many ways, what is happening in Europe at the moment is a by-play to what is happening on a global scale, and Brazil in 1992 is sure to see a battle of visions. On the one side will be a vision of the world in which countries and continents may, by making some slight adjustments to their economic strategies, essentially carry on with business as usual. On the other side will be the Green vision, one which has *listened* to the messages from a collapsing global environment and collapsing human economies. The Green plan for Europe, like the Green plan for the world, is not a plan just for emperors. Nor is it a plan for little people. It is a plan which must be engaged by all people if it is to be successful.

Over the last decade the Green movement has become the most rapidly growing movement the world has ever seen. In west Europe, where Greens have been elected to national and European parliaments, progress has not always been without difficulties.[Von Uexkull] But the new light which ecological thinking can cast on the predicament of humankind makes Green ideas very powerful.[Andreis] The majority of the democracy movements in east Europe grew out of environmental campaigning groups, and their courage is replicated in other groups throughout the world where democracy is limited if not absent.[Jordan, Ecoglasnost]

Greens everywhere have been arguing for over twenty years

that the only political agenda which matters is the one which tackles the ecological crisis — the failing power of the environment to support unthinking human activity. Greens also point out that ecological sustainability is not only the *goal* of our endeavours but also the *route* to resolving many human dilemmas. We have got used to thinking of the environment as a cause or a tool of war; but as we move into times of great uncertainty, we would be foolish to ignore the power of the environment to act as a diplomat. For example, the route to a broader peace in the Middle East may best be found through a conference on water security in the region. Similarly, NATO and the European Community may be able to find a face-saving way out of their institutional impasses by being obliged to subsume their organizations, (together with the Warsaw Pact and COMECON countries) into, say, the CSCE structure, because it is there that environmental standards, emission targets and so on are most sensibly agreed and monitored.

There is no doubt that Europe faces massive problems, but the solutions will be found not only in Brussels, Prague, Moscow or Washington, but also in Brazil and in every human community, no matter how small or how large. It is in all these places that the rays of light cast upon our continent by the particular perspective of each contributor to this book come together to shine a bright Green beam of hope into the future.

Sara Parkin
Port Charlotte, Isle of Islay
August, 1991

Notes

1. Mike Rowles, *Union or Dis-union*, Green Party briefing paper on the USSR, 31 January 1991.
2. Jim Rohwer, 'The Way the West Has Won', in Dudley Fishburn, *The World in 1990*, Economist Publications, 1989.
3. Organization for Economic Cooperation and Development, *The State of the Environment*, OECD, Paris, 1991.

4. Herman Daly and John Cobb, *For the Common Good*, Green Print, 1989.
5. The Ecologist, *A Blueprint for Survival*, Penguin, 1972.
6. Michael Renner, *National Security: The Economic and Environmental Dimensions*, Worldwatch paper 89, May 1989.

* Author references in square brackets are to articles in this book.

Jacques Grinevald

Europe and the Biosphere's Global Ecology

'Until recently historians and students of humanities, and to a certain extent even biologists, consciously failed to reckon with the natural laws of the biosphere, the only terrestrial envelope where life can exist. Basically man cannot be separated from it; it is only now that this indissolubility begins to appear clearly and in precise terms before us. He is geologically connected with its material and energetic structure.'

Vladimir I. Vernadsky[1]

'From now on we have to see the Earth, which seemed to us so immense, in its constraints. We live in a closed system, totally dependent on the Earth and on one another, both for our life and for that of future generations. Everything that divides us is infinitely less important than that which ties us and the peril that unites us.'

'Message from Menton', Le Courrier de l'Unesco,
July 1971

Global ecology deals with the world, what Aristotle called the 'sublunary' world: the world of the Earth with its spheres and its elements — water, air, fire and earth. The environment in which we live, this terraqueous globe, is a finite and limited world, a 'closed world', as the ancients thought, and not the 'infinite universe' of modern thought which Alexandre Koyré speaks of in his 1957 book *From Closed World to Infinite Universe*. We do not *live* in the immense universe of astronomy, but rather in this privileged terrestrial environment, protected by the gaseous envelope of the atmosphere, as if at the bottom of an ocean of air (Torricelli), an environment that the science of global ecology, following Vernadsky, calls the Biosphere.[2] The 1980s saw a mobilization of international scientific cooperation: this is currently expressed in the vast project of interdisciplinary and holistic research known as the International Geosphere Biosphere Programme: A Study of Global Change (IGBP), officially launched at the general assembly of ICSU (International Council of Scientific Unions) in Berne, Switzerland in September 1986.

The essential message of the 'environmental revolution' (Max Nicholson) is to remind us of certain basic truths. 'Ecological awareness' implies a 'theology of the Earth' (René Dubos); it is expressed in this fundamental idea[3] of biospheric or global ecology, which is also a deep ecology, in the sense given to this concept by the Norwegian philosopher Arne Naess. The Earth does not belong to us: 'the world began without humanity and will end without it' (Claude Lévi- Stauss). In the same way as all other living species, past, present and future, humanity is totally bound into the evolution of the biosphere of planet Earth.

It is useful to recall that it was in his theory of the Earth, which prefigures certain ideas of biogeochemistry, that Lamarck introduced the modern term of biology. 'Terrestrial physics,' he wrote in his *Hydrogéologie* (1802), 'divides into three essential parts, the first of which must embrace the theory of the atmosphere, meteorology; the second, that of the external crust of the globe, hydrogeology; and the third, that of living beings, biology.'[4]

Buffon, Lamarck's protector, similarly began his *Histoire naturelle* with the theory of the Earth. To the great scandal of the religious and intellectual authorities of his century, Buffon progressively discovered the immensity of geological time. He

WATERSTONE'S

21/11/93 19:53   E   0   1064
  1 @   4.99 0747405689   £   4.99
            GRIDLOCK
  1 @   9.95 0946097291   £   9.95
          GREEN LIGHT ON E
  1 @   7.99 1856750450   £   7.99
            UNKNOWN
SUBTOTAL
SALES TAX @ 0.00%   £   22.93
TOTAL   £   0.00
TENDER CASH   £   22.93
CHANGE   £   30.00
                           £   7.07

266 EARLS COURT RD LONDON SW5 9AS
TEL: 071 370 1616 VAT NO: 238554836

already emphasized the close link betwen life and Earth, noting in a volume published in 1765:

> The particular constitution of animals and plants is related to the general temperature of the Earth's globe, and this temperature depends on its situation, that is, the distance between it and the Sun. At a greater distance, our animals and plants could neither live nor vegetate; water, sap, blood and all other liquids would lose their fluidity; at a lesser distance, they would evaporate and dissipate into vapours: ice and fire are the elements of death; temperate heat is the first germ of life.[5]

Although ignorant of the greenhouse effect of the atmosphere, this reflection of Buffon prefigures the viewpoint of comparative planetology on our terrestrial Biosphere.

As a science of the complexity of nature's economy, ecology continues, as Charles Elton has written, the tradition of natural history.[6] This naturalist tradition speaks to us of the 'living world', this 'habitable Earth' that the Scottish doctor James Hutton, at the dawn of modern geology, imagined — beyond the mechanical metaphors of the Newtonianism of his day — as an 'organized being', a living organism that repaired itself and assured the self-regulation of its steady state. Like Buffon and Lamarck, Hutton imagined the abyss of geological time, so contrary to the biblical chronology of western Christianity. The 'immense time' of the 'system of the Earth' is so incommensurable, he concluded, that in our scientific research 'we find no vestige of a beginning, no prospect of an end.'[7]

James Hutton (1726-1797), who presented the first version of his *System of the Earth* to the Royal Society of Edinburgh in 1785, but only published the two first volumes of his famous *Theory of the Earth* ten years later, supported the thesis of a medical doctor at Leyden,[8] published in 1749 as *Dissertatio physico-medica inauguralis de sanguine et circulatione microcosmi*. Following a scientific analogy of preindustrial Europe,[9] well illustrated by the frontispiece of a disciple of Harvey's titled *Oceanus macro-microcos-*

micus,[10] Hutton compared the hydrological cycle in the terrestrial macrocosm with the circulation of the blood in the living microcosm. This metaphor of the 'living Earth' and its cycles has come down across the centuries, despite accusations of mythology, vitalism and finalism put forward by orthodox western science and its mechanistic paradigm. With new scientific arguments, and the space age's perspective of comparative planetology, the ancient image of Mother-Earth as a 'living organism' — the biosphere in Vernadsky's sense — has been significantly revived today by the Gaia hypothesis and 'geophysiology' of James Lovelock.[11]

As a medical doctor, but also a chemist, farmer, agronomist, geologist, metaphysician, and undoubtedly one of the greatest philosophers of the Scottish and European Enlightenment, an intimate friend of Joseph Black, James Watt and Adam Smith, Hutton illustrates a deeply ecological 'natural philosophy'. If the 'body wisdom' of Doctor Hutton's Earth has been ignored by the ideology of industrialization, it represents none the less a remarkable historical step in the discovery of the Biosphere's natural cycles, as the Russian geologist Segei I. Tomkeieff,[12] a disciple of Vernadsky who emigrated to England, has remarked.

The holistic tradition of ecology, before even acquiring its present name (coined as is well known by the German naturalist Ernst Haeckel in 1866), had always considered the living Earth, Nature — what is unhappily called nowadays the environment — as a 'whole pervaded by the breath of life'. This formula is found in the first pages of Alexander von Humboldt's (1769-1859) admirable *Kosmos*; Humboldt was one of the fathers of our ecological vision of the world as well as of international cooperation in the Earth sciences. His great book, as well as his *Essay on the Geography of Plants* and his *Aspects of Nature*, is a classic in the history of ecology. Darwin, Vernadsky and the ecologists have always accorded Humboldt an exceptional admiration and recognition. Between Hutton and Vernadsky, there was the whole development in the 19th century of a 'Humboldtian science', of which the French agronomist Jean-Baptiste Boussingault (1802-1887) and the Russian scientist Vasily Vasilievich Dokuchaev (1846-1903) were just two eminent representatives among many others less well known in the history of ecology.

James Hutton is rightly saluted today by James Lovelock — himself a great doctor of the Earth. In the prehistory of the Gaia hypothesis, in the little known scientific tradition leading from Hutton to Lovelock,[13] the two other chief European figures that mark the birth of global biospheric ecology are the great Russian scientist Vladimir Ivanovich Vernadsky (1863-1945), the true founding father of the holistic concept of the Biosphere and the new science of biogeochemistry; and George Evelyn Hutchinson, the English biologist born in Cambridge in 1903, who moved to the United States in 1928, and founded at Yale University the great school of scientific ecology which integrated into traditional naturalist ecology the ecosystemic theory that issued for a decisive part from the biogeochemical and energetics approach of the author of *The Biosphere*.

Studying the structure and functioning of the Biosphere and of ecosystems, as they have been named following Tansley (1935) and Lindeman (1942), ecological science is the most interdisciplinary and holistic of the sciences of nature. In this sense, it really does represent an alternative paradigm, different from that of the dominant western science, which is essentially reductionist and mechanistic. The systemic perspective of theoretical ecology, founded in the inter-war years and subsequently enriched by cybernetics, general systems theory and open systems thermodynamics, proposes a new synthesis, beyond the academic division betwen biosciences, geosciences and human sciences. Thus the global science of ecology studies the reciprocal interactions between life, the totality of living beings, the biota (at a given biogeological epoch), and the surface of the Earth considered as a 'living planet', unique of its kind in the cosmos.

From the beginnings of the thermodynamic revolution, with Fourier and Carnot in 1824, the theory of heat introduced the question of the Earth's energetics.[14] It preoccupied many scientists, notably those specialising in energy,[15] and some philosophers such as Bergson. Since Timiriazeff,[16] Vernadsky, Alfred Lotka and the Hutchinson-Lindeman school, the most scientific ecologists strongly emphasize the thermodynamic aspect of the biosphere's ecosystems.[17] The debate on entropy and coevolution of life and planet is still a burning scientific issue, above all since the Romanian-American economist Nicholas Georgescu-Roegen has brought to light the 'bio-economic aspects of entropy'.[18] This entire history of relations between thermodynamics and theoretical ecology (still too little known to development economists!) well shows that ecology is also a cosmology, inseparable from a physical theory, in this case the Carnotian thermodynamics that arose from the European industrial revolution.

The thermodynamic revolution, starting from the engineering genius Sadi Carnot's (1796-1832) *Reflections on the Motive Power of Fire and on Machines Fitted to Develop That Power* (1824), radically transformed our physical theory of nature's economy. For a long while the Academy of Sciences was simply dazzled. However, with Fourier (whose memorandum of 1824 originates the concept of the greenhouse effect) and Sadi Carnot, the heat of the industrial revolution invaded the science of the universe, even if classical culture, mechanism and the ideology of industrialization repressed its epistemological and philosophic implications. The thermo-industrial revolution in the west, which has transformed reserves of fossil fuel and mineral resources into waste and pollution, according to the second law of thermodynamics, has repressed what we can and should call, with Georgescu-Roegen and Michel Serres, the 'Carnotian revolution'.[19]

Not understood in its time, and repressed by western neoclassical economics and the ideology of progress and growth, the Carnotian revolution has still not finished revealing its multiple implications, not only for the theory of biospheric evolution, but also, with enormous social and political implications, for the ecological question of humanity's economic development, in other words the integration of our 'industrial metabolism' into the great natural cycles of the Biosphere.[20] By the very fact of development (demographic, technological, economic and scientific), and its evolutionary acceleration on a world scale, we are from now on collectively coresponsible for the 'fate of the Earth' (Jonathan Schell), i.e. of the Biosphere.[21]

The emergence of the holistic concept of the Biosphere, a genuine scientific and philosophical revolution begun by Vernadsky in inter-war Europe, is inscribed in the totality of the great historical adventure — also a geographical and intercultural adventure — of western Europe's relations with the Earth. The term biosphere significantly appeared at the dawn of the 20th century. It came not from biology, but from geology. It was coined by Eduard Suess (1831-1914), professor of geology at Vienna University. In the conclusion of his little book *The Formation of the Alps* (1875), Suess represented the structure of the terrestrial globe as composed of concentric interconnected envelopes. On the surface, the lithosphere, hydrosphere and atmosphere are thus connected to a biosphere, 'eine selbstandige Biosphäre'.[22] Suess took up this idea of the biosphere, without defining it very explicitly, to emphasize this time the 'interconnection of all life' in the last chapter, titled 'Life', in the third and final volume (1909) of his great book *The Face of the Earth*.[23] Admired throughout Europe, this book fired the enthusiasm of the geological and geographic community. Alfred Wegener (1880-1930) made much use of it to revolutionize Earth science with his controversial theory of continental drift. But the 'Wegener revolution' (J. Tuzo Wilson), as we know, only triumphed in the late 1960s thanks to plate tectonics. In the same way, industrial civilization has not yet accepted the Vernadsky revolution, for it is to Vernadsky and not Suess that we owe the biogeochemical and cosmic vision of the Biosphere which represents a new paradigm for the developmental crisis, planetary and ecological, of the 'human phenomenon'.

In Paris in the 1920s, two admirers of Suess each took up the notion of the biosphere, but with very differing intentions and theoretical perspectives: Pierre Teilhard de Chardin (1881-1955), then professor of geology at the Catholic Institute (before leaving for China), continued developing to the end of his life a whole evolutionist and anthropocentric philosophy of the biosphere. However, pervaded by a typically Eurocentric religion of progress, Teilhard's geobiological doctrine of the biosphere in no way corresponded to the global biospheric ecology developed in parallel by Vernadsky. Unfortunately, it is Teilhard who largely contributed to the diffusion and confusion of the term biosphere! For his part, while an emigrant in France in the wake of the Russian civil war,[24] the eminent mineralogist Vernadsky gave a series of lectures at the Sorbonne which were published in 1924 under the title *La Géochimie*. As a sequel to this book, Vernadsky wrote another and more speculative work, this time explicitly called *The Biosphere*, published in Leningrad in 1926, then in a revised and expanded French version in 1929.[25] This book of Vernadsky's, with its stupendous intellectual boldness, undoubtedly marked one of the great turning-points in human scientific thought. It is certainly a classic of 20th century European thinking.Vernadsky's works on biogeochemistry and the theory of the Biosphere were unfortunately not appreciated at their true value. The author of the first scientific monograph on the Biosphere was ahead of his time. And later, partly due to the cold war, the very name of Vernadsky was forgotten after his death. In 1968, the Unesco conference on the Biosphere and its resources[26] marked the end of this incredible neglect. The Vernadskyan concept of the Biosphere, like Lovelock and Margulis' concept of Gaia, are however far richer and at bottom very different from the internationally accepted concept of global environment! It is high time, as evidenced by the symposium organized by the USSR Academy of Sciences in March 1988, to pay homage to Vernadsky,[27] and to rediscover the immense intellectual inheritance, in part unpublished, that he left at the end of the Second World War to his country, to Europe and the world community.

The meeting between Vernadsky, Teilhard de Chardin and the mathematician and philosopher Eduard Le Roy (1870-1954), Bergson's successor at the Collège de France, was both one of the most remarkable and one of the least well known in the history of contemporary ideas. Their discussions bore on the evolution of life in the geological history of the Earth, on the cosmic aspect of the Biosphere and consciousness, on the geological role of the development of the 'phenomenon of man' and its future on the global scale. In the mid 1920s this brilliant scientific and philosophical trio introduced the concept of noosphere, which includes that of the technosphere,[28] but this was interpreted in as varied a way as that of biosphere. The terminological and conceptual confusion has still not disappeared, quite the contrary. It would however be useful, faced with the 'urgency of the worst case' (Cioran), to take up this debate on the biosphere and the noosphere.[29]

Despite the respectable 'European' tradition that we have just evoked, the interdisciplinary and holistic science of global ecology is still embryonic, full of uncertainties, but with an international currency more important than ever, as evidenced by the research undertaken in the context of the International Geosphere Biosphere Programme. Significantly, the precedent of the International Geophysical Year, in 1957-58, marked by the launch of the first artificial satellites and thus the beginning of the space age, still neglected the Biosphere. Even the International Biological Programme that followed ten years later did not succeed in imposing a global biospheric perspective in the attention that began to be paid to the ecosystems on which the very existence of humanity depends. The 'environmental revolution' since 1970 has often surrounded the word 'ecology' with a semantic and media inflation without for all that providing a coherent global vision of the integration of the economy of human societies into the great planetary equilibria of the Biosphere.

The great lesson of ecology, and in fact of all natural history, is to impress on us the limits of human existence,[30] the awareness of our belonging to the evolution of the Biosphere, i.e. to the extraordinary adventure of planet Earth in the cosmos. Global ecology, centred on the holistic concept of the Biosphere, truly represents an alternative paradigm, very different from the 'natural philosophy of modern biology' as defined in Jacques Monod's *Chance and Necessity* (1970). The debate between holism and reductionism that was so acute in the 1920s is not purely academic; it bears on the crisis of western civilization that has arisen from the historical and cultural adventure of our old Europe. Molecular biology with its exploits in genetics, or the physics of particle accelerators, i.e. the scientific and technological Europe of CERN,[31] may well lead to the belief that holism is definitely dead, but this is not the case at all. The whole great ecological tradition, and more precisely the biospheric or Gaian tradition as we may say today, defends a certain organic, holistic idea, the unity of nature in its diversity.[32]

Modern science, inseparable from the technological advance of medieval society in western Europe, and marked by the revolution of Galileo and the Newtonian synthesis, developed within the religious culture of the west; it shares its beliefs and its founding myths. This is what the medievalist Lynn White (1907-1987) showed clearly throughout his work on the social history of technology, and especially in his resounding lecture of 26 December 1966 on 'The Historical Roots of Our Ecologic Crisis'.[33] The mechanistic conception of modern science and technology is deeply rooted in a certain western Judeo-Christian idea of creation as the work of the divine architect-engineer-mathematician, with man, the privileged creature shaped in his image, destined to become 'master and possessor of nature' (Descartes). It is time for our civilization to give way to the evidence: 'the time for arrogance has passed' (Romain Gary). Planet Earth, as a Biosphere, is not our 'spaceship': the Earth has not waited for the genius of the west to function and assure the perpetuation of life for four billion years! The beauty of the Earth defies our imagination.

What modern Europe has called science is simply a reductionist paradigm, arithmomorphic and mechanistic, which is neither neutral nor universal nor objective. Technoscience in its western canons is in no way the 'brain' of the Biosphere but simply the world vision of a power-based civilization. Our old European ambition to conquer the Earth — which alas! risks succeeding — is associated, historically and culturally, with a paradigm of death, that 'thanatocracy' which the French philosopher Michel Serres and many recent ecological, pacifist and feminist scientists have spoken of.[34]

The techno-scientific philosophy of conquering Europe, so terribly reductionist, has rejected holism because it is concerned to divide in order to rule, to measure in order to master. The philosophy of western science, from Descartes and Bacon through to Hiroshima and Star Wars, has been a politics and strategy of war, of reason of state par excellence. We have still not escaped from this statist and technocratic ideology of 'domination of nature'. From the rise in late medieval times of the model of machine and engineers, due largely to the military, the religious and rational Weltanschauung of the west conceives our relationship to the world on the model of war, inquisition and violation, as explained by the feminist critique that associates the European scientific revolution with 'the death of nature' (Carolyn Merchant). This critique takes on a whole new sense in the light of the new biospheric paradigm of Gaia, the holistic scientific theory that significantly takes up the mythological symbol of the ancient Greek goddess of the Mother-Earth.

As the sage Evgraf Korolenko (1810-1880), in the old Russia, loved to say to his young nephew Vladimir Vernadsky, 'the Earth is a living being'. We form part of it, the same as millions of other species, many of which moreover are still unknown to us. The Europeans, if they possess a specific cultural responsibility within the international community, by very reason of the geographic and scientific adventure of the west, can and must witness today to this major transformation of human consciousness that is our co-responsibility in the evolution of the biosphere. The philosophical, ethical and spiritual implications of global ecology, as well as Gaia's economic and political implications, are immense and truly staggering. For global political ecology, it means the end of industrialism.[35]

Notes

1. V.I. Vernadsky, 'The Biosphere and the Noosphere', *American Scientist*, January 1945, 33(1), pp.1-12.
2. See Nicholas Polunin and Jacques Grinevald, 'Vernadsky and Biospheral Ecology', *Environmental Conservation*, 1988, 15(2), pp.117-122. Mitchell B. Rambler, Lynn Margulis, René Fester, eds., *Global Ecology: Towards a Science of the Biosphere*, Boston, Academic Press, 1989. J. Grinevald, *The Industrial Revolution and the Earth's Biosphere: A Scientific Awareness in Historical Perspective: Selective Bibliographical Notes* Bern, Swiss Academy of Sciences, ProClim, 1989.

3. J. Grinevald, 'On a Holistic Concept for Deep and Global Ecology: The Biosphere', *Fundamenta Scientiae*, 1987, 8(2), pp.197-226.

4. J. B. Lamarck, *Hydrogéologie ou Recherches sur l'influence qu'ont les eaux sur la surface du globe terrestre; sur les causes de l'existence du bassin des mers, de son déplacement et de son transport successif sur les différens points de la surface de ce globe; enfin sur les changemens que les corps vivans exercent sur la nature et l'état de cette surface*, Paris, chez l'auteur, au Muséum d'Histoire Naturelle, An X (1802), p.8.

5. *Oeuvres philosophiques de Buffon*. Texte établi et présenté par Jean Piveteau, Corpus général des philosophes francais, Prais, P.U.F., 1954, p.36.

6. See Donald Worster, *Nature's Economy. A History of Ecological Ideas*, Cambridge University Press, 1977, 2nd edn, 1985. Frank N. Egerton, 'The History of Ecology', *Journal of the History of Biology*, 1983,16, pp.259-311 and 1985,18, pp.103-143. Roger Dajoz, 'Eléments pour une historie de l'écologie. La naissance de l'écologie moderne au XIXe siècle', *Histoire et Nature*, 1984, 24-25, pp.5- 111. Robert P. McIntosh, ed., *The Background of Ecology: Concepts and Theory* Cambridge University Press, 1985. Ludwig Trepl, *Geschichte der Ökologie*, Frankfurt, Athenäum, 1987. Pascal Acot, *Historie de l'écologie*, Paris, P.U.F., 1988. Jean-Paul Deleage, *Une science devenue monde: histoire de l'écologie*, Paris, La Découverte, forthcoming.

7. James Hutton, 'Theory of the Earth, or an investigation of the laws observable in the composition, dissolution, and restoration of land upon the globe', *Transactions of the Royal Society of Edinburgh*, 1788, 1(2), p.304; and *Theory of the Earth with Proofs and Illustrations*, Edinburgh, 1795, vol.I, chap.I, p.200.

8. See François Ellenberger, 'Les origines de la pensée huttonienne: Hutton étudiant et docteur en médecine', *Comptes Rendus de l'Académie des Sciences*, Paris, 1972, 275, pp.69-72; 'La métaphysique de James Hutton (1726- 1797) et le drame écologique du XXe siècle', *Revue de synthèse*, 1972, 67-68, pp.267-283; 'La thèse de doctorat de James Hutton et la rénovation perpétuelle du monde', *Annales Guebhard*, 1973, 49, pp.497-533. Arthur Donovan and Joseph Prentiss, 'James Hutton's Medical Dissertation', *Transactions of the American Philosophical Society*, 1980, 70(6), pp.1-57.

9. See Walter Pagel, 'William Harvey and the Purpose of Circulation', *Isis*, 1951, 42, pp.22-38. Yi-fu Tuan, *The Hydrological Cycle and the*

Wisdom of God: A Theme in Geoteleology, University of Toronto Press, 1968. Otto Mayr, 'Adam Smith and the Concept of the Feedback System: Economic Thought and Technology in 18th Century Britain', *Technology and Culture*, 1971, 12, pp.1-22. S. Tood Lowry, 'The Archeology of the Circulation Concept in Economic Theory', *Journal of the History of Ideas*, 1974, 35, pp.429-444. J. Grinevald, 'Le monde comme architecture hydraulique', *CoEvolution* (Paris), 1982, 10, pp.30-33.

10. Philip Jacob Sachs von Lewenheimb (1627-1672), *Oceanus macromicrocosmicus*, Wratislaviae, 1664. Quoted in Lynn Margulis and James Lovelock, 'The Atmosphere as Circulatory System of the Biosphere — The Gaia Hypothesis', *The CoEvolution Quarterly*, 1975, 6, pp.30-40; 'Is Mars a Spaceship, Too?', *Natural History*, 1976, 85(6), pp.86-90; 'Atmosphere and Evolution', in John Billingham, ed., *Life in the Universe*, Cambridge, Mass., MIT Press, 1981, pp.79-100. Hutton takes up the analogy between the circulation of the blood and 'the revolution of the globe' in his *Theory of the Earth*, 1795, vol.2, p.546.

11. James Lovelock, 'Gaia as Seen Through the Atmosphere', *Atmospheric Environment*, 1972, 6, pp.579-580. J. Lovelock and Lynn Margulis, 'Atmospheric Homeostatis by and for the Biosphere: The Gaia Hypothesis', *Tellus*, 1974, 226(1-2), pp.2-9; 'Homoeostatic Tendencies of the Earth's Atmosphere', *Origins of Life*, 1974, 5, pp.93-103. L. Margulis and J. Lovelock, 'Biological Modulation of the Earth's Atmosphere', *Icarus*, 1974, 21, pp.471-489. J. Lovelock, *GAIA: A New Look at Life on Earth*, Oxford University Press, 1979, 2nd edn, 1987; 'Gaia: the World as Living Organism', *New Scientist*, 18 December 1986, 112(1539), pp.25-28; 'Geophysiology: a New Look at Earth Sciences', *Bulletin of the American Metereological Society*, 1986, 67(4), pp.392-397; *The Ages of Gaia: A Biography of Our Living Earth*, Oxford University Press, 1988. J. Donald Hughes, 'Gaia: An Ancient View of Our Planet', *The Ecologist*, 1983, 13(2), pp.54-60., Dorian Sagan and Lynn Margulis, 'The Gaian Perspective on Ecology', *The Ecologist*, 1983, 13(5), pp.160-167. Elisabet Sahtouris, *GAIA: The Human Journey from Chaos to Cosmos*, New York, Pocket Books, 1989.

12. S. I. Tomkeieff, 'James Hutton and the Philosophy of Geology', *Transactions of the Geological Society of Edinburgh*, 1948(2), pp.253-276

(Reprinted in *Proceedings of the Royal Society of Edinburgh, 1947-49,*, 1950, 63B, pp.387-400). See also S. I. Tomkeieff, 'V. I. Vernadsky', *Nature*, 1945, 155, p.296.

13. See James Lovelock, 'Prehistory of Gaia', *New Scientist*, 17 July 1986, 11(1517), p.51; *Gaia: A New Look at Life on Earth*, op.cit., 2nd edn, 1987; *The Ages of Gaia*, op. cit.; J. Grinevald, 'Sketch for the History of the Idea of the Biosphere', in P. Bunyard and E. Goldsmith (eds), *GAIA, the Thesis, the Mechanisms, and the Implications*, Camelford, UK, Wadebridge Ecological Centre, 1988, pp.1-34; *James Hutton et Gaia: la Terre comme macrocosme*, forthcoming; *La Biosphère de la planète Terre: naissance de l'écologie globale*, in preparation.

14. J. Grinevald, 'L'effet de serre de la Biosphère: de la révolution thermo-industrielle à l'écologie globale', *Stratégies énergétiques, Biosphere et Société*, University of Geneva, faculty of law, 1990, 1, pp.9-34.

15. See Juan Martinez-Alier, *Ecological Economics: Energy, Environment and Society*, Basil Blackwell, Oxford, 1987.

16. Climent Timiriazeff (1843-1920), 'The Cosmic Function of the Green Plant', *Proceedings of the Royal Society of London*, 1903, 72, pp.424-461.

17. See David M. Gates, *Energy Exchange in the Biosphere*, New York & London, Harper & Row, 1962. Harold J. Morowitz, *Energy Flow in Biology: Biological Organization as a Problem in Thermal Physics*, New York & London, Academic Press, 1968. G. E. Hutchinson et al., *The Biosphere*, A Scientific American Book, San Francisco, Freeman, 1970. Ramon Margalef, *La Biosfera: entre la termodinamica y el juego*, Barcelona, Omega, 1980.

18. Nicholas Georgescu-Roegen, 'Bio-economic Aspects of Entropy', in J. Kubat and J. Zeman (eds), *Entropy and Information in Science and Philosophy*, Prague, Academia, and Amsterdam, Elsevier, 1975, pp. 125-142; *The Entropy Law and the Economic Process*, Cambridge, Mass., Harvard University Press, 1971; *Energy and Economic Myths*, New York, Pergamon Press, 1976; *Demain la décroissance: entropie, écologie, économie*, introduced and translated by Ivo Rens and Jacques Grinevald, Lausanne, Editions Pierre Marcel Favre, 1979; *Energia e miti economici*, introduced by Stefano Zamagni, Torino, Boringhiere, 1982. J. Grinevald, 'Le sense bioéconomique du développement humain: l'affaire Nicholas Georgescu-Roegen', *Revue européenne des sciences sociales et Cahier s Vilfredo Pareto*, 1980, 51, pp.59-75. J. C.

Dragan and M. C. Demetrescu, *Entropy and Bioeconomics: The New Paradigm of Nicholas Georgescu-Roegen*, Milano, Nagard, 1986. Narindar Singh, *Economics and the Crisis of Ecology* (1976), 3rd edn (revised), London, Bellew Publishing, 1989. J. Grinevald, *Vernadsky and Lotka as Sources for Georgescu-Roegen's Bioeconomics*, 2nd Vienna Centre Conference on Economics and Ecology, Barcelona, 26-29 September 1987 ('Vernadsky y Lotka como fuentes de la bioeconomica de Georgescu-Roegen', *Ecologia Politica* (Barcelona, Icaria Editorial), 1991, 1, pp.99-112.

19. J. Grinevald, 'La révolution carnotienne: Thermodynamique, économie et idéologie', *Revue européenne des sciences sociales et Cahiers Vilfredo Pareto*, 1976, 36, pp.39-79.

20. J. Grinevald, 'L'effet de serre de la Biosphère', op. cit.

21. See Hans Jonas, *Das Prinzip Verantwortung*, Frankfurt a.M., Insel Verlag, 1979. Nicholas Polunin, 'Our Global Environment and the World Campaign for The Biosphere', *Environmental Conservation*, 1982, 9(2), pp.115-121; 'Genesis and Progress of the World Campaign and Council for the Biosphere', *Environmental Conservation*, 1984, 11(4), pp.293-298. J. Grinevald, 'Safeguarding the Biosphere', *Peace Review*, 1989, 1(2), pp.27-32. Jonathan Weiner, *The Next One Hundred Years: Shaping the Fate of Our Living Earth*, New York & London, Bantam Books, 1990. Michel Serres, *Le contrat naturel*, Paris, Francois Bourin, 1990.

22. Eduard Suess, *Die Entstehung de Alpen*, Wien, W. Braunmuller, 1875, p. 159.

23. Eduard Suess, *Das Antlitz der Erde*, 3 vols, Prague, Wien, Leipzig, 1883-1909. Translated into English as *The Face of the Earth*, London, 1904-1924.

24. See Kendall E. Bailes, 'Science, Philosophy and Politics in Soviet History: The Case of Vladimir Vernadsky', *Russian Review* 1981, 40(3), pp.278-299; and his posthumous *Science and Russian Culture in an Age of Revolutions: V. I. Vernadsky and his Scientific School, 1863-1945*, Bloomington, Indiana University Press, 1990.

25. V. Vernadsky, *La Géochimie*, Paris, Félix Alcan, 1924; *La Biosphère*, Paris, Félix Alcan, 1929. On Vernadsky's ideas, see in particular Andrei Lapo, *Traces of Bygone Biospheres*, Moscow, Mir, 1982, 2nd revised edn 1987. Studies on Vernadsky in Soviet literature have undergone a real renaissance in recent years, still too little recog-

nized abroad.

26. Victor Kovda et al., 'Contemporary Scientific Concepts Relating to the Biosphere', in *Use and Conservation of the Biosphere*, Paris, Unesco, 1970, pp.13-29.

27. N. Polunin and J. Grinevald, 'Vernadsky and Biospheral Ecology', op. cit.

28. J. Grinevald, *The Forgotten Sources of the Concept of Biosphere*, Annual Meeting of World Council for The Biosphere and Joint Planning Session with International Society for Environmental Education, Les Avants sur Montreux, Switzerland, 18-22 June 1985; 'Le développement de/dans la biosphère', in *L'homme inachevé*, Cahiers de l'I.U.E.D., 17, Geneva and Paris, P.U.F., 1987, pp.29-44. Rafal Serafin, 'Noosphere, Gaia and the Science of the Biosphere', *Environmental Ethics*, 1988, 10(2), pp.121- 137.

29. See William C. Clark and R. E. Munn (eds), *Sustainable Development of the Biosphere*, Laxenburg, IIASA, and Cambridge University Press, 1986. 'Réconcilier la sociosphère et la biosphère', *Revue internationale des sciences sociales* (Unesco), 121, 1989. Nicholas Polunin and John H. Burnett (eds), *Maintenance of the Biosphere*. Proceedings of the Third International Conference on Environmental Future, Edinburgh University Press, 1990.

30. Armand Petitjean, 'La pensée des limites', introduction in *Quelles limites? Le Club de Rome répond...*, Paris, Seuil, 1974, pp.11-29.

31. See J. Grinevald, A. Gsponer, L. Hanouz, P. Lehmann, *La Quadrature du CERN*, preface by Robert Jungk, Lausanne, Editions d'En Bas, 1984.

32. J. Grinevald, 'L'écologie contre le mythe rationnel de l'Occident: de la diversité dans la nature à la diversité des cultures', in *La pensée métisse*, Cahiers de l'I.U.E.D., Geneva and Paris, P.U.F., 1990, pp. 195-212.

33. L. White, 'The Historical Roots of Our Ecologic Crisis', *Science*, 1967, 155, pp.1203-1207. For the bibliography on this debate, see Lynn White, *Les racines historiques de notre crise écologique*. Dossier établi par Jacques Grinevald, forthcoming. Robin Attfield, *The Ethics of Environmental Concern*, Oxford, Basil Blackwell, 1983. Roderick Frazier Nash, *The Rights of Nature: A History of Environmental Ethics*, Madison, University of Wisconsin Press, 1989. Sergio Bartolommei,

Etica e ambiente, Milano, Guerini e Associati, 1989.

34. J. Grinevald, 'L'histoire des sciences et la raison d'Etat', in *La Science et la guerre*, Bruxelles. Groupe de recherche et d'information sur la paix. Dossier GRIP no. 97,98,99, 1986, pp.23-67; 'The Greening of Europe', *Bulletin of Peace Proposals*, 1991, 22, pp.41-47.

35. See Peter Bunyard and Edward Goldsmith (eds), *GAIA, the Thesis, the Mechanisms and the Implications*, op. cit., and *Gaia and Evolution*, ibid., 1989. Peter Bunyard, 'Gaia: The Implications for Industrialized Societies', *The Ecologist*, 1988, 18(6), pp.196-206. Edward Goldsmith, 'Towards a Biospheric Ethic', *The Ecologist*, 1989, 19(2), pp.68-75. Patrick McCully, 'The End of Industrialism', *The Ecologist* 1990, 20(5), pp.162-164. Andrew Dobson, *Green Political Thought: An Introduction*, London, Unwin Hyman, 1990.

Johan Galtung

Mapping Green Politics for Europe

There is a Green spectre not only in Europe East and West, North and South, but all over the world. To grow from no Green parties to 25, represented in 11 parliaments, in less than ten years is no minor achievement. Evidently there was a need, a vacuum to be filled. The Green movement had found its political articulation, in democratic competition with other parties. That Green movement and parties are still in a minority is no wonder: fundamental critique of the dominant order is rarely a majority pursuit. And where — except in dictatorships — did power come immediately?

Movement and party are related, but never the same. The movement gives voice to *values*, loud and clear, in speech, writing and above all in imaginative action of the Greenpeace variety. The party is one of the many carriers of these values, participating in the electoral system and increasingly present in local and national elected bodies. For the movement the task is to give clear voice to values and problems, to make diagnosis, prognosis, and to set ultimate goals. For the party the task is to come up with therapies, with remedies, with acceptable solutions. And solutions are never so pure as the values. They never fit the diagnosis completely; they are more likely to be 70 per cent solutions, not 100 per cent. Moreover, solutions for any problem usually have side-effects, not only in the sense of exacerbating other problems already on the Green list, but of bringing in completely new, so far unthought-of problems, like the ozone hole as a consequence of the discovery of CFC in 1928. There is never a one-to-one mapping between problems and solutions in human and social affairs; there is always a complex web relating everything to everything else. Hence politicians easily become cynical and movement people moralistic, two proven ways of escaping complexity. Neither is compatible with Green epistemology: think and act globally and holistically at the personal, local, national and regional levels.

The values of the Green movement are easily listed:

- In **Nature space**: ecological balance, honoring all life, not only human life, enhancing nature also for its own sake, not only protecting imbalances against further deterioration.
- In **Human space**: priority to such basic needs as food, shelter and clothing for all, rejecting cynical 'utilitarian' calculations like 'the greatest good for the greatest possible number'; with equal emphasis on such nonmaterial needs as a sense of identity and meaning, individual and collective freedom, as on the material needs for food, shelter, clothing.
- In **Social space**: equal rights for all regardless of age, gender, race, class and nation; participation in democracies with referendum and initiative as obvious as elections; emphasis on subsidiarity with everything that can be done at the local level done at that level; nonviolence.
- In **World space**: equal rights for all countries and nations regardless of age (as country), race, position in the international division of labour; people's participation in a democratic United Nations with a Second Assembly, emphasis on subsidiarity down to the national and local levels; nonviolence.
- In **Culture space**: promoting values of respect for all life, fully enjoying equity, diversity and symbiosis on this one Earth, struggle against ideas of chosen peoples or of one true religion/ideology, including the Green one!

In one sentence: *the Green movement is a modern movement preparing people for life in a world society on a small planet.* In no way does this mean a full rejection of the market economy, an age-old, tested institution. The socialist economies of Eastern Europe and East Asia were wrong in depriving people who want to exchange something of the right to do so; the capitalist economies are equally wrong in seeing the market system as both un-problematic and self-repairing. What we need is *ethically conscious and conscientious market behavior,* with individuals aware of the consequences of economic behaviour for the values listed above, and buying and selling accordingly. Growth is not good enough; we want *solidarity in development; growth at the expense of nobody.*

The task of the Green parties is to mark this message clearly, attractively, in the party landscape. In Europe that landscape can no longer be mapped by a line running from left to right. Like any map there is also up and down, there are at least two dimensions.

Quite close to each other, on the horizontal axis, are the classical European parties that still gather votes: the pink social-democrats to the left and the light or dark blue conservatives to the right. A century of political struggle has made them similar, with labour parties accepting most of capitalism in return for conservative parties accepting some of the welfare state in an economy that is social, not socialist. Change of government along this axis elicits little excitement. People know that most will remain the same except maybe in Britain, and in the US where the choice is only between two conservative parties, one dark blue and one light blue, with extreme rightism lurking in the background.

This tacit coalition has made countries rich per capita, at the expense of ecological degradation everywhere; grinding misery also inside such rich countries as the US and Britain; a materialist individualism that has made so many people lonely, alienated alcohol and drug abusers; massive social injustices with child abuse, old people invited to practise euthanasia, women still oppressed in most places, other racial and ethnic groups treated with contempt, fear, repression and the construction of war machines apt for genocidal warfare, self-seeking peacekeeping, rapid development, and massive state terrorism.

Red and pink — light and dark blue? In reality these are the grey parties of managers, of technocrats, leaving a layer of toxic dust on whatever they touch, nature as well as human beings, fitting us all as cogs into their well-greased social machines, destroying the generous natural base off which we all have been living since time immemorial. Children of the naive idea of progress from the eighteenth and nineteenth centuries, these parties go on destroying, with some marginal repair work here and there.

Of course people revolt; poor people, poor countries, poor people in poor countries, the suppressed and subjugated all over. Nature revolts, in her ways, like Mother Earth, Gaia, trying to shake us off because of our lack of respect and understanding. Gaia's self-appointed human brain starts looking more like a viral disease, like some kind of AIDS. There are problems of control. The grey parties deep down fear that things are getting out of hand, all the time appointing more study groups and commissions as the problems exacerbate, and synergetically so.

It is not strange that brown, neo-fascist parties emerge from this fertile soil. They share the basic assumptions of the grey parties, materialist individualism in social space and materialist nationalism in world space. They love economic growth and the corporate and bureaucratic megamachines. But they find democracy too tolerant and too slow, giving voice to far too many. Nature is there to serve us, and the social and world spaces are giant stages where only the fittest will survive and *tant pis* for the rest. Those who do not like the game will suffer the consequences and the iron fists of a strong police in social space and a strong military in world space. This is the culture of fascism, deeply rooted in European individualist competition.

This political map gives us pink to the left, light blue to the right, brown below and green above. With 15 per cent to green, another 15 per cent to brown and 70 per cent divided between the grey parties nobody has a clear majority in the Western European (and some other) democracies. Coalitions will emerge, and have already done so. The light blue parties will have too much to lose in an alliance with the brown; the shadows of conservative cooperation with fascism and nazism are still with us. Dark blue individuals will join, however. The pink parties will, willy-nilly, cooperate with the green, individuals will join. Highly unlikely is any cooperation between green and brown as this is where the real political difference is located on the map for the 1990s and beyond.

Highly likely, however, is a grand coalition, the elephant's wedding between the grey parties, legitimized as a bulwark against the brown, in reality equally or more against the green. Brown is somehow illegitimate in good circles; green is not. Consequently, green is more dangerous.

What this means is that the years ahead will not be easy going after the initial gains have been made. Old parties do not enjoy newcomers of any kind. And yet there are possibilities, although the outcomes will rarely be so pure as purists will demand, if better than pessimists fear.

One important formula here lies in the holism of the Greens versus the sectoral thinking of the others. There is much environmental thinking, talking, even action in the world today. But environment as an isolated sector makes little sense. What is the meaning of cleaner air and water for people who live miserable lives, materially and spiritually impoverished? Green political thought does not accept the idea of using only the environmental degradation produced by socialism and capitalism as a way of attacking these two systems, avoiding such words as inequality and injustice, poverty and repression, as if rain forests were more important than human beings. They are both important, as are the social and world structures being shaped and reshaped every day in the struggle against environmental degradation and human impoverishment, and the formidable violence used by state and corporate forces to maintain the system.

What do these principles mean for European politics, for Europe in the world, for European security? Quite a lot; and it is not going to be easy.

Let me make a first start with the environment. Eastern Europe shows clearly the specificity of socialism: their environmental degradation, just like their repression, hit themselves, unlike the system run by and from the US which hits and represses others worse than themselves, e.g. in Latin America. *Nothing teaches the lessons of ecology so effectively as being a victim of one's own mismanagement.* But without democracy and the guaranteed right of protest and organized action this knowledge is dead. The structure is highly self-preserving: the worst hit cannot protest, those who can protest are not the worst hit. Morale: Europeans must stop doing damage to other people's environment, and defend themselves effectively against the damage we do to ourselves.

But why should Europeans do that? We know perfectly well that most Europeans see themselves as superior to others, including Americans and Russians. The Judeo and Greco-Roman traditions make us see ourselves as a chosen people, of individuals gifted in art, science and philosophy, with a special talent for statecraft: a blessing for the world. What is West is universal according to this type of thinking, including the Christian idea (shared by Islam) that their religion is universal; the liberal and marxist belief that Western history is the universal model of history; and the belief of most Westerners that Western science is universal. Even to be colonized by us, to be environmentally damaged is seen as a blessing in disguise, since the victims become a part of us, at the bottom or even below the table, but at least close to it. Like the peasant daughter raped by the king.

I do not think we shall make much progress unless such beliefs are confronted head on. In other words, a major part of our task lies in cultural space. There is the negative aspect of creating more balance in our view of Europe, this strange continent that enslaves people all over the world, yet (or precisely for that reason) designs and adopts the most beautiful conventions of human rights. But there is also the positive aspect of enhancing the appreciation of pluralism, for instance by learning from the immigrants in our own midst. Learning does not mean accepting everything; the over- arching concept should be the *dialogue of civilizations.* The Green movement should understand the significance, close to primacy, of culture. Our culture, and not only our religion but all our myths and symbols, defines our economic and military systems and underlies our political decisions — with all three also feeding back into the culture and shaping it further.

Misery is incompatible with Green politics. Misery is suffering due to deprivation of basic needs. *Misery is a scandal*, as the liberation theologians point out. There are many approaches to the giant human task of eliminating misery: by creating jobs, by monetary support, by support in kind, by having people produce themselves what they need for direct consumption. Green is compatible with all four approaches: support as return for work done and as a human right; support as money and in kind. We need them all, but we certainly don't need misery and the ideologues that justify it.

This also applies to misery in world space. The basic way out must be through production for one's own consumption and through exchange, meaning trade and economic cooperation. Just as much as individuals need space, literally speaking, to grow their own food, nations and local communities need the same. To receive aid only makes sense as an emergency measure or to launch the young human being/nation as 'pocket money', to get started. Lest this may sound too old-fashioned, let me hasten to emphasize the point that others must not occupy that space by buying up everything under the pretext of developing it, thereby making national and local self-reliance for basic needs impossible.

Of course we need market and trade, and of course market behaviour has to be enlightened by something more than short-term self-interest. Even the most conservative have understood this for nature space, but with the danger that the result may become some kind of eco-fascism, putting eco-values above all others. Green politics is to work for all these values simultaneously, synchronically. Rather make some progress on all of them than a giant leap in one space — at the expense of other spaces.

Geo-politically this points to the equality of nations, and the best institution, with all its shortcomings, is and remains the United Nations, removing however the position of permanent members of the Security Council with a veto. If there is one commodity we do not need in the world, then it is superpowers. Rather, Green politics would support the disintegration of them all, by backing independence movements and decentralization movements in the United States as well as in the Soviet Union, in Japan (where the giant firms are becoming bigger than ever), as well as in China (Tibet, and the 64 per cent of the land inhabited by the less than 5 per cent non-Chinese), in India and certainly in the giant now taking shape, the European Union as the next stage of the European Community.

As a general formula: build confederations, keeping government and parliament national and local, cooperate whenever possible and desirable, but do not build irreversible unions, freezing economic and political formulas that may be dead a decade or two later. More particularly, cooperate economically and culturally but keep basic political decision-making national and local; and make the military increasingly defensive, even nonviolent and increasingly local. The path of big superpowers equipped with superweapons and deployment capabilities for vast regions, even for the world, leads only to disaster for themselves and others after some deceptive spells of glory. History has much to teach us in that regard.

On the other hand, cooperative, confederal regions hold much promise, like the Nordic Council, the European Community, ASEAN. Europe is one obvious example, and there are excellent institutions to build on: the UN Economic Commission for Europe, the Conference for Security and Cooperation in Europe, the Council of Europe for economic, security and cultural matters respectively, all potentially pan-European. A political forum on top of this should not be problematic, granting representation for the many European minorities. The basic point is to promote equitable cooperation and to prevent the formation of superpowers.

One foundation for national, regional and world society is the local society and more particularly the municipality, found all over the world; maybe as many as one million of them. Let each one have two, three or four sister municipalities scattered around the world, and not only for ceremony but for all kinds of cooperation. Let schools, companies, professional groups, age, gender and minority groups cooperate across the borders, to spin a tight web of positive relations all over the globe.

In this setting development assistance can be from people to people, and always on a reciprocal basis; always giving poor countries a chance to help shape the rich, not only vice versa. Neither the cultural imperialism of missionary activity, in spite of all the good deeds, nor the economic penetration of the latter-day variety, 'official development assistance', belong in a world of equity and harmony. They are both left-overs from an epoch hopefully coming to an end with the West in general and Europe in particular as a self-appointed guardian and policeman for the whole world.

Finally, the problem of security in this evolving global community. A world government with strong military forces is not the solution; in their self-righteousness they may become extremely dangerous like the police in a police state, as with the US-led coalition in the Gulf war. Rather, set the global structure right and liberate certain peoples from the obsessive idea of being chosen for missions above others, and we would have eliminated at least a good percentage of the causes of conflict and violence. Above that have the youth of the world join in UN peacekeeping forces, with hand weapons for self-defence only; and as UN volunteers for development and environment service. And below that prepare the municipalities, the districts, the nations for self-defence with ever more defensive weapons, increasing the nonmilitary capacity for defence, scaling down to zero the offensive capability. Unrealistic? Problematic? Certainly. We have to make our experiments and learn from them. But considerably more realistic than the present balance of terror and world police formulas, enacted by a handful of countries possessing the means of major state terror.

Jacqueline M. McGlade

The Seas and Shoreline as Part of the European Biosphere

The casual observer of the seashore can always find children caught up in the excitement of investigating rock pools. Lifting up seaweed, finding crabs, fishes and shrimps, watching barnacles and anemones sweep the water with their 'arms', whilst periwinkles slowly bustle along the rocks. And from the inundation of the sea and spray comes the appearance of order as brown seaweeds give way to green sea lettuce.

But as a marine biologist paid to interpret this order, to me the patterns seem to disappear in a nadir of unrelated facts. Why does the abundance of one fish species apparently fluctuate so dramatically, whilst others continue at such a constant level? Why do some fish species form schools when others are solitary? Why do some animals reproduce in areas where their young became rapidly dispersed in the seas around them? And why do some animals feed voraciously on their own young?

The naturalist Charles Darwin recognized the complexity of the living world when he wrote in the concluding paragraph to his famous text *The Origin of Species*, 'These elaborately constructed forms, so different from each other, and dependent on each other in so complex a manner, have all been produced by laws acting around us.' The problem is that because so little of the sea around us is open to view, we end up having to use proxies to gain an understanding of its complexity. One example comes from the birds that inhabit our shores.

Every year millions of birds flock southwards over the sandy wastes of Norfolk and the eastern shores of the British Isles, to shelter from the winters of northern Europe. These transient members of the maritime ecosystem are not only a graceful addition to the shoreline, but also a barometer of the health of the local maresphere. On sandy beaches and mud-flats one can see oystercatchers, ringed and Kentish plovers, knots, dunlins, sandpipers and sanderlings, along rocky beaches turnstones and redshanks, and over marshes and inland fields lapwings, golden plovers, curlews, whimbrels, dotterels, snipes and stints. On far-flung islands and rocky cliffs are the homes of puffins, auks, terns, fulmars and gulls. All vying for space and food, their absence reveals the fragile balance between wasteland and valuable habitat.

These birds act as roving predators feeding on fish and invertebrates. Scientists estimate that seabirds can remove up to 30 per cent of some fish resources. So when in addition humans remove large quantities by commercial fishing, the outcome to both birds and fish can be devastating. In 1989, two scientists from the Royal Society for the Protection of Birds reported in the magazine *New Scientist* (22 July) that thousands of seabirds had failed to rear their young on the Shetland Islands north of the Scottish mainland. The evidence in 1990 was even worse. Virtually no chicks had survived, and in the case of the arctic tern it was thought that there were no fledglings at all. In 1980 there had been 32,000 pairs of terns; today only about 8,000 remain. Given the fact that the first bad breeding season occurred six years ago and that arctic terns only reproduce after they are four years old, it is unlikely that the population, now reduced after three years of poor breeding, will be able to withstand such a drastic decline in the numbers of sexually mature individuals. But what was the cause of the demise?

Starvation. A large part of a seabird's diet is sandeel, a small pelagic fish commonly portrayed in the beaks of puffins. Chicks in particular seem to rely on these fish, although it is noticeable that the puffins have now apparently changed part of their diet to rocklings, thereby saving themselves from the brink of repro-ductive failure. But other species have not been so adaptable, and the impact on them has been devastating. Arctic skuas have not reared any young on the mainland of Shetland, and kitti-wakes throughout the area have failed to produce any young for the sixth successive year.

The ornithologists blame the fishing industry for extracting too many fish from the area, and it would seem that there has been a noticeable decline in the landings of sandeel. However, without incontravertible evidence of overfishing, the UK government will not ban fishing for sandeels. In fact the burden of proof lies outside the capabilities of the models that are used, because they do not explicitly deal with fluctuations and uncertainties in the recruitment of young fishes that have been produced in different years. In the case of the sandeel, scientists re-estimated the recruitment of young sandeels from the 1989 year class downwards from 21 billion to 1 billion. If real, then the effects of this decline on the bird communities will be devastating, as well as economically depressing for the Scottish fishing industry. But to understand how these local losses are likely to affect the whole system, we have to look back over time.

Eighteen thousand years ago the northeast Atlantic was a very different place to be. For one thing it was much colder, and because the polar ice cap extended over much of the North Sea, there was a much smaller expanse of open sea. Any signs of the luxuriant vegetation and tropical fauna that had existed half a million years before had long since gone. Since then, recolonization of northern Europe's seashore has come mostly from the mid-Atlantic, helped by incursions of water from the Gulf Stream.

Nowadays, scientists recognize three biogeographical regions which overlap in the seas around Europe: the Arctic, the Boreal and the Mediterranean-Atlantic. The Boreal region is centered on the North Sea, and includes the Baltic Sea and the area up along Norway and out across to Iceland. The western part of the English Channel and up to the Orkney Islands falls into the Lusitanian province of the Mediterranean-Atlantic region. The provincial boundaries for plankton (organisms that live in the top few centimetres of the sea) are somewhat different with Mediterranean waters extending northwards as far as Orkney. Within this complex web of boundaries we can find many species at the limit of their ranges, including sea cucumbers, anemones, starfish, seaweed, wolf fish, brittle stars and hydroids.

In recent years, satellite pictures have enhanced our knowledge of biogeography by allowing the movement of water masses to be continuously tracked. We can also observe the presence of other large-scale phenomena such as shelf-sea fronts. These are not unlike those of the weather system, occurring as a result of temperature differences of up to 1°C per metre arising from differential mixing within water masses. The most surprising observation is how constant the location of shelf-fronts is from year to year, and that once formed they can remain virtually static throughout the season. The waters in frontal areas have a high nutrient loading, because of mixing. Phytoplankton production is therefore enhanced and this in turn provides a rich source of food for fish and then birds. Unfortunately, the sandeel decline occurred in a frontal area, where the waters are exploited by a range of other Boreal species such as saithe, which are often less accessible to the bird community. Regeneration of the sandeel population may not occur, because it would involve not only building up a large enough spawning population, but also the displacement of other species.

For nearly 40 years, phytoplankton and zooplankton have been monitored in the North Sea. The results show that the biomass of both declined from the 1950s to 1980, but that since then, the trend has reversed. Scientists attribute the change to long-term alterations in climatic factors and possibly the influx of extra nutrients from activities on land. Unfortunately these forms of change are rather subtle, and often go unnoticed with the result that when dramatic alterations occur in the ecosystem we are all surprised. For example, in May 1988 a particularly devastating toxic bloom of *Chrysochromulina polyepis* dominated the Skagerrak, killing nearly all marine life to a depth of 15 metres, including commercial fish species valued at approximately £150 million.

At least four different types of dinoflagellate poison are known to occur around our coasts; these are Paralytic Shellfish

Poison (PSP), Diarrhetic Shellfish Poison (DSP), Venerupin Shellfish Poison (VSP) and Ichthyotoxic Poison. Algae can also form massive blooms that inhibit degradatory processes, because of the bacteriocidal acrylic acid that they contain. Deposition of these blooms on the sea-floor can also prevent recirculation, leading to a loss of oxygen and subsequent loss of life. The actual cause of these blooms is not really known. Many bloom-forming organisms deposit resting cysts or protected seeds in the sediments below the seas, which can act as a potential source of future outbreaks. However, scientists from Norway concluded that part of the problem in 1988 resulted from industrial and agricultural discharges.

The dangers of ecological change are always present, but most European governments are not prepared to face up to their implications. Take, for example, the fact that five million tonnes of sewage sludge and industrial waste, and 50,000 different chemicals, are dumped into the North Sea every year. It is not surprising that the analogy of an open sewer is used repeatedly. But the level of monitoring of these inputs is inadequate to give us sufficient information about the likely impacts on the ecosystem. Yes, the general awareness of the problem has increased, and yes, many European governments did sign and ratify an agreement to decrease inputs of pollutants. But no, we do not have an understanding of where those inputs go, nor even a comprehensive range of biological material upon which to monitor the progress of clean-up programmes. Neither do we have a complete model of the North Sea that encapsulates the three-dimensional flows of water masses, let alone an understanding of what a few points stranded in space and time might actually mean. But one thing we do know is that advances in the analysis of nonlinear systems have shown ecosystems to be moulded by the dynamics of the 'accidents' contained within them. Our research efforts should therefore be redirected towards gaining a deeper understanding of the processes governing ecosystem evolution and functioning, rather than simply keeping active by accumulating more data.

The problem is that many of our government policies do not voice a common theme. For example, in 1989 the United

Nations called for a worldwide ban on drift nets, and Italy put forward a similar proposal at the Conference on Security and Cooperation in Europe for fisheries in the Mediterranean. However, the proposal was rejected by Britain, because it was argued that the ban might one day be extended to the North Sea and Atlantic, where it would affect future British designs on fishing (British vessels do not currently use drift nets, but the French fleets have increased their drift-net vessels from three to 35 to try and revive the tuna fishery). Given the overwhelming evidence of deaths of marine mammals caused by these nets, the stand taken by Britain seems to be absolutely contradictory to its supposed environmental policy to 'follow through the British initiatives at the third North Sea Conference on protecting porpoises and dolphins and cooperate on the site and species protection with other North Sea states.'

Similar discrepancies occur in setting pollution standards. A wide range of human activities are known to be potentially harmful to marine ecosystems, including fishing, dredging, dumping or pipeline input of contaminants, shipping, and oil extraction. The majority of studies to determine the biological effects of contaminants have been undertaken in coastal areas, but unfortunately, the results from these field investigations have often been ambiguous, with the result that many governments tend to ignore claims that increased nutrient loading or pollution is having any identifiable effect on the ecosystem.

What governments forget is that ecosystems can change in different ways. Sometimes the alterations occur as part of a gentle progression, at other times disaster seems the only description possible. What constitutes a disaster is hard to define because ecosystems appear to have their own independent Richter scales which radically affect the timing of recovery. For example, on a short timescale there are episodic events such as the distemper virus outbreak in seals, which reduced the population in 1988 to very low numbers, but from which recovery could take place over one or two generations. On a longer timescale we see succession, and sometimes the creation of new ecological systems, such as colonization of the spoil heaps from mining. To set standards means that we have to have an understanding about the processes that have been damaged.

Environmental quality objectives have been set for estuaries all around the North Sea, including i) protection of all existing uses of estuaries such as disposal of effluents, commercial fishing, nature conservation, water sports, tourism, navigation, extraction of material for agricultural and industrial use; ii) the maintenance of benthic communities to sustain fisheries; and iii) passage for migratory fish. There are 14 determinants of standards relating to the main body of water in the estuary, including heavy metals, temperature and dissolved oxygen.

The scientific support for this list should be a source of concern to us all. A large number of studies on toxicity of contaminants on aquatic organisms have been carried out, but few relate to marine organisms. They include widespread use of the mussel in the international Mussel Watch programme, and one or two fish and shellfish species including cod and clams. From these and other freshwater studies, our environmental quality standards have been set.

Worse still is that most of the toxicity studies in the past have only looked at the effect of single contaminants, and only recently have investigators begun to examine the more likely situation in which organisms are exposed to combinations of toxicants. Although no general rules appear to describe the uptake of toxicants in the presence of other toxicants, it can be said that accumulation of combinations can be influenced by i) inhibition of detoxifying enzymes which can alter the uptake or loss of xenobiotics; ii) action upon biological surfaces, thereby affecting the permeability of membranes to other toxicants present; iii) physiological effects, such as increasing the flow of blood through the gills of fishes, thereby increasing the uptake of toxicants; and iv) the formation of complexes. In most cases reported it has been observed that for mixtures of the commonly occurring constituents of sewage and industrial wastes (viz. ammonia, phenol, cyanide, copper, zinc, cadmium, nickel, chromium, mercury, and other metals and substances), the lethal toxicity may be additive in the short term, and markedly more additive in the longer term, but generally within a two-fold limit.

In a scientific status paper prepared for the 1984 North Sea Conference it was concluded that because the North Sea had a high exchange of water with the north Atlantic no substantial build-up of pollutants would occur, compared to other areas such as the Baltic and Mediterranean. The sources of pollution were mostly given as rivers, the Rhine-Meuse constituting about 50 per cent of the total pollution input, but overall coastal discharges were considered less important, even though they could be locally very damaging. As to the possible causal links between pollution and fish abnormalities, scientists at the meetings agreed that it was speculative to link the two together from the results on hand. Four years later this rather non-committal response to pollution was abruptly changed by the outbreak of exceptional algal blooms off Norway and in the Baltic, and the viral epidemic in seals and dolphins.

Our appreciation of the sea and coastline has been shaped over the millenia, and with it has come the idea of a community made up of interconnecting parts. In fact it was from the work of the marine biologist Möbius on oyster beds in the North Sea that we now make the distinction between a community and a collection of independent organisms sharing the same physical space. Möbius's ideas spread to botany, and then later into much of ecology.

One cannot help but see, then, the connection between this scientific work on community structure and the great social works of Patrick Geddes, the marine biologist from Aberdeen, who in 1886 bought a slum and converted it into the first self-governing hostel in Britain. But such a philanthropic view does not always characterize the activities of the marine industries. In fact ask anyone who makes a living from the sea about their feelings towards it, and one quickly gains a picture of a community waged in battle between government departments and the natural variability in productivity of the seas. This situation is exacerbated because these communities are often cut off from mainstream affairs, with a way of life not easily shared or understood by most of Europe.

The problem that then arises is an intellectual one. The major influences of the twentieth century have given us many theories about natural resource scarcity, with the result that conservation is now irrevocably joined to resource management. Inside this framework, the dynamics of change, including the way in which natural populations renew themselves, have been subsumed by a crude economic shaping which sets long-term investment virtually equivalent to short-term financial gain. Rewards can be prescribed in such a system of maximizing the yield of a resource, or developing a total rent for an industry. Intervention, by default, is thus a necessary role for any government committed to conservation of renewable resources.

In most of today's institutions there is the belief that the effects of intervention can be predicted. This supposition arises because the current models allow managers to simulate and in a crude way anticipate the future. Implicit then is the idea that the models can successfully imitate not only the observed changes in the system, but also the processes that will direct its forward evolution. This supposes that the elements within a system will not change their behaviour, i.e. future states are already contained and defined in the present system.

But this is unrealistic. First the inner dimensions of such a model would have to contain so much working details that in practice it could not be developed, and second the outer dimensions could not correspond with the fact that complex living systems are open and hence exchange energy and matter across their boundaries. Unfortunately, science has led us into a situation in which we are trapped by our own knowledge. We might think that we know what a living system is doing, but rarely do we understand why or even how it is doing it.

Simple inexactness does not fully describe this problem, for the uncertainty is not merely the spread of data around some average condition that we know with confidence, but rather the result of systemic errors. So that even in a quantitive science like physics, achieving certainty relies largely on managing the different sorts of uncertainty affecting many operations.

When science is used to provide input for the policy process, as in fisheries and marine pollution control, the problems of managing uncertainty are more severe. First, the original data are rarely as controlled as in a laboratory. Well-structured theories, common in many branches of science, are conspicuous by their absence. Furthermore, the research is interdisciplinary, involving fields of varying states of maturity and with very different practices in their theoretical experiments and social dimension. Scientists must use inputs from fields which they are unfamiliar with, so that they find it difficult to make sensitive judgements. The result is a dilution of quality control of the research process and a weaker quality assurance of results.

The situation is compounded by the fact that scientists rarely receive training in quality assessment; they therefore develop a healthy prudence about passing a judgement on the results of others. Unfortunately, in an interdisciplinary policy-related area of research, such tact and reticence can be very counterproductive because criticism (the lifeblood of science) does not occur in sufficient strength. We therefore need new ways to evaluate scientific work to provide clear, explicit and public guidelines for analysis and communication.

The problems of uncertainty in policy-related research are increased by their public dimension. Science is judged by the public, including bureaucrats, on its performance in such sensitive areas as hazardous wastes, radioactive fallout, food additives and genetic engineering. All these involve much uncertainty, as well as inescapable social and ethical aspects. Simplicity and precision in predictions or even in safe limits are not feasible, yet policy-makers tend to expect straightforward information as input to their own decision-making process.

In such circumstances, the maintenance of confidence among policy-makers and the general public becomes increasingly strained, with the scientist often caught in the middle. The scientific adviser knows that a prediction such as a one in a million chance of a serious accident or health incident should be hedged with statements of many sorts of uncertainty. If these are expressed in prose, the statement becomes tedious and incomprehensible to the lay user, but if they are omitted or even given in some simple statistical representation, then the same adviser can be accused of conveying a certainty unwarranted by the facts. Predictions of danger will appear alarmist if nothing happens in the short term, whilst reassurance can be condemned if it retrospectively turns out to be wrong. But if a scientist prudently declines to provide definitive advice when asked, then science is regarded as obstructionist and not performing its public functions.

Obviously all uncertainty cannot be removed, but it must be clarified. Institutions and managers should explore the long- and short-term scenarios of responses by the marine ecosystem to different management policies and strategies. This replacement of a single prediction sinecure by a vision of probable future states is not only more realistic when dealing with living systems, but also a necessary safeguard in our highly connected and integrated global system. Institutional perspectives should not simply be a reflection of their ability to implement rules and practices.

But it has to be acknowledged that the sciences of clean-up and survival are less well matured cognitively than those of the laboratory. They have a different social and intellectual style, and because the results are not restricted to an elite group but relate directly to people's worries as human beings, it is unlikely that these sciences will ever be dominated by dogmatic consensus. The processes controlling the regulation and bureaucracy of the environment must therefore be given over to an extended peer community of concerned individuals. Popularizing issues, such as the loss of resources or increasing contaminant levels around our coasts, will allow individuals to enter into the debate more easily. If local sustainability of our marine environment is to have any real meaning, governments must open up the arena in which they are willing to obtain their advice, and change their intellectualized icon to a gestalt in which monetary values are allocated to the regenerative processes that keep our oceans functioning.

Ecoglasnost

The Rise of the Ecology Movement in Bulgaria

On 8 March 1988 a Public Committee for the Ecological Protection of the city of Russe was founded in Sofia. With the establishment of this committee more than 400 representatives of the Bulgarian intelligentsia aimed at focusing public attention on the disastrous ecological situation in Russe, and of helping, as far as they could, those who were suffering the consequences of the pollution.

Since the early eighties, in the sky above the city a cloud began to emerge with increasing frequency, carrying chlorine and other health-endangering chemical compounds. These gasses emanated from the chemical plants near Giurgevo in Romania. While the situation was worsening, the anxious public received from the authorities in charge the vague explanation that this problem was international and thus very complicated, but that they were doing everything possible for its favourable settlement. But time passed with no visible results. Losing all hope, some of the citizens began to leave the city for other parts of the country, irrespective of the difficulties created by the local authorities.

In the autumn of 1987 and during the winter of the following year, demonstrations began to break out in Russe, organized by the desperate citizens of this city. As public protest demonstrations are something quite uncommon even for contemporary

Bulgarian conditions, the very fact that these were taking place in Russe indicated that the tragedy there was reaching its culmination.

It was in these circumstances that the Committee for the Protection of Russe was founded, its purpose being to help its countrymen. However, its establishment was followed by an immediate and sharp reaction from the highest government levels and on the part of the security forces.

Strong pressure was exerted especially upon the leading members with the aim of forcing them to withdraw immediately from the Committee. Although this did not give the expected results, the lack of organizational and political experience reduced the Committee's activity to a minimum of defending its right to existence.

Nevertheless, even by the very fact of its establishment, the Committee managed to exercise enough influence on the highest government levels, so that within a few months the latter reached an agreement with the Romanian side on the cessation of the gas pollution.

The aroused public activity could no longer be detained. People began to realize that the problem of Russe, although very severe, was not the only one of its kind, and that the economic development of the country was very often carried out at the expense of irreversibly damaging or even destroying the environment which is vital for normal human existence.

On the other hand the problem of Russe revealed the fact that the executive bodies established from above for the protection of the environment, very often placed their parochial interests above those of society. In this respect their actions are just as detrimental to the environment as the actions of those who pollute and destroy it through their industrial activities.

This conception and the experience gained by the Committee for the Protection of Russe led to the founding by a few of its members, in the winter of 1989, of a 'coordinating group' for the Public Movement of Ecological Glasnost. On 11 April the same year, the Independent Society for the Ecological Protection of the Population, known as Ecoglasnost, was founded in Sofia. The founding members signed a constituent protocol and accepted an organization chart and a policy statement of the Society.

One of the foremost tasks of Ecoglasnost is to collect, analyse, and spread information on the ecological situation in Bulgaria as a whole, and on any individual ecologically harmful event, as well as on the level, nature and sources of the pollution of water, food, soil, air and the causes for it.

It goes without saying that for this purpose Ecoglasnost only resorts to and makes full use of all legal means.

Ecoglasnost expresses concern for various ecological problems, cautions and alerts, and works for the advancement of ecological culture not only of the people but also of those who rule.

Within the limits of its capacities Ecoglasnost supports the people in their struggle for the betterment of the ecological environment. The Society has offered its support to the inhabitants of the Studentska municipality in their demands to abolish the scientific-industrial pharmaceutical complex from the territory of their municipality. This enterprise carries out organic synthesis and releases into the atmosphere and the sewerage system substances which endanger the health of the inhabitants of this district.

Ecoglasnost directs inquiries to the responsible government bodies regarding the existing pollution sources about which the public has little or no information at all: regarding the problems with the deposits of radioactive waste on the territory of Bulgaria, about the radiation background of the country, the characteristics of imported phosphorites, etc.

The Society focuses the attention of the people and the government on the possible environmentally unfavourable effects caused by the realization of various industrial projects such as the hydrocomplexes of Rila and Mesta. These projects foresee the transfer of the Rila water resources into the Upper Thracian lowland, thus bringing the level of the water to a height of 1200 metres. There is a well-grounded argument that this would lead to a disastrous distortion of the ecological balance of the Rila mountain region.

Ecoglasnost has initiated the signing of a petition, which

demands an immediate termination of all work connected with the realization of these projects, their submission for public discussion and evaluation by an uncommitted panel of experts.

This is the reason why the demands for an unlimited ecological glasnost are an underlying factor in the programme of the Society, which enables it to join the struggle for the radical restructuring and democratization of the social order in Bulgaria. That is why the Society supports every individual or organization which fights with legal means for further expansion and deepening of the general process of democratization.

Many people sympathize with Ecoglasnost, but deeply rooted fears, hard to overcome, stand in the way of converting Ecoglasnost into a widespread social movement.

On the other hand government officials from all levels, as well as the representatives of their subordinate 'social organizations', do not conceal their negative attitude towards Ecoglasnost, and never miss the opportunity to impose their standpoint that the Society is illegal and therefore nonexistent.

But in accordance with the actual legislation in Bulgaria, every non-profit organization becomes legal through the very fact of its foundation, under the condition that it does not promote violence or propagate racist, fascist or any other form of anti-democratic ideology. In order that Ecoglasnost should be able to perform its activities with greater efficiency, its members have decided that the Society should be registered as a legal entity, which grants it the right to acquire property. Therefore both the Public Committee for the Ecological Protection of Russe and Ecoglasnost have prepared all necessary documents and handed in their applications to be registered.

Government officials and their subordinate 'social organizations' keep identifying the issue regarding the registration of a legal entity with the one regarding the legitimacy of the independent public societies. In this case no mention could be made of any lack of basic juridical knowledge. This peculiar display of incompetence only proves that the authorities have no legal grounds to hinder the activity of the ecological movements.

By confusing the problems, the authorities are trying to convince the public about something they themselves do not believe in, i.e. that regardless of everything they have certain legal grounds for their negative attitude towards the independent public societies, and in particular towards Ecoglasnost.

From all that has been said, it becomes obvious that the motives for such an attitude are strictly political, not juridical.

Nevertheless, the fairly brief and not very rich history of the ecological movement in Bulgaria enables us to draw some general conclusions:

1. More and more people are beginning to realize that an impending ecological catastrophe can be avoided only through the active efforts of all citizens, and that it is their right and responsibility to fight for its prevention.
2. For this purpose the public can and must establish independent ecological organizations and movements.
3. The principles of democratization and pluralism fully comply with the markedly social character of the ecological movement, and they determine its overall structure.
4. The more the authorities hamper this process, the more the ecological movement will depart from its specific activity and immediate aims, and thus become more and more political.
5. Such a development would be harmful to the ecological movement, although it could hardly lead to its dilution: there could be certain unpredictable consequences for the government structures, because a hidden danger exists that the movement may transform from an 'opponent partner' into an 'unconstructive opponent' without its social influence diminishing.

J. Vavrousek and others

Ecological Policy in Czechoslovakia

1. Formulation of the Problem

The quality of the environment has sharply deteriorated on practically the whole territory of our state over the past decades owing to human activity. In some areas the situation is critical. Besides the generally known problems related to the pollution of the air, surface and ground waters (including drinking water sources) there is a gradual degradation of soil, the reduction of the vitality of forests and their destruction, and the extinction of a great number of plant and animal species. Foreign and hazardous substances are accumulating in the environment. The water regime of landscape ecosystems is being disturbed and their ability to cope with negative changes in living conditions is declining. Any further continuation of the present trend would therefore cause a further sharp aggravation of existing ecological problems.

The immediate cause of the continuing destruction of the environment in Czechoslovakia is the excessive and inconsiderate extraction of natural resources, extensive emission of wastes, and arbitrary interference in the landscape — failure to observe ecological and aesthetic laws. Deeper causes include especially the inefficient economy which does not sufficiently respect the natural conditions of the Earth, consumes excessive amounts of raw materials and energy, uses ecologically unsuitable technologies and manufactures products with poor ecological parameters. The directive management of the national economy directly led to the wastage of natural resources and to the destruction of the environment. A negative role was also played by the classification of data on the state of the environment, its causes and consequences. The institutional provision of environmental control was totally inadequate. Resources allocated to environmental care in no way corresponded to the scale and significance of the problems, and were moreover used almost exclusively for subsequent remedial measures which only limited some of the consequences of ecologically unfavourable technologies, and did not prevent the damage. The sad state of the environment in our country is the heritage of the totalitarian political system where legislative, executive and judicial power was concentrated in the hands of a narrow ruling group at the top of the hierarchy of the Communist party which in fact excluded all corrective feedback. The attitude of people to nature and to the environment was loaded with arrogance, recklessness, indolence and exploitation.

Contributing significantly to the destruction of the environment (namely of air) in the Czech and Slovak Federative Republic was also transboundary pollution from the territories of other states which mainly affects the northern areas of Bohemia and Moravia, the Orava area and the High Tatras.

The destruction of the environment is one of the causes of the relative and absolute deterioration of the state of health of the population and the stagnation or shortening of the mean life expectancy — as compared with advanced countries we are thus being deprived of five to seven years of life. This state of affairs has its impact on the disruption of the social structure of the affected areas and the growing estrangement of the individual and of society which is unable to provide the basic conditions of human existence. In some places, namely in the Northern Bohemian region, in Prague, the Ostrava-Karviná basin, in Bratislava, in Ziar nad Hronom and Ruzomberok there is tension bordering on an explosion. The urgency of the demand for a substantial improvement in the quality of the environment in our country is also demonstrated by the results of public opinion polls where respondents rank this problem among the most pressing. Economic damage and losses caused by the depleted environment are constantly increasing and now equal at least 7 per cent of the total volume of the national product. The Czech and Slovak Federative Republic significantly contributes to the pollution of the environment in other countries (the 'export' of hazardous waste products is higher than their 'import') and contributes to global climatic changes which in turn has a negative effect on the international position of the state. The further deterioration of this position will result from the country's probable failure to fulfil the internationally adopted commitment to reduce by 1993 the emissions of SO_2 by 30 per cent as compared with 1980. The Council of Europe has already agreed to reduce the emissions of this hazardous substance by 50 to 70 per cent.

Problems linked with the deterioration of the quality of the environment require systematic and effective solution oriented to the gradual and speedy 'ecological optimization' of processes taking place in society and to a strategy of sustainable development. The experience of a number of advanced countries, such as the USA, the Federal Republic of Germany, Japan and Holland, show that ecological motivation may also become a significant stimulus for further economic growth based on a qualitatively higher level of production and consumption.

State environmental policy may become the means of coordinating the effort for improving the quality of the environment in Czechoslovakia. Practically all advanced countries have not only formulated ecological (environmental) policies but are also implementing them with great effort and remarkable speed. A joint ecological policy is also being created by supranational groupings, such as the European Community which is now implementing its fourth action programme (since 1972). Our lag behind the advanced countries in this area is thus 15 to 20 years.

State ecological policy proceeds from an analysis of the state of the environment in our country, the evaluation of the health, social, ethical, economic and political consequences of changes in the quality of the environment and the identification of internal and external (international) factors affecting the quality of the environment, this in continuity with the evaluation of actual and potential risks. It formulates the goals which Czecho-slovak society wants to attain and suggests the strategy for such attainment.

The scale and depth of problems related to the destruction of the environment and the considerable inertia of the economy requires that effort, financial and other resources be concen-trated, possibly even at the cost of delaying the growth of material consumption, so as to attain a substantial improvement in the quality of the environment within this decade. We have a moral obligation to limit the negative impact of the disrupted environment on people's health — especially on the health of children — to the shortest possible period. The basic precondi-tion for this is to introduce a substantial change in the approach to the solution of the given problem.

The state should assume overall responsibility for the quality of the environment on its territory. This does not mean direct responsibility for eliminating the individual sources of environ-mental destruction, which was what the state attempted, albeit hesitatingly and unsystematically, within the directive system of management. This responsibility must be indivisibly linked with production, consumption and other activities which affect envi-ronmental quality. Organizations and individuals must be aware of this responsibility because only thus can they be expected to make the desirable change in their behaviour. The state must, however, create such conceptual, legislative, economic, institu-tional, educational, information, resource and other conditions which will stimulate organizations and individual citizens to save energy and raw materials, to take care of the environment, to remove 'old' sources of pollution, and to punish those who waste natural resources and pollute the environment. Environmental control must be based on the autonomous activity of towns, communities and districts (or areas) proceeding from a detailed knowledge of local conditions. It is the role of the state and of its institutions to make ample room for the initiative and entrepreneurial activity of all citizens while at the same time regulating activities taking place in society.

State environmental policy can only be effective when it becomes an integral component of the overall concept of the development of Czechoslovakia and part of European and world policy oriented towards improving the quality of the environment on a regional and global scale. The ecological problems of Czechoslovakia cannot be resolved in isolation from the solution of all other substantial problems which our society faces and without active participation in the international effort for overcoming the threat of a global ecological crisis.

The formulation and gradual implementation of state ecological policy is not a one-off process. It must take place continuously on the basis of close cooperation between the two republics and with the participation of ecologically oriented voluntary organizations, political parties and movements, and primarily with the active support of the public.

2. Goals of Environmental Control

The goals of environmental control proceed from the right of citizens of this country to live in a healthy and good environment and from the general obligation to protect the environment.

The fundamental goal of state ecological policy is to restore the dynamic equilibrium between society and the environment and thereby to create preconditions for people's all-round physical and mental development and for maintaining the wealth of nature to the maximum possible extent. The attainment of this goal is the indispensable, albeit not sufficient, condition of the long-term oriented, qualitative, and permanently sustainable development of our country as well as being a contribution to the attainment of harmonious relations between human society and its environment on the European and global scale. The philosophy of permanently sustainable development was formulated by the World Commission on Environment and Development in its report 'Our Common Future', which was adopted by the 42nd UN General Assembly in 1987.

Following up on the basic goal are the following interdependent specific goals:

a) the protection of human wealth and well-being oriented
   towards protecting people from dangerous chemical, physical and biological factors in the environment, creation or
   preservation of an aesthetic and undisturbed environment;
b) conserving nature's wealth, especially the plant and animal
   genofund as the basic condition of ecological equilibrium in
   nature, the wealth of non-living nature, this both as a goal in
   itself and as a means for meeting the needs of present and
   future generations;
c) the prevention of cultural and economic values having an
   unfavourable impact on the environment;
d) the protection of life-giving systems of the planetary biosphere dependent on the sensitive balance of interactive
   physical, chemical and biological processes whose disturbance by human activity is manifested, e.g. in the destruction
   of the ozone layer or global warming. For the attainment of
   the above goals it is primarily necessary to:

• substantially improve the quality of the human food chain by
  providing safe drinking water and food with a high nutritive
  value not contaminated by harmful substances;
• to minimize the extraction of renewable and especially non-
  renewable natural resources by reducing not only the relative
  but also the absolute consumption of raw materials, including water, by better use of auxiliary and secondary raw
  materials, the recultivation of mining areas and systematic
  care of renewable resources;
• to limit the introduction of solid, liquid and gaseous harmful
  substances and waste energies into the environment by
  reducing the volume and hazardousness of produced pollution and by improved utilization (recycling), possibly at least
  by the harmless and selective depositing of wastes, by reducing emissions of waste heat, noise and vibrations, ionizing
  and non-ionizing radiation;
• to minimize the amount and hazardousness of foreign substances deliberately introduced into the environment in the

form of pesticides, manufactured fertilizers, salting materials, etc., and to consistently monitor the introduction of foreign or newly developed organisms into the environment;

- to restore and maintain the ecological stability and aesthetic value of the landscape, primarily by ecological husbandry, the introduction of alternative methods of husbandry, the restoration of healthy forests, the reconstruction and maintenance of systems of ecological stability and the elimination of drastic interference in the landscape, especially that which is related to technocratic investment projects;
- to improve conditions in cities and villages for the healthy and the physically disabled population by creating functional and aesthetically valuable settlements, this by the comprehensive regeneration of villages and towns, better architectural concepts of new construction, better maintenance, etc.;
- to provide a better protection of nature both in protected areas and in the economically intensively used landscape, this including the protection of livestock;
- a reduction in the volume and danger of the transboundary transport of harmful substances across the borders of our state, as well as the 'export' of such substances by air and water flows, and the 'import' of such substances from sources on the territory of other countries (based on negotiations);
- to provide effective aid to other countries (namely the developing countries) in environmental control, mainly oriented to education, counselling and information activities.

The said goals should be attained primarily in a decentralized manner, at the level of enterprises, villages, towns, districts and other autonomous and self-governing units, where perfect knowledge may be expected of concrete conditions; moreover, decentralized systems are more flexible and less vulnerable. The irreplaceable role of state institutions is limited to the creation of overall concepts and strategies of environmental control, the coordination of processes of implementation, and activities which relate to the whole and which exceed the possibilities of autonomous units. Federal and republican governments, ministries and other state authorities cannot replace responsible, involved and initiative approaches and actions of individual citizens, voluntary organizations, local bodies of self-government and the management of production and other enterprises and institutions.

3. Principles of Environmental Control

Environmental control proceeds from the following principles:

a) comprehensiveness — the endeavour for an overall improvement in environmental quality in the Czech and Slovak Federative Republic and on a global scale, not only as concerns improving the quality of the individual components of the environment which in practice often means shifting problems, e.g., separation of fly ash often leads to improvement of environmental quality but the incorrect storage of ash contaminates soil and ground water and often means secondary pollution of the air;

b) direct responsibility for environmental pollution, i.e., polluters bear direct responsibility for the pollution of the environment, they shall pay damages and are responsible for the reuse or harmless depositing of the waste products of their activity. Polluters are also obligated to provide information on the real or potential impact of their activities on the environment;

c) prevention — preventive measures are preferred wherever they are technically and economically feasible. Preventive activities oriented to the restriction of emissions at source are more effective and usually less costly than subsequent clearing or compensation measures. To attain this goal it will be necessary to apply the best practically available production and consumer technologies with minimal negative impacts on the environment;

d) minimization of negative impact — orientation to increasing quality of products and services allows the needs of users and consumers to be better met and minimizes negative impact on the environment.

The said principles will be projected into generally binding legal regulations and into the overall strategy of resolving existing and potential ecological problems.

4. Strategy of Environmental Control

The purposeful combination of two mutually complementary strategies should be used for the attainment of the set goals of environmental control.

A) **Subsequent and compensation measures** (the *ex-post* strategy) mainly oriented to the elimination or at least the attenuation of existing 'old' polluters by building waste water treatment plants, plants for the treatment of combustion and other waste gases, controlled waste heaps and waste disposal or recycling facilities, to the partial compensation or restriction of damage caused by the destruction of the environment by the elimination of 'wild-cat' dumps of hazardous wastes, the liming of forests and lakes, the organization of school camps in natural surroundings, etc.

The advantage of this strategy is the possibility of reducing relatively quickly part of the negative loading of the environment using tried technologies. Its disadvantage is the basic impossibility of removing all significant factors which disturb the environment, rapidly growing demands on financial and other resources reducing the overall efficiency of the economy and the high consumption of raw materials and energy for the production and operation of the required installations. This results in a vicious circle which deepens the imbalance between nature and society.

B) **Preventive measures** (the *ex-ante* strategy) aimed at attaining the ideal of relatively closed cycles of production and consumption with minimal negative impact on the environment.

The advantage of the said strategy is the preclusion of phenomena leading to the destruction of the environment and the efficient solution of ecological problems in the process of the innovation of products and technologies, the reconstruction, modernization and new capital construction, and of other processes taking place in society. Its disadvantage is unsatisfactory preparation owing to insufficient environmental education, unsystematic and badly managed research and development, insufficient production capacity and inadequate structure, and often the absence or unavailability of environment-friendly products and technologies.

The suggested ecological policy uses the advantages of both stated strategies while suppressing their disadvantages. In the first period, i.e., to the end of the millenium, this policy will mainly be oriented to the accelerated implementation of subsequent and compensation measures, primarily with regard to 'old' sources of environmental pollution where low-waste technologies cannot be expected to be introduced and which cannot be closed down. In the first phase, insofar as market mechanisms do not indicate the appropriateness of individual production technologies, the focus should be on the municipal area, i.e., by constructing municipal waste-water treatment installations, etc. In instances where the polluter cannot be identified, responsibility passes to state institutions (this mainly applies to certain old hazardous waste dumps).

The intensive preparation for the implementation of preventive measures (*ex-ante*) will take place in parallel with the above-stated measures and will include the implementation of tried or accepted innovations. This strategy should gradually prevail, by the turn of the millenium at the latest.

State environmental policy must purposefully orient all basic factors directly or indirectly affecting the quality of the environment, and therefore comprises:

a) the orientation of science and technology to a deeper recognition of relations between nature and society, the preparation and introduction of environment-friendly production and consumer technologies, and the development, production and marking of all environment-friendly products through

all phases of their service life;
b) changes in the structure and orientation of the Czechoslovak economy with emphasis on closing down or rapid limiting of the manufacture of highly power- and raw-material-demanding production processes and processes which inadmissably disturb the environment, the introduction of environment-friendly production and technology innovations, and the endorsement of technologies based on renewable power and raw-material resources;
c) ecological husbandry in the landscape oriented to the endorsement of the natural capacity to maintain the state of dynamic balance in changing conditions;
d) providing systematic information on the state of the environment, its consequences, causes and development;
e) broadening and deepening environmental education and the education of all social groups;
f) cooperation with voluntary environmental organizations and giving all-round support to their activity.

The first prerequisite of the implementation of state environmental policy is the introduction of such a set of generally valid legal regulations which will stimulate the rapid improvement of the quality of the environment and will determine the respective sanctions (including penalization). These legal norms shall include the compulsory evaluation of ecological parameters and ecological parameters of certain product categories so as to provide for the observance of valid regulations. Also in this area it will be necessary to restore the principles of the legal state which, as against the present state, will no longer operate bad laws, the existence of many exemptions and very often also the violation of valid laws. In the transitory period obsolete laws will speedily be amended to span the period of the drafting of new and missing laws while respecting legal regulations valid abroad, especially in the countries of the European Community. Environmental bodies will have to determine binding time schedules for the speediest removal of exemptions.

Another prerequisite for resolving existing ecological problems and for preventing the development of new ones will be the drafting of a system of institutional environmental control at the level of the federation, regions (or districts), towns and communities. It must incorporate a control system, e.g. integrated environmental inspection.

The support backbone of state environmental policy should be economic instruments based on the principles of market economy. Economic instruments limiting the exploitation of natural resources and punishing disturbance of the environment include: deposits, taxes and fees for the use of natural resources, fees and fines for the discharge of wastes into the environment, fines for prohibited negative interference in the landscape, ecological taxes or customs fees for products with unsuitable ecological parameters. The respective environmental payments will be projected into increased prices of energy, raw materials and products in production or use causing extensive disturbance of the environment. This will be done in order to stimulate consumers to reduce energy consumption. The assessment of the economic effect of existing and projected enterprises shall take into consideration not only ecological projects under existing regulations but also expected future costs.

Economic instruments endorsing activities and products aimed at improving environmental quality comprise allocations and subsidies, advantageous credits and loans, including credit cost payments and credit guarantees, tax and return reliefs, import and export permits and customs reliefs.

The transition period to the full functioning of the market economy will be a critical period. This will roughly be to the year 1993. In that period it will be necessary to use to a certain extent directive rule by state authorities at federal and republican levels. This will not only include the closing down of inefficient and environmentally harmful production units but also the state's participation in the implementation of economically more demanding measures which exceed the immediate real possibilities of concrete polluters and where it is not feasible to fully implement the principle of direct responsibility for pollution. Total costs of improving the quality of our environment cannot as yet be determined, but by analogy with the neighbouring states it may be estimated in tens of billions of crowns per annum, part of which will have to be paid in hard currency.

All measures aimed at improving the quality of the environment must be founded on broad international cooperation aimed at gaining knowledge of the development of the environment on a regional and global scale, seeking ways towards attaining permanently sustainable development.

Carlo Jordan

Greenway 1989-90, The Foundation of the East European Green Parties

Between the September 1989 annual meeting of Greenway held in East Berlin, and that held a year later in Riga — in still-soviet Latvia — the political landscape of Eastern Europe took on new colours. In particular Green, the colour of the movement for survival into the new millenium.

Greenway — the East European network of Hungarian, Czech and Polish environmentalists — was founded in Hungary in 1985. Through informal networking by way of the Greenway newsletter and annual conferences, the embryonic Green grass-roots movement in Eastern Europe succeeded in building up contacts that though informal were nonetheless very encouraging, against the marginalizing policy of the late-Stalinist regimes and their omnipresent secret services. Against the Stalinist practice of violating basic human and civil rights, such as freedom of association and information, and freedom to travel, the Greenway networks managed between 1985 and 1990 to establish connections in an East-West direction, from East Berlin to Samara (formerly Kybichev) in Russia and the Ukraine, and in a North-South direction between the Baltic and the Balkan countries of Romania, Bulgaria and Yugoslavia. An important part was played in this by our self-published and distributed samizdat, which could not even be sent in the post, but had to be smuggled across the frontiers.

Annual conferences were obstructed by travel bans, especially on East Germans and Romanians, and by banning of visitors into Poland and Hungary. And yet each year at least smaller conferences were organized, in churches or mountain refuges, even under the extreme regimes of East Germany and Czechoslovakia. In the more liberal countries of the 'socialist camp' such as Hungary and Poland, Greenway conferences were even held at universities.

But the East European secret services were omnipresent even here. Prosecutions, interrogations and imprisonment were quite 'normal' experience in many countries for participants in these Green conferences. After the world's ostensibly best secret service, the East German 'Stasi', was disbanded, at the central round table at which the GDR Greens actively participated, their very extensive documentation on the Berlin Greenway meeting of 1989 was published.

The First Green Parties in Poland and Lithuania

The following extract appeared in the Stasi's 'Information on the so-called Greenway workshop of 1 October 1989' (Berlin State Security, department 20):

> In connection with the appearance of known foreign participants, immigration bans were imposed on a total of 27 persons. These included the leading representative of the environmental organizations in the People's Republic of Poland, Zygmunt Fura, from whom guiding initiatives were anticipated.

Zygmunt Fura had already taken the 'guiding' initiative for the East European Green movement in December 1988, in Cracow, with the foundation of the first Green party in this part — the larger part — of Europe. Despite the present difficulties of the Polish Greens, Fura's service was to have given the signal for the foundation process in eastern Europe, and he will go down in history as its pioneer and initiator. The Poles were followed by the Lithuanians, who on 15 July 1989 called the second of east

Europe's Green parties into life.

At the Greenway conference in Berlin, organized by the Green-ecological network Arche in a Protestant church in Friedrichsfelde, the Stasi made clear their special interest in the founding initiative for a Green party in the GDR. They sought to obstruct this foundation with all means, such as slander and imprisonment.

> At the same time, informants in key positions in 'Arche' succeeded in coming to the fore and making their influence felt in the assembly, preventing the efforts of Jordan and Bogisch to publicize their conception of the foundation of a 'Green party' or 'Green list' during the meeting.

But even at this time the Stasi were no longer able to halt the initiative for a Green party in the GDR. The Polish signal was taken up even under this seemingly all-powerful late-Stalinist regime.

As a result of the years of work by the GDR grassroots movement and its conversion into a citizens' movement for a better environment uniquely broad in German history, travel freedom, free elections and the disarming of the Stasi and the Stalinist 'Socialist Unity Party', the Green Party of the GDR was founded in November 1989, at the Bekenntniskirche in Treptow (East Berlin). At the same time and place, and with the same aim in mind, the Grüne Liga (Green League) was created to organize projects, actions and campaigns.

Green Movement and Citizens' Movement

The collapse of the total power or at least claim to power of the Stalinist regime over all spheres of social and individual life, is not explicable simply in terms of the new policy of glasnost and perestroika introduced by Gorbachev after 1985. At the grassroots of our east European societies, in the early 1980s, new social movements sprang up for demilitarization, protection of the environment, liberation of women, and of cultural, sexual and regional minorities – but also for the affirmation of national identity against an enforced foreign domination, for national self-management and independence.

The new non-violent approach of these essentially Green movements in eastern Europe 'disarmed' the organs of re-presssion, the police and secret services of our uniquely militar-istically organized societies. Small groups achieved for their constituencies enlightenment about the real conditions of life and the rapidly accelerating destruction of the basis of existence. In the 1940s and 1950s, the national movements of the Baltic against the annexation of their countries by the Soviet Union in the wake of the Hitler-Stalin pact were brutally suppressed by the Stalinists. Any of the so-called 'enemies of class and people' who survived were banished to Siberia, from where only few re-turned. In East Germany, Poland, Czechoslovakia and Hungary, it was the same for the social movements up to the 1980s. Uprisings were repressed. Initiators and activists were expelled from normal professional life and many people emigrated to the West. These traumatic experiences, and the everyday suppres-sion by the powerful security apparatus, created a deep anxiety in people's consciousness and behaviour.

Only the new and gentle movements – against the militariza-tion of everyday life and an economy that, following Stalinist concepts, was oriented overwhelmingly to heavy industry and increasingly damaging the foundations of life – encouraged people across all strata of society to get involved with the small Green initiator groups, to voice their demands and claim a social identity.

The special role of the Green movement in eastern Europe, with its small grassroots groups and new kinds of actions such as human chains, peace marches, warning weeks, networking of different initiatives, supplied the model for the larger citizens' movements that followed.

In this way, many different initiatives mingled in the political transformation of eastern Europe – from originally small grass-roots initiatives there spontaneously grew broad citizens' movements — which as a new political force were united against the old one-party rule and thus compelled the first free elections.

In these citizens' movements, such as Solidarity in Poland after martial law, the Democratic Forum in Hungary, Civic Forum in Czechoslovakia or New Forum in the GDR, and the people's fronts in the Soviet republics, a popular will was formed against the total one-party rule in these countries.

At the same time as the loss of power by the Communist parties, however, a process of differentiation of this popular will set in. Already in this new situation, the broad anti-totalitarian citizens' movements displayed the outlines of the new party landscape in the parliamentary system that was coming to be. Those citizens' movements, including the Greens, that grew out of a grassroots democratic initiative, found that in the process of political structuring that was unfolding in the various east European countries, they did not necessarily enjoy a majority position.

Precursors of the citizens' movements such as Bärbel Bohley and Ingrid Koppe in East Germany based themselves on fluid tendencies which no longer chose to form themselves into parties. But the processes of formation that were actually going on show the autonomous dynamic and persistent integration force of party-forming structures. The citizens' movements themselves could only be imperfectly institutionalized, and with growing demands vanished into parliamentary work or themselves became parties.

The Green parties, with their structures open to the new movements, might still offer the best partners for the citizens' movements.

The New Green Parties

At the Latvian Greenway conference in autumn 1990, we could state that the east European process of founding Green parties was complete.

In January the Latvian Green Party followed the Estonian to complete the picture in the Baltic states. In Byelorussia, Yugoslavia, Czechoslovakia, Hungary, Bulgaria and Russia there are now also Green parties. The most recent foundation is the Ukrainian Greens, in September 1990. The final straggler, just as in the general European process for security and cooperation, is the last bastion of orthodox communism in eastern Europe, Albania. All Greenway attempts to make contact with Albania have until now remained unanswered.

In the Baltic states and Byelorussia, Slovakia, Slovenia and East Germany, Green deputies have been elected to the national parliaments. In Estonia the well-known Thomas Frey entered the government as environment minister. The decision to take part in government, a decision not unchallenged among the Greens, was expressed as follows by the Estonian Greenway speaker: 'In Eastern Europe in particular, the Greens must take responsibility and not leave governing to the bloody bureaucrats.' The Slovenian Greens were actually able to appoint three ministers, in a republic that is still within Yugoslavia. In the former East Germany, the Greens have Mathias Platzek as Brandenburg's environment minister.

In the most highly populated countries, Russia and the Ukraine, the Green way is still being pursued via the democratic citizens' movements. The situation in Poland is hard to assess, as not only have three competing Green parties emerged, but also, according to the Polish spokesperson, these are splintered into 140 different organizations. In the Czech lands, the Green party did not arise out of the longstanding environmental movement in Bohemia, but rather, according to the Czech Greenway spokepeople, from people unknown to the Green movement who founded it at the breakthrough time. Contrary to expectations, this party was unable to win seats in parliament, and will establish a connection to its proper roots — the environment movement — by way of a lengthy process of self-discovery.

Romania is a country in which because of the extreme Dracula-regime of Ceaucescu, the ecology party did not arise from any real movement. Besides, Romanian and Bulgarian Greens have still to battle with the restoration of the old powers in a transformed socialist form.

But despite all national difficulties, it became clear at the

Latvian Greenway conference that the Greens in Eastern Europe are the only comprehensive new political force, and are working together over the inflammatory nationalism of the East in the direction of a common and nonviolent course for protection of the conditions of life.

The Tasks Ahead

With the far-reaching peaceful revolutions in many countries of eastern Europe, the power of Stalinism has been broken. But Stalinism was not only an anti-democratic concept based on total power over the entire state and society. From this derived also the characteristic way in which this totalitarian power dealt with people, economy and environment. The result is that whole regions of eastern Europe and Russia to an extreme degree are today a kind of desert.

Stalin's madness led to such gigantic projects as the 'plan for transformation of nature'. The gigantic heavy industry, which absorbed almost the entire available labour of these societies, was not just designed to serve the military-industrial complex that grew ever more monstrously in the Cold War, but extended to a plan for diverting whole rivers from their course, as had been done in Siberia, Central Asia and Romania — even shifting mountains.

The Green movement in eastern Europe, and its political wing, the new national Green parties, have the historic task of demolishing the deadly structures erected over the past 40 or 70 years, and rebuilding them in harmony with nature. The Greens are the only political force that already put forward under the old regime their social-ecological critique of the life-threatening industrial structures.

Other political forces in eastern Europe, for example the reawakening Social-Democrats, all too often base themselves on the short-term interests of the mass of those employed in large-scale industry. But the general problem lies in the structures erected one-sidedly on heavy industry.

This is why the Greens in eastern Europe campaign for the phase of political foundation to be speedily followed by an economic foundation. Society's self-organizing potential, which has been oppressed for decades, must be freed again. Ecological reconstruction needs the promotion of small and medium-size enterprises, with energy- and resource-sparing production, in decentralized settlement and communications patterns, so as to foster those goods that are really required for the living world.

If this reconstruction is speedy, then it will also be possible to stem the outflow of population to western Europe. A new regional identity is therefore an important task for the Greens.

However, even this industrial reconstruction should proceed with caution. One of the subjects discussed at the Greenway conference in Latvia was how through international network contacts we can prevent the import of toxic wastes that are no longer acceptable in western Europe. But the impending ecological catastrophe will face the Greens with their greatest challenge.

What can be done with the areas of Ukraine and Byelorussia that have been poisoned by radiation from Chernobyl? Where can the people go? For ecological catastrophe is also the fundamental cause of social catastrophe, such as the mass unemployment in the former centres of heavy industry and industrialized agriculture.In some areas, a Green turn has been introduced already, for example stopping the Stalinists' European plan for Danube navigation and canalization. This was achieved by the Hungarian and Slovak environmental activists and the Duna Kor initiative against the power plant. The Romanian Greens also declared at the Greenway conference that their concern was to re-naturalize the greatest river delta in Europe, that of the Danube, and put an end to Ceaucescu's concrete canal. This would go a long way towards saving the Black Sea.

But all this also needs international aid — which is also a task of the Greens, the movement of our century for survival into the new millenium.

How far we in eastern Europe have advanced will be seen at the Greenway conference in Hungary in autumn 1991!

Greenway office:
Gorkeho 6
81101 Bratislava
Czechoslovakia

Greenway newsletter:
Mara Silina
Ozoleiema str. 18-36
226058 Riga, Latvia

Zsuzsa Beres

Hungary in Transition: The Ecological Issue

Today, Hungary is experiencing a period of transition, both economic and political. The old system has collapsed, but as yet there seems to be no clear-cut vision for the future apart from the aim to establish a free-market economy and to keep up, at all costs, the servicing of Hungary's massive, 20 billion dollar foreign debt.

Whilst the government is concentrating on complying with the demands of the IMF and the World Bank, not enough has been done to curtail a free-for-all situation in privatization, and almost nothing to prevent the inflow of environmentally destructive capital and technologies. Some of the country's national assets are also at risk. Western investors have already set eyes on historical buildings and prime real estate, and, for instance, the formerly Communist party-owned provincial daily newspapers have been snapped up by Springer. The Western press moguls have already appeared on the scene, and after buying into Hungary's most prestigious national dailies, they are now ready to move into radio and television as well.

The grassroots movement now emerging in Hungary is still too frail and not powerful enough to match the challenge of big business. Moreover, vitally needed information on major issues such as the debt crisis, nuclear energy, dangerous waste, and environmentally hazardous investment projects such as the

Vienna-Budapest EXPO are still inaccessible to the public.

Outlining the government's programme, Hungary's newly elected prime minister, Jozsef Antall, said in his programme speech in parliament on 22 May 1990 that his government regarded the cause of the environment as possessing strategic importance. It must be noted that the whole government programme, in fact, starts off with a general discussion of the environmental issue in high-flown terms. The new government wishes, Mr Antall said, to allot priority to the protection of the environment — as against a short-sighted economic mentality. To this end it will create the necessary legal regulation, lest the transforming of the economy increase the risk of environmental damage. The cause of the environment must be separated at every level of management from direct production interests.

Mr Antall also promised new comprehensive environmental legislation, and expressed the government's intention to establish close cooperation with the environmental institutions of the EEC. In addition, Hungary's new environment minister, Sandor K. Keresztes, has promised to cooperate with the grassroots Green organizations.

As most critics of the government programme pointed out, the principal problem with it is that it proffers no concrete policies for realizing a myriad of extremely appealing promises, neither does it put forth any concrete ideas on how it will handle any conflict situations as and when they arise.

This also holds true for the environmental issue. Eight months after entering office, the government has failed to come up with a concept for environmental protection, nor is there a clear-cut idea as to the role the Ministry for the Environment would play in such a concept.

On the other hand, at the end of December 1990, environment minister Keresztes sacked deputy under-secretary of state Zoltan Illes, the only Green activist given a high-ranking ministerial post following the general election of March 1989.

From the former regime, whose industrial and environmental policy devastated the environment in Hungary, the new government has inherited the following, extremely serious situation:

- Air pollution in Budapest and major industrial centres has reached untenable proportions. (Lead content of the air in Budapest is 15 to 20 times higher than the permissible level, and 95 per cent of children suffer from respiratory disorders.)
- Our waters are polluted. (Some 84 million cubic metres of untreated industrial waste water still end up in Hungary's rivers and lakes every year. Consequently, the discharge of organic pollutants, heavy metals, oil and its derivatives, and dissolved salts has increased accordingly.) In many rural communities, drinking water is distributed to infants in plastic bags.
- The soil is also contaminated, due mainly to the excessive use of artificial fertilizers. Heavy metal contamination is also a serious problem. In autumn 1990 there was a scandal involving a Hungarian chemical plant responsible for soil contamination with mercury on an alarming scale. Another shocking discovery was the soil contamination left behind by the Soviet army, whose deadline for pulling out of Hungary is June 1991.
- We must also bring into focus the problem of dangerous wastes. One million tons of dangerous waste is produced each year in Hungary, and the problem of what to do with it is unresolved. There are over 2,000 illegal waste dumps in the country. Municipal waste is unsorted, so that highly poisonous substances (e.g. dioxin) are released by incinerators.

One specific promise the new government has made is to make all information related to environmental issues public. This is extremely important as previously, under the former regime, the public had absolutely no access to information of any kind on issues that affected their basic human rights to a healthy environment.

At present, there are two controversial issues on which the ruling party, the Hungarian Democratic Forum, has been rather evasive up until now, but on which it will shortly have to act.

First, the Gabcikovo-Nagymaros hydroelectric power plant, a joint Czechoslovak-Hungarian investment project and the last in the Stalinist vein. Spearheading a campaign of protest and action against the project, the Danube Circle drew the world's attention to its potentially catastrophic ecological impact. In 1989, Hungarian environmentalists achieved the first major breakthrough when the then Hungarian government axed the Hungarian side of the project.

It now seems, however, that the new Czechoslovak regime still wants to put the Gabcikovo plant into operation. There will be further negotiations between the two countries after the elections in Czechoslovakia, but the possible outcome is not yet clear. Were the Gabcikovo plant to enter into operation, this would have extremely serious consequences for the environment, with a special threat to both countries' drinking water reserves. (The most important bank-filtered groundwater is stored in alluvial formations along the Danube and Tisza rivers. Theoretical supplies of groundwater from this one source are estimated to be around 7.5 million cubic metres per day, with 87 per cent coming from the Danube's catchment area and 13 per cent from the Tisza's.)

Second, the problem of nuclear energy. Whilst grassroots Hungarian Democratic Forum activists have joined in action against more nuclear power stations, the government seems to be taking a different line. To fill in the background: Hungary already has a nuclear power plant in the town of Paks, from where the country gets 40 per cent of its electrical energy. This, in our view, signifies too great a dependency on a single source of energy. Moreover, there is the unresolved problem of nuclear waste. At the moment the burned uranium rods are sent back to the Soviet Union. This, we Greens feel, is not only morally wrong, but also politically precarious as the Soviet Union may go back on this at any time — perhaps precisely under pressure from popular movements. There is, in addition, no place to dump other nuclear waste. The former government's plan to create a nuclear dump in the southern Hungarian community of Ofalu was frustrated by that community's resolute struggle for three years.

The government is now looking for Western offers to build further nuclear power plants in Hungary. It seems likely that

France may win the contracts to realise these plans. We therefore turn to the European Greens in general and to the French
Greens in particular to take joint action against this project.

The problem of nuclear energy will have to be tackled within
the framework of the government's new general energy programme. A major issue is whether Hungary will need more
energy in the future, and if so how it would be obtained. The
problem of efficiency can no longer be evaded, for at present
Hungarian industry uses twice as much electrical energy per unit
of product as, for example, neighbouring Austria.

The women of Hungary have played a negligible role in the
major political changes of the past two years. With the present
conservative backlash in almost all walks of life (a centre-right
government coalition espousing christian-democrat ideals now
sets the conservative scenario), considerable effort is being
made to pressure women back into their 'traditional' roles.
Women in this country are not present in any important
decision-making body and thus have almost no representation
of their special interests. Women are, however, involved in some
of the Green groups, although they are mostly not as yet aware
of their potential power in an ecological movement. Indeed, at
this stage, the majority refuse to accept the need for a 'feminist
perspective' in Green politics, unwilling as they still are to
acknowledge the need for some fundamental changes in this
regard. Hungary's women are tired, overworked, guilt-ridden.
They are fed up with the paternalist emancipation of the
Communist era and, if anything, many would prefer to get back
to home and hearth and give it a rest for a while. (It may not even
be a choice any more for many women, with massive unemployment expected to hit working women especially hard.) Clearly,
at this point women can only be motivated via concern for their
families. Indeed, they have organized a number of angry marches
in the part of Budapest worst hit by air pollution. Women in the
fledgling feminist movement, very small at present, are, on the
other hand, showing intensive interest in ecological issues and
the special role women could play in the ecological movement
(Feminist Network, Green Women, Ariadne-Gaia Foundation).

What we now need is to break out of isolation, find access to and exchange information, to join in with network cooperation and link campaigns with others grappling with similar difficulties.

Jeremy Leggett

Energy, Global Warming and Europe in the New Environmental Politics*

Recently, the London Dumping Convention (LDC) adopted measures for industrial wastes which sit uncomfortably with current measures for the wastes of the energy business. The LDC adopted the precautionary principle. Where global warming is concerned — if the world's climate scientists are to be believed — adopting the precautionary principle would require a global cut in carbon dioxide emissions from human activities of more than 60 per cent.[1] The LDC intends to outlaw, globally, all dumping of industrial waste at sea by 1995. Who, in 1991, can imagine a world in which the Global Climate Convention (for which negotiations began in February 1991) could or would countenance outlawing, globally, all dumping of energy-related waste in the atmosphere by 1995?

Yet are the scientific imperatives which drive the LDC's law making, or lead the chemical industry to now talk openly about the prospect of waste elimination and clean production,[2] significantly more advanced than the scientific imperatives formalized in 1990 by the Intergovernmental Panel on Climate Change (PCC) concerning the greenhouse gases in energy wastes? They are not.

We are living in a world in which a dynamic tension is built into environmental politics, a tension between our emerging willingness to stop using the oceans as a dumping ground, and the emerging unwillingness in influential quarters on the world stage to interrupt the steady flow of energy-related greenhouse gases into the atmosphere. This is a tension which — I shall argue in this essay — holds within it the capacity to change the face of environmental politics in the 1990s.

I use two frameworks: the present environmental politics, in which for example we hold as axiomatic that environmental considerations factor into our lives far more than ever they did in the early 1980s, and the future environmental politics, in which for example the prospect of the precautionary principle applying to atmospheric pollutants as well as marine toxic pollutants enters the realm of the feasible. I shall argue that there is currently a wide gulf between the two political frameworks, but that the gulf (while not *certain* ever to be bridged) is *far from unbridgeable*. I shall also argue that, indeed, the seeds of the future environmental politics are there to be seen in the present politics.

Building from my analysis, I will make two main points. The first involves simple environmental expediency: that if we are to be sure of guaranteeing environmental security to the generations to come in the face of the global warming threat, we have no choice but to *actively encourage* a switch of framework to the future environmental politics. The second involves economics: that in the future environmental politics, the successful industries, corporations, and governments will be the most prescient; the most able to face up to the challenge of change; the most able to countenance paradigm shifts rather than bolt-on peripheral adjustments in environmental practice; in short, the most willing to look for ways out of the energy-squandering, fossil-fuel-dependent, potential suicide pact which passes for normality for most people in the energy business today.

Profound changes will be taking place in the energy economy of Europe, western and eastern, during the early 1990s. The third and final section of the essay considers these specific changes in terms of their opportunities for promoting or suppressing the new environmental politics.

Global Warming in the Present Environmental Politics

A principal pillar of environmental politics is the discovery and articulation of problems by scientists. Over the last decade, and particularly the last two years, there has emerged a remarkable, and indeed unprecedented, broad consensus among climate scientists. Summarizing the now well-known IPCC scientists' Working Group report in plain language, this consensus holds that if we continue with business-as-usual in terms of pouring greenhouse gases into the atmosphere — or indeed anything remotely approaching business-as-usual — then the world is very likely heading for ecological disaster in the decades to come.

Close to 60 per cent of the anthropogenic greenhouse gas build-up can be ascribed, either directly or indirectly, to the energy sector. Fossil-fuel use over the last century, and particularly in the postwar years, has resulted in an atmospheric CO_2 concentration of 350 ppm (parts per million) today. For thousands of years before mass coal- and oil-burning began, the concentration averaged around 280ppm.

The IPCC logic can be summarized using a hierarchy of certainty. *Known*: the radiative forcing capability of the greenhouse gases — simple physics shows us that they have the ability to force up the Earth's surface temperatures. *Measured and proven*: the unprecedented build-up of the greenhouse gases in the atmosphere. *A very safe bet:* unprecedented global warming in consequence.

But by when, and how unprecedented? Here the scientists have to use an honest but easily misrepresentable form of words, 'according to present models', with appropriate statements emphasizing uncertainty. And it is here that those wedded to the energy status quo, and/or those willing to gamble with the environmental security of generations to come, focus their arguments for stalling policy responses.

Permit me to dwell on the stakes here. The temperature mountain awaiting us if the vast majority of the world's climate modellers, and all the world's best climate models, are right, is some 10 to 100 times steeper than any previous long-term natural rise in global average temperature during the time humans have walked the planet. I submit, as a long-time researcher of the environmental history of the planet, that the geological record screams a warning to us of how unprecedented, how ecologically unsustainable, that temperature mountain is. To risk running into it is, in a very real sense, a decision to borrow environmental capital from future generations to an extent that may imperil their very future.

But there are uncertainties in the models which predict future global warming. Cause for solace — as so many would have us believe — or cause for added alarm?

Many of the uncertainties concern feedbacks. There are more than 20 known feedbacks, which, in a warming world, can either amplify global warming (positive feedbacks) or dampen it (negative feedbacks). Fourteen of the feedbacks are known or strongly suspected to be positive in a warming world of the kind anticipated in the decades to come, in the absence of anti-greenhouse policies. Only a minority of these feedbacks are incorporated in the global climate models on which the scientific community bases predictions of the magnitude and speed of global warming. The IPCC scientists make it clear that, though our lack of detailed knowledge of these important facets of the climate system do not allow their quantification in models, our knowledge base is sufficiently robust to permit an important qualitative conclusion about risk. *Given that there are a significant number of positive feedbacks, the scientists in the IPCC conclude that the uncertainties are 'likely' to make the warming even worse than the already unprecedented warming predicted in the computer models of all the world's main climate modelling centres.*[3] More than 300 of the world's best climate scientists — mostly in government — were involved in compiling the IPCC report. More than 600 climate scientists endorsed their view at the World Climate Conference, and 'urged' cuts in greenhouse gas emissions.[4]

These are not good odds if you are a gambler. There is a real prospect in a business-as-usual world of global warming of a speed and magnitude capable of posing profound threats to ecosystems and real threats to the very future of civilization. The

Appendix describes a scenario which could lead to a runaway greenhouse effect, and the end of human civilization. *In my opinion and experience, a MAJORITY of the world's best climate scientists would not dismiss this scenario as a possibility, and a SIGNIFICANT MINORITY believes this kind of scenario (not necessarily with the exact mix of snowballing feedbacks I describe) a probability.* Hence, the 'uncertainties' of climate prediction amount to a completely unacceptable risk. Debates over the perceived economic costs of policy responses take on a new perspective when viewed in this context, because there is no way of providing for comparison a meaningful measure of the costs of inaction, or minimal action: they could in principle be infinite.

It is my belief that in the course of the IPCC process the worst-case analyses (plural), such as the example in the Appendix, have not been adequately articulated for policymakers and the public. It is rare to meet a policymaker who understands this side of the global warming coin, though all are well versed in the latest calculations from the White House school of economics as to how many billions of dollars any policy response is likely to cost. There is still a common view, for example, that there could be long-term 'winners' from global warming. In fact, any serious study of the IPCC report will show that global warming in a world which does not attempt meaningful policy responses is in principle open-ended, and that in such a world — sooner or later — the short-term 'winners' such as the putative grain-growers of Siberia would come, metaphorically, to drown in a burgeoning collage of losers. Many will dismiss this as environmentalists' doom-mongering. But this is an opinion which can be field-checked. I consistently find a bleaker tone among scientific practioners in private than (for the most part) I hear from conference platforms.

Given that there is a broad consensus among scientists perceiving high threat, and a significant minority who perceive extreme threat, it is instructive to ask how the scientific prognosis translates into perceptions — and actions — in the public, policymaking, and industrial realms.

The minority of scientists who perceive low threat (or even

advantage) with the enhanced greenhouse effect is a small one, and if the scientific pedigree of the doubters is limited to those of world class, the doubters can be counted on the fingers of one hand. Yet, in the current environmental politics, their influence is extreme.

Public perception of the threat from global warming is in general relatively low compared to other environmental issues. In Greenpeace's tracking of public opinion in the UK, for example, less concern is expressed over global warming than many other environmental issues of the day.[5] In some measure this is undoubtedly due to the way the media deal — collectively — with the scientific doubters. The modus operandi which gets space in the print media, or is designed to make good television or radio, is the format which pits a 'believer' against a 'doubter'. The result is a public which in general perceives two warring camps of scientists: critically, more-or-less equally populated camps. A travesty, in other words. Coupled with the complexity of the issue (a depressingly high proportion of the public still confuse ozone depletion and global warming), the result is a metaphoric collective shrug by ordinary citizens.

However, those with shares in the oil multinationals, and/or other interests in a stout defence of the energy status quo, should not necessarily take heart. Public opinion can change very fast on these issues: witness the original emergence of the ozone issue. It is in this context that, personally, I am so disappointed with my scientific colleagues' collective shyness of the worst-case analyses. Their coyness, of course, is another area which defenders of the status quo cannot rely on in perpetuity. Environment ministers at the World Climate Conference did not even deign to append the Scientists' Declaration to the Ministerial Declaration. I sense a community of professionals which is slowly being awakened from its innate conservatism by ever-growing evidence of disenfranchisement such as this.After all, the scientists have issued what even Mrs Thatcher called 'an authoritative early warning system',[6] a warning which can be likened to humankind being collectively at the wheel of a car, driving through a dense mist towards a very steep and dangerous slope an unknown distance away. The mist represents the scientific uncertainties, the slope represents the effects of the predicted global warming. And it could very well prove to be a bottomless precipice if the worst-case analyses prove correct. Little wonder, then, that the scientists used the word 'urge' to describe the need for cuts in emissions in their statement at the World Climate Conference. Yet some governments (with the USA, the USSR, and the Saudis in the vanguard) wish to actually *increase* the speed of the car — to put still more carbon dioxide into the atmosphere each year. Others merely wish to maintain speed. This group includes the EC, with its collective decision to freeze emissions: freezing emissions will simply send concentrations of carbon dioxide in the atmosphere still higher into dangerous, uncharted territory. Few countries have yet declared their intention to ease off the accelerator by adopting the so-called Toronto target of a 20 per cent cut in emissions by 2005: a policy which would still send concentrations higher into uncharted territory, but less quickly than a freeze. As yet, no government has even acknowledged that there is a brake in the car — a brake which translates into stabilizing the atmospheric concentration of carbon dioxide at or near 350 ppm (a level already 20 per cent above the level it averaged for thousands of years before this century).[7]

This gap between the scientists' articulation of the problem, and the policymakers' collective response, can only be described using adjectives such as interplanetary. The longer it exists, the more it is likely to nudge the scientists into the field of advocacy. If it does, an important new political dynamic will have emerged. As the Brazilian minister of science commented, in frustration, in the closing session of the World Climate Conference, 'You can't alter science to suit the interests of oil-producing countries.'

How about perceptions of the extent of the global-warming threat among policymakers? In my experience, garnered in person-weeks of lobbying at IPCC meetings and in ministries in a dozen countries, the concern among policymakers is far greater than ever the public would imagine. Of course, there are strong regional variations: in Washington, the generalized level of concern is much lower than in, say, Amsterdam, Tokyo, or

Canberra. In the UK, for example, 200 'opinion formers' — the majority of them policymakers — were asked in a 1990 survey for Greenpeace to name the single most important environmental problem. Global warming was highest at 26 per cent.[8]

The level of threat perception among policymakers has not yet, of course, translated into effective policymaking at the global level. The Ministerial Declaration at the recent World Climate Conference failed even to commit governments to freeze their greenhouse gas emissions. This was not for want of many governments trying. Rather, it reflected the vigour with which the Saudi Arabians carried the torch for the self-interest of the foot-dragging nations in the negotiations. The generally robust nature, globally, of policymakers' assessments of the global-warming threat may yet contribute to the unlocking of a few logjams as the UN Conference on Environment and Development nears. (The Climate Convention, with or without the all-important measure of a protocol cutting carbon dioxide emissions, is due to be negotiated in time for the 1992 UNCED in Brazil.)

What of threat assessment in industry? Here, I distinguish two categories of response. One is the public face of threat-appraisal, particularly by the coal, oil and auto industries. Taken at its face value, this holds that there is little to fear, and even if there is, not yet — not until we have narrowed down the scientific uncertainties. But I believe this is a very transient position. Industry people are no less able to hear and understand the world's climate scientists than are policymakers, and I believe that there is a latent body of those who see the global-warming threat as real and immediate. These people, the optimistic environmentalist must hope, will have the courage to speak out, even in the current corporate climate, in sufficient numbers to contribute towards nudging the current environmental politics in the direction of a new energy paradigm. Certainly, if my scrapbook of off-the-record soundings is anything to go on, there are a lot of crises of conscience being wrestled with out there in the energy business.

But in the interim, we are left with a sorry picture. My perception from the environmentalists' front lines is largely a

picture of strident lobbying by energy industries in defence of
the status quo, mixed with cynical opportunism. I believe we are
looking today at a corporate world still largely locked into a past
which now is patently incapable of delivering a viable future.
This corporate world offers us token greening such as its
conversion to lead-free petrol, while still persisting in trying to
persuade us that we need tigers in our tanks. It is capable of
manufacturing prototype vehicles which can do more than 100
mpg, but still persists in mass advertizing to persuade us that
human status — and even sexuality — are linked with the ability
to burn petrol at less than the OECD average of a quarter that
figure. We have a gas industry which seeks to persuade us that
it can produce much less carbon dioxide per tonne-equivalent
than coal, but obstructs efforts to find out how much methane
escapes from its production and distribution infrastructure.

As for the lobbying, a propaganda flier released by the
cohorts of industry lobbyists at the final IPCC meeting in
Sweden in August claimed to represent the interests of thousands of oil, coal, gas and chemical companies in 20 different
countries. Environmentalists have not been surprised by the
kind of concerted opposition to cuts in carbon dioxide emissions which we now see from the many vested interests. Grim
precedents to the initial response of the corporate world in
defence of its perceived interests are to be found in the behaviour of the chemical industry throughout the Montreal process.
Let me offer one illustration. It comes from the negotiations for
the Ministerial Declaration at the World Climate Conference.
The Saudi strategy in these negotiations soon became clear: to
excise the words 'carbon dioxide' from the entire statement,
replacing them with 'greenhouse gases'. (No mention in the
Ministerial Statement, no reason for a protocol to the Convention.) They all but succeeded. During this process, I saw frequent
and brazen shuttling by a senior oil industry lobbyist between
the US and Saudi desks, as did the hundreds of delegates from
the hundred-plus countries present.

Imagine how this looked to the many low-lying island nations,
whose very physical and cultural survival is at stake if the IPCC
scientists are right. No wonder that in the final session, when

many countries read statements into the minutes making it clear that they had signed on to the Ministerial Declaration only under sufferance so as to ensure that negotiations commence in February 1991, one minister said, 'We refuse to become codicils to this monster.'

Future Environmental Politics as the Extent of the Global Warming Threat Dawns

There is, of course, a potential future environmental politics which is capable of delivering the new global energy infrastructure able to guarantee humankind surviving the greenhouse threat. Let me start by describing that new global energy infrastructure. It must be one capable of delivering 60 to 80 per cent cuts in global carbon dioxide emissions, and of factoring in equity — the fact that 25 per cent of the world's population, in the industrialized nations, have emitted 80 per cent of the greenhouse gases currently in the atmosphere. It involves a paradigm shift in thinking about energy: a profound switch from supply-side to demand management, and a concerted effort in fuel-switching to avoid greenhouse gas emissions. The new global energy infrastructure involves a world which saves energy to the fullest extent of its technical ability, and a world well on its way to providing all its energy from renewables. Such a world — it cannot be denied — will be dismissed as environmentalists' cloud-cuckooland by many in the energy business today. But such people would be advised to consider the possible constraints of their present frame of reference. Have they fully understood the position of the world climate scientists? Have they thought through the extent to which they may be mortgaging their grandchildren's future by defending the energy status quo?

We know that we can in principle achieve the new global energy infrastructure with *existing* technology, let alone the kind of technology we could develop if we put serious budgets into the routes to survival, instead of starving them as we have all these years at the expense of fossil fuels and nuclear. We know that we can — in principle — produce electricity, and heat of any temperature useful to humans and their industries, virtually any place on the planet, any time we want. This is a technical *fact*. We can do it, furthermore, using a *range* of existing renewable resources such as solar thermal, solar photovoltaic, wind power and biomass. Of course, currently we only produce a small percentage of world energy this way. But all that is required, in the very last analysis, is a will to face up to the challenge of change, and to accept the management problems involved with bringing the necessary paradigm shift in energy policy to fruition. It becomes easier to perceive this paradigm shift in a world in which we mine to the bottom the vast reservoir of untapped energy efficiency which we know exists in industry, commerce, the home, and transport.

The importance of human societal feedbacks in changing frames of reference to this kind of extent in the years to come has, I submit, not been adequately appreciated. Picture the following scenario. First, governments send the right signals to industry and consumers by agreeing to cuts in emissions. This might, for example, involve a decision by the governments of the world to adopt Toronto targets (of a cut in carbon dioxide emissions of 20 per cent globally by 2005), or something like them, at the UNCED. Such a decision, in this political model, acts as a trigger for the events that follow. Other triggers are feasible, of course. One such might be a chapter of unforeseen environmental catastrophes which become widely ascribed by scientists to the enhanced greenhouse effect.

How likely is it that the world's governments will agree Toronto targets at UNCED? On the evidence of the IPCC process, the World Climate Conference, and the early stages of the climate talks, governments such as the USA, USSR, and Saudi Arabia are bringing to the climate convention negotiations a determination to stall any progress towards agreeing cuts, much less targets. But a growing number of governments have already agreed targets unilaterally. Importantly, there is emerging confidence that such decisions, contrary to protestations of the White House, offer net economic benefit irrespective of geopolitical context. The German government's Enquette Commission has recently provided important ammunition in this field. Conceivably, if the foot-dragging governments are not persuaded to shift position before UNCED, they may yet be left isolated.

What extraneous factors might provide new political dynamics in the climate negotiations? Between now and UNCED, science is likely to have little new to offer. Definitive advances in understanding of the climate system, the IPCC report makes clear, are not likely for maybe a decade or more.[9] In the interim, as the IPCC report also makes clear, there may be scientific 'surprises': a greenhouse equivalent of the ozone hole, for example, being guaranteed to translate into a strong new political dynamic. We should remember that the world's climate science community is a somewhat chastened one, arguably much shaken by its broadly collective rejection of the CFC threat before the Antarctic ozone hole was discovered. Nature itself may hold wild cards — another drought in the American midwest, for example, or an announcement by the nuclear navies that they have data showing wholesale melting of ice across the Arctic.[10] Already there is much anecdotal science for the tabloids: 1990 was the hottest year ever,[11] making the six hottest ever all in the last decade; coral reefs are bleaching on an unprecedented scale across the Caribbean;[12] cyclone intensity has been building in the South Pacific in recent years:[13] none of which is proof of a signal from the enhanced greenhouse effect, but worrying nonetheless.

Let us assume the trigger for the new environmental politics arrives. It may be a climate convention introducing cuts in emissions at the UNCED, or it may be a later event. The trigger sends signals both to public and industry that there *is* a coherent problem, if a complex one, and that governments are summoning the necessary will to take the first steps to deal with it. A set of political dynamics then begin to build: dynamics subject to profound societal feedbacks. Consumers in the industrialized economies, in growing numbers, exert pressure for anti-greenhouse choices. They begin to favour greenhouse-friendly products, they modify their consumer behaviour in ways which show in consumer surveys.

The industry response is initially product-focused. But innovative companies soon begin to market the greenhouse- friendliness of their production *processes*. This feedback loop expands the number of modified consumers, and the number of anti-greenhouse producers. It may or may not be reinforced by the course of nature — in growing public concern over droughts, floods and the like — or by scientific developments.

These developments stimulate the emergence of a genuine political currency among politicians, who begin to outbid each other in ever more 'outrageous' anti-greenhouse promises. In some countries, the first stages of such a process can be sensed: in Australia and New Zealand, for example, both government and opposition support Toronto targets. This process feeds back into continuing growth of the modified-consumer class. This class may even move in some numbers to a 'minimalized' mode of consumerism, should environmental groups and Green parties succeed in sowing the ethic that consumers should 'buy greenhouse-friendly, but only when you have to: remember we can't shop our way out of the greenhouse effect,' thus tightening markets and corporate competition, so fuelling further the drive in industry towards anti-greenhouse production.

Industry by this time is discovering by experience that, managed correctly, the new energy efficiencies are not costing them the earth, and that renewables such as solar-thermal have reached an 'explosion point', in which their economic advantages over fossil fuels and nuclear are such that multi-billion dollar industries are in the offing.

The successful companies begin to be seen in the eyes of shareholders as the ones with the prescience to see the writing on the greenhouse wall. A snowballing process emerges. It is based in part on market forces, but genuine, level-playing-field market forces. The market has been steered by measures such as carbon taxes and fiscal inducements which will be a natural product of the new 'political currency' in anti-greenhouse politics. A paradigm shift in global energy infrastructure, viewed by many in 1990 indeed as the laughable cloud-cuckooland of environmentalists, emerges from the new environmental politics.

There is a major qualification in all this optimism. The belief of the great majority of the world's climate scientists is that, at some stage in the future, the signal of the enhanced greenhouse effect *will* emerge from the natural noise of climate in a world with a business-as-usual (or only peripherally modified) energy infrastructure. Then it *will* set in train the kind of political dynamics I have described here. But it would likely then do so in an atmosphere of panic, with every prospect of being too late. The IPCC scientists present graphic charts of the increasing difficulty of the emissions reduction task with every month that goes past, and every new tonne of carbon dioxide which goes up into the atmosphere. The future environmental politics can be brought about by admitting the need for a new global energy infrastructure now, and accepting that need as a global management challenge — even though it is a challenge absolutely without precedent in human history.

The more energy practitioners who accept that need today, the quicker we can manage the task, and the more chance we have of bequeathing our grandchildren a viable future. That is the reality for the energy business today. I do not believe there has ever been a more important issue in human affairs.

Energy, Global Warming and the New Europe

Significant developments in energy are in the offing in greater Europe in the early 1990s. If the world's climate scientists are right about the extent of the global warming threat, these events will assume a long-term importance which far outweighs their apparent present significance: they hold within them the power to contribute significantly towards the dawn of the new, anti-greenhouse, environmental politics, or to promote substantially the likelihood of its suppression.

In western Europe, significant features of the energy landscape are the internal energy market (target date December 1992), the October 1990 EC decision to freeze community-wide carbon dioxide emissions by 2000, the decision of several EC countries to enact unilateral cuts in carbon dioxide emissions, and the emerging prospect of a Pan-European Energy Charter.

In eastern Europe and the USSR, the energy landscape is dominated by the move towards market economies.

The European internal energy market, with its commitment
to increase exchanges of electricity and gas within the community, and its extended system of price transparency, cannot fail
in its present guise to disadvantage small- and medium-sized
suppliers of cogeneration and renewables, or to favour supply-
side policies over demand management. It is likely to foster
increased energy consumption in all sectors, perhaps especially
transport, and hence increased greenhouse-gas emissions, particularly if it delivers lower energy prices.[14] An additional uncertainty concerns harmonization of environmental costs (such as
those rising from global warming) being factored into energy
pricing. It could be worse yet if harmonization in the internal
energy market turns out to involve a uniform environmental
standard which is appreciably less stringent than the best standards currently available. The internal energy market, at least in
its present form, then only assists in deepening the energy
suicide pact.

Much the same dismal prognosis applies to the Pan-European
Energy Charter, conceived originally as an energy trade and
cooperation bloc from the Atlantic to the Urals, and essentially
designed to open up Soviet gas and oil resources to the west in
exchange for transfers of energy technology, technical assistance and expertise. Discussions of the exact format for the
Charter are ongoing at the time of writing.

In objectives and conception, current EC energy plans sit uncomfortably with the rhetoric of the governments who accept
the IPCC scientists' conclusions — particularly those, like Germany, who have backed their rhetoric with the first promises of
cuts in emissions. The main ways for policymakers to bring
emerging EC energy policy more in line with the bulk of the EC's
political rhetoric are clear. They should involve harmonization
of technical standards at the best available levels, and legislation
to support it — including such measures as minimum efficiency
standards Europe-wide for the full range of main domestic,
industrial and transport energy users: from buildings to individual appliances such as fridges, via industrial motors and automo-

biles. In the current EC document on barriers to an internal market there is not even a reference to the barriers involving trade in energy-saving goods.[15] Subsidies should be introduced to favour the wide dissemination of energy efficiency into the market. Taxes should be introduced which at least attempt to factor in environmental costs (always remembering that such costs could in principle be infinite).

Yet no such measures fully grasp the nettle of the IPCC conclusion that immediate cuts in carbon dioxide emissions of more than 60 per cent are needed to stabilize concentrations in the atmosphere. For such cuts to be achieved, an overnight reduction in the use of fossil fuels of more than half would be needed: an impossibility, at least in the current frame of reference. What is needed, however, is for governments to acknowledge that there is now an imperative for a wholly new global energy infrastructure based on efficiency and renewables, and for them to take measures which show they are heading in that direction as fast as they humanly can.

This, of course, is a million miles away from the current energy thinking in Europe. For example, renewables currently provide 4.1 per cent of the Community's primary energy needs, and 95 per cent of that is hydro. The Community continues to stint R&D in efficiency and renewables, in favour of fiscally flogging the dead horse of nuclear. In 1988, the eight EC countries who participate in the International Energy Agency spent three times more on nuclear R&D than they did on renewables and energy efficiency combined.[16]

A study for the Dutch government on the costs of deep cuts in carbon dioxide emissions (50 to 80 per cent globally) concludes that bringing such cuts about would require investment costs in the OECD of $18 billion per year, 0.4 per cent of GDP. In eastern European countries, the equivalent costs would be $27 billion per annum, 1.6 per cent of GDP.[17] Put this way, and given the stakes, the price to pay seems small. These kinds of sums equate for example to adding less than $1 to each barrel of oil produced, or increasing annual global insurance expenditures by just a couple of percent.[18]

The opportunities which the collapse and restructuring of the former centrally planned economies offer to fashion a sustainable energy economy are substantial. Intensive demand management is needed in eastern Europe even more than it is in western Europe. If the gap between the energy intensity of eastern Europe and western Europe (imperfect even as western Europe's is) was reduced by just 50 per cent, 540 million tonnes of oil equivalent would be saved each year by 2000, and 600 million by 2010. This is equivalent to the total oil production of the USSR (the world's number one oil producer) and the equivalent of 5 to 6 per cent of global carbon dioxide emissions.[19] Savings such as these look all the more environmentally imperative when it is considered that (former) East Germany, Czechoslovakia and Poland use coal for 69 per cent of their primary energy needs, much of it the brown coal and lignite which is responsible for some of the worst of Europe's pollution.[20] Coal generates more carbon dioxide per gram-equivalent burned than does oil, and — provided leakage from production and distribution infrastructure is kept to a suitably low figure — much more than gas. (In western Europe, oil dominates primary energy, and in the USSR gas dominates.)

It would behove western Europe to invest in the energy economy of eastern Europe, even in the narrowly economic frame of reference. But adding the environmental imperative to this, the statement becomes axiomatic.

Whether or not such investment — literal and metaphorical — comes to pass is one of the litmus tests for whether or not humankind has the collective will to escape the global warming threat. It is encouraging that there are apparently so many such litmus tests. It is discouraging, given that surviving the greenhouse threat may well require a paradigm shift in energy thinking in the 1990s rather than a slow evolution, that so many of these litmus tests will be upon us so soon.

Notes

1. *Climate Change: The IPCC Scientific Assessment. Intergovernmental Panel on Climate Change, Report to IPCC from Working Group 1*. Edited by J. T. Houghton, G. J. Jenkins and J. J. Ephrams. World Meteorological Organization and United Nations Environment Programme, Cambridge University Press, 1990.

2. 'Borrowing the Land of Our Children', Jean-Marc Bruel, *Chemistry and Industry*, 19 November 1990, no.22, p.734.

3. As note 1, Policymakers Summary, p. xxvii.

4. *Final Conference Statement, Scientific/Technical Sessions, Second World Climate Conference*, Geneva, 6 November 1990. This document was the result of a week's work by more than 600 scientists (747 participants — but many of them without the scientific pedigree of the IPCC participants: my subtraction of 147 from the figure is an estimate). It was not appended to the Ministerial Declaration of 7 November 1990.

5. In a sample of more than 1,000 questioned by the British Marketing Research Bureau for Greenpeace, 19-25 October 1990, less than 50 per cent professed themselves 'very concerned' about the greenhouse effect. For pollution of rivers and the sea, for example, more than 75 per cent were very concerned.

6. 'We have an authoritative early warning system: an agreed assessment of some 300 of the world's leading scientists of what is happening to the world's climate... a report of historic significance... what it predicts will affect our daily lives.' Margaret Thatcher, 15 May 1990, speaking at the opening of the UK Meteorological Office's new climate research centre on the morning of the completion of the IPCC Report.

7. The atmospheric concentrations of carbon dioxide can be assessed up to 160,000 years into the past using trapped bubbles of air in polar ice cores. The average figure during interglacial periods is 280 parts per million (ppm). The figure today is 350 ppm. The linear annual buildup of carbon dioxide in the atmosphere has been measured at a number of observatories since the International Geophysical Year in 1957. The pre-industrial atmosphere contained 575 gigatonnes of carbon (GtC), the present atmosphere contains

750 GtC. There are 4,000 GtC in recoverable coal and oil alone.

8. The representative sample consisted of 200 people from industry (48), media (24), the city (18), civil servants (24), trade unions (28), MP's (10) and lords (28), interviewed in July 1990 by IFF Research Ltd. Asked whether environmental concern would increase over the next few years, 90 per cent of respondents said that it would.

9. As Note 1, Policymakers Summary p. xxxi.

10. In September 1989, the Arctic ice was reported to be thinning dramatically. The UK Scott Polar Institute released a report based on sonar measurements from British nuclear submarines, showing that the ice in an area north of Greenland had thinned from an average of 5.3 metres in 1976 to 4.5 metres in 1987. This was, however, a relatively small area of the total Arctic ice. The status of the whole ice cap is known only to the scientists of the nuclear navies.

11. *Testimony to the US Senate on Global Temperatures*, P. D. Jones, Climatic Research Unit, University of East Anglia, 11 October 1990.

12. *Testimony to the US Senate on Coral Bleaching*, T. J. Goreau, Research Scientist, Discovery Bay Marine Laboratory, Discovery Bay, Jamaica, 11 October 1990.

13. 'Recent Environmental Changes on Pacific islands', P. D. Nunn, *Geographical Journal*, vol.156, p.125, July 1990.

14. Brand, M. and Jochem, E., 'The Internal Energy Market: The New Coalition Against Energy Efficiency and Environmental Concerns?' *Energy Policy* 18, October 1990, pp.694-701.

15. *The Internal Market*, COM (88) 238, EC, Brussels, October 1988.

16. OECD figures quoted in Stirling, A., 'Energy Without Frontiers: A Single European Energy Market in the Age of Environmental Awareness.' *Greenpeace International*, January 1990.

17. McKinsey and Company Inc., 'Background Paper on Funding Mechanisms', prepared for the Ministerial Conference on Atmospheric Pollution and Climate Change, Noordwijk, 6-7 November 1989.

18. Goldemberg, J., 'Policy Responses to Global Warming', in Leggett, J. K. (ed), *Global Warming: The Greenpeace Report*, pp. 166-184, Oxford University Press, 1990.

19. Brendow, K, 'The Energy Efficiency 2000 Initiative', paper presented at the International Energy Conference, Royal Institute of International Affairs, London, 4 December 1990.

20. Russell, J., *Environmental Issues in Eastern Europe: Setting an Agenda*. Royal Institute of International Affairs, Special Publication, 1990.

*The first two sections of this essay are an edited version of a paper presented at the Fifth International Energy Conference, 'Energy and the New Europe: the Global Dimension', held at the Royal Institute for International Affairs, London, 4th December 1990.

Appendix

One worst-case scenario involving the 'likely' dominance of amplifying feedbacks in a warming world

Global average temperatures go up faster from the 1990s through the 2010s than they have ever done before during the tenure of humankind on the planet.[1] The world continues to warm as concentrations of carbon dioxide continue to build up in the atmosphere[2] and other — new — greenhouse gases such as HFCs are emitted.[3] The warming oceans prove less capable of taking carbon dioxide down from the atmosphere in the way they do today.[4] Luck is not with us. The 'plankton multiplier' feedback[5] comes in, just as many scientists believe it did during phases of rapid warming at the end of the last ice age.[6] In fact, it is more severe than in those past times, because increased fluxes of ultraviolet-B from human-induced ozone depletion have harmed high latitude plankton populations.[7] So more carbon dioxide is left in the atmosphere, unabsorbed by the oceans, and the temperature goes up still further. By now, ecosystems are experiencing an increase in soil and plant respiration over photosynthesis.[8] Hence, more carbon dioxide still is released to the atmosphere. The consequent rise in temperatures causes the tundra to melt faster than expected. More carbon dioxide — and now huge quantities of methane, a more potent greenhouse gas — are emitted to the atmosphere from the spreading wetlands and increased oxidation of organic matter which result.[9] The world's temperatures go up further still. By this time, the warming is being amplified above rates currently predicted by climate models[10] because clouds have begun to work against us: the net negative forcing of clouds in the modern world switches to a positive feedback as more high- altitude clouds form than is the case today, trapping more heat in the atmosphere.[11] By now the result is profound aridity at many latitudes. This means that far from vegetation prospering as a result of the carbon dioxide 'fertilization effect',[12] it suffers, and because there is less photosynthesis to draw carbon dioxide down from the atmosphere, even higher carbon dioxide concentrations build up. So the temperatures go yet higher above projected levels. Today's children are now in their fifties and sixties — some of them the policymakers of the day. Some regions of the world, as would be expected given the natural regional variability of climate, have warmed only little. Most, however, are suffering profound ecological traumas. Such has been the effect of the warming that the 'short-term winners' — areas where the climate has grown more equable and the crop yields have risen — are also now deteriorating as a result of a drastically blighted world economy. And the bad luck continues. Tropospheric chemistry has started to work against humankind. The hydroxyl radical[13] is now under severe stress as a result of the additional quantities of methane in the atmosphere. More nitrogen oxides and carbon monoxide accumulate by default, generating significantly more ozone[14] in the troposphere than is the case today. And by now the Arctic is appreciably warmer. At this time, the feedback which is to do the most damage of all is awakened. On the Arctic continental shelf, submarine methane hydrates[15] start to release additional huge quantities of methane. The measurements of the new World Climate Monitoring System detect the unprecedented escalation of concentration in the atmosphere. Finally, sweeping emergency policies are brought in to cut greenhouse gas emissions worldwide via the United Nations. But that is no use. A runaway greenhouse effect has been generated.

References

These refer to page numbers of the *IPCC Report* where the science of the feedbacks is described, and to the relevant sections of *Global Warming: The Greenpeace Report*, published recently by Oxford University Press. See tables 1.3 and chapters 1, 2, 3 and 5 of the *Greenpeace Report* for explanations of the scientific concepts used above. 'Positive', 'negative' or 'uncertain' refers to the likely future course of the feedback described, according to the IPCC conclusions.

1. As is highly likely, according to the IPCC climate model predictions.
2. Recall that the IPCC scientists calculate that *emissions* must be cut by more than 60 per cent to stabilize *concentrations* in the atmosphere.
3. As ICI, DuPont and others intend to do despite knowing that these gases are thousands of times more potent as greenhouse gases than carbon dioxide, molecule for molecule, and could contribute up to 10 per cent to global warming according to IPCC calculations.
4. *IPCC* 1.2.7.1.1. positive; *Greenpeace* p.33.
5. *IPCC* 1.2.7.1.2. positive; *Greenpeace* pp.33-34.
6. As note 5.
7. *IPCC* 1.2.7.1.5. positive; *Greenpeace* p.38.
8. *IPCC* 1.2.7.2.2. positive; *Greenpeace* p.37 and see chapter 5.
9. *IPCC* 1.3.4.2. uncertain; *Greenpeace* pp.39-40.
10. i.e. more than the 0.5 degrees centrigrade per decade predicted at the upper end of the range of values predicted by the IPCC.
11. *IPCC* 3.3.4. uncertain; *Greenpeace* pp.31-32 and see Chapter 1.
12. *IPCC* 1.2.7.1.3. uncertain; *Greenpeace* pp.35-36.
13. *IPCC* 2.2.3. uncertain; *Greenpeace* p.32.
14. The hydroxyl radical is the atmosphere's 'cleansing agent', scavenging as it does methane, carbon monoxide, nitrogen oxides and other gases by oxidizing them. The interaction of some of these gases with sunlight forms ozone, a greenhouse gas, in the lower atmosphere.
15. Methane hydrates are ice-like solids comprising a network of water crystals with methane gas trapped under pressure within. Geologists have shown that an unknown but huge quantity of methane is isolated from the atmosphere in these hydrates. Warming can destabilize them under permafrost and in shallow high latitude seas. The IPCC reserves judgement on the magnitude of this problem. See the *Greenpeace Report* pp.40-41.

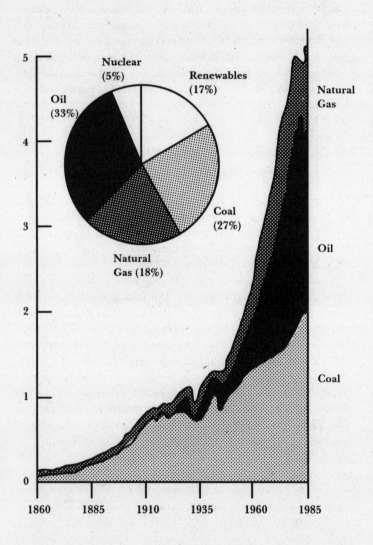

Figure 1: Growth in fossil fuel consumption since the Industrial Revolution, and current world energy consumption. Source: British Petroleum, Worldwatch.

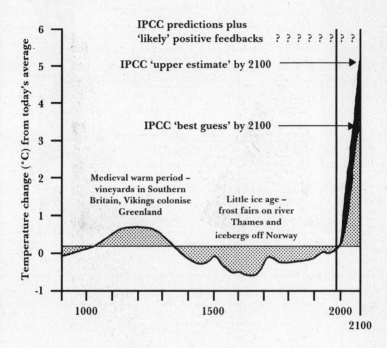

Figure 2: Generalized global average temperatures during the last 1,000 years, compared to IPCC predictions for the next century. The averages depict a range of analyses from sediment- and ice-cores. The grey peak is the 'best guess' of the IPCC scientists. The black peak is the upper range of the estimates from the IPCC models. As the IPCC scientists observe, however, the likelihood of positive feedbacks — many of them unaccounted for in the climate models — means that the real temperature is 'likely' to be even higher than that predicted. (From *Global Warming: The Greenpeace Report*, Oxford University Press, 1990; and based on *Global Changes of the Past*, International Geosphere Biosphere Programme Report no. 6, July 1988, and *Global Climate Change*, UK Department of the Environment, May 1990, modified to include the IPCC scientists' results.)

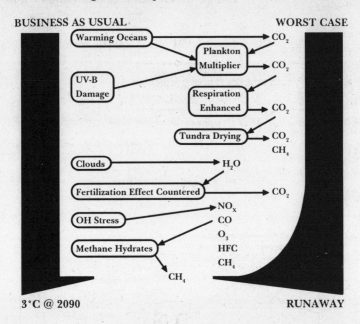

Figure 3: Flow chart of one worst-case scenario illustrating the 'likely' dominance of amplifying feedbacks in a warming world. For further explanation, see Appendix 1.

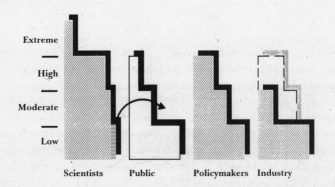

Figure 4: Schematic illustration of perceptions of threat from global warming by scientists, the public, policymakers and industry. For further explanation see text.

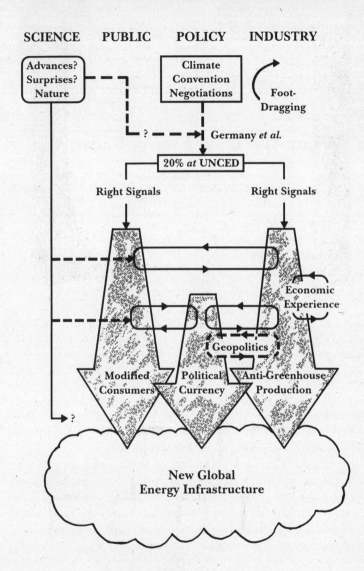

SCIENCE   **PUBLIC**   **POLICY**   **INDUSTRY**

Figure 5: Flow chart of one political model which could prove capable of delivering a paradigm shift in global energy infrastructure in the years to come. For further explanation see text.

Wilhelm Knabe

What We Can Learn From the Trees

> Single and free
> Like a tree
> Sisterly united
> Like a wood.
> That is our dream
> What we want to be.
>
> (Turkish poem)

For our survival in a time of growing pollution, destruction and armament, ecological visions are needed. In this situation ecologically minded people try to learn from those organisms which have survived for such a long time. What strategies have they used? Are these strategies still working after the Industrial Revolution? And what can we learn from them?

Ecologically minded people try to learn from the grass, to learn from the trees. While the grassroots movement has passed along some knowledge about the special features of this plant group, their big sisters and brothers have not been considered that much. They should be described in more detail therefore. The trees, what can we learn from them?

1. Long Life Versus Annual Reproduction

Trees have developed the capability to survive for centuries on the same spot. A generation ago people in Germany could still look at majestic linden and oak trees more than a thousand years old, and a gnarled specimen of Bristlecone pine *(Pinus aristata)* in California is believed to have grown up when the Egyptians erected their pyramids four thousand years ago. Such a long lifespan of individuals is one survival strategy of trees in contrast to annual plants which die after their first flowering season. A tree is using the chance to fruit and spread its seed many times and not just once.

The natural age of man is not as long as that of trees, but much longer than that of most mammals. The natural strategy to prolong the lifespan of individuals has been fostered by medicine and social security, by good nutrition and medical care. The need for early and copious reproduction however was reciprocally reduced. We should remind: trees and people — a long life needs protection, as great differences really occur between both groups.

2. Making Friends With a Tree Means Learning for Survival

STOP reading now for a minute. We cannot learn from trees in an abstract way as in a university course. You have to find your tree. Is there one you have planted yourself? Visit it and see how large it has grown so far. Later you may come back, but now search for the oldest tree in your city. How to find it? Well, look around, see some documents and ask people. Who knows most about trees or about the history of your city? You will find interesting individuals who you will like to meet again. But you may also find nobody who knows anything about trees in your city. Then ask for the oldest forest and go to this place. Wander around and look for the tallest tree, never mind the species, and visit it. It might be old enough to be your grandfather.

Meeting a friend

Meeting a person the first time you shake hands. You cannot do this with a tree. But you can lay your hands on the stem and close your eyes. So you touch your friend and you make the first discovery. Your hands feel the structure of the bark. Hold it just a minute and then let your fingers carefully slide over the bark, the tree's skin. Later on you will be able to determine a species just by the bark, but now you only need to feel this special skin of your friend and memorize the smoothness of the beech or the rough ribs and snarches of the oak you have chosen. You learn to use your hands in a different way than usual. You will train new abilities which are necessary for survival, the full use of all your senses. Start with the hands. They are such wonderful explorers. What you learn by touching a tree will help you also to express emotions to your human friends. This wordless expression of your feeling is especially valuable for communication between individuals of different nations in Europe to overcome the language barrier. Now open your eyes and look at the bark, which you just felt. Then look up to the crown and down to the stem base. You must know whom you made contact with and by doing this you train your second sense, your eyes.

But now again STOP reading and go out to see your friend. The weather should not matter. Take the clothes you need and get out. Do what you just read.

Be quiet and open your mind

You have touched the tree and looked at it. Now sit down and lean your back against the stem. You get support and can relax, even if it is cold. Be silent and start to listen, not to the Walkman you left at home, but to the sound of the forest. You may hear the birds singing, leaves telling their little stories to the wind or big branches moaning under the pressure of a storm. Being quiet and listening belong together. By listening to the tree you learn what you may have lost a long time ago, the ability to listen to what other people have to say, which is a must for fruitful communication. And isn't it this lack of communication between people and nations which causes so much trouble, and which almost split the German Greens? By listening to the trees we not only sharpen our ears, we learn to understand better what somebody else means, wishes, or fears. And this is absolutely necessary for survival, for any peaceful development.

3. Rooting Deep and Growing High

If you look up above to the crown of your friend, you can imagine how hard it was to grow so high. Year after year it made slow progress. The tip grew higher and higher, the branches formed the crown and the stem became thicker and longer. You begin to realize one other main characteristic of trees which makes them different from other plants, their great height which requires a deep and wide rooting system. Height growth is the main way of competition between individuals of the same species or another one with similar requirements and growth rythm. The fastest tree will win and overtop the other, thus creating the base for further growth and reproduction. That could be regarded as the 'struggle for life' in Darwin's theory. We will see that this is just one side of the coin, while cooperation with other organisms is equally essential for the survival of species. The roots should not be forgotten in spite of the fact that most people just walk on the ground and do not take notice of them. Healthy roots perform not only the uptake of water, mineral salts and nitrogen compounds from soil, but are also the only means to withstand wind and storm over a whole lifespan. No matter how high they may grow, trees will never lose contact with mother earth, with nourishing soil, whereas people retreat into artificial, concrete blocks where many of them lose any contact with nature. This means in politics that Europe will only grow if people remember their roots and find the specific region they belong to, the city or village they care for.

4. Living from Renewable Resources

Sitting in the forest you realize another fact. Trees have the capacity to grow from the surplus energy of our sun. The process by which light energy is trapped and used to synthesize reduced carbon compounds from carbon dioxide and water is called 'photosynthesis'. Its importance cannot be overemphasized, because all the energy in our food is directly or indirectly stored by the process of photosynthesis and most of the energy used to operate our factories comes from fossil fuels which were stored by photosynthesis in the distant past. Hence forests are forerunners of an ideal solar society which depends only on solar energy.

The formula:

$$6 CO_2 + H_2O + light/chlorophyll \rightarrow C_6H_{12}O_6 + 6 O_2$$

carbon dioxide + water + light/chlorophyll → glucose + oxygen

describes the transformation of light energy into chemical energy, which is used afterwards for many purposes.

If you turn the process around and read the formula backward, you win energy, maybe thermal or kinetic, which you can realize just by breathing. Look at the green leaves and deliberately exhale. (Inhaling follows unconsciously.) Let your mind follow your breath to the leaves which eagerly take out the CO_2 just exhaled to build up organic material while they give out oxygen for all the living beings — like you — which need it. Thus you are connected with all the plants of this planet just by breathing. This new experience will help you to develop a new attitude towards trees and nature, urgently needed for your survival. I should like to say: We are allowed to use those plants we need for food, shelter or heat, but we should use them with respect.

Most pre-industrial cultures followed the same way of using renewable resources — woods, leaves, grass, bark, etc. — for their home, shelter and clothes. We certainly need to increase the use of renewable resources in a Green Europe. Those people who recommend nuclear energy as a future source and economic base should consider that no living community on earth except man has ever used nuclear energy as a means of survival. Hence safety arguments against radioactive waste are supported by the history of evolution. Beside this general argument, nuclear energy has been so strongly connected with centralized systems, aggressive marketing and the increase in energy consumption that neither energy conservation nor regenerative energies got a real chance.

5. Recycling of Limited Resources

The building up of organic material by green plants must be counteracted by another process, its decomposition into CO_2, water, and mineral salts. This process is also called mineralization of organic compounds. Soil animals mechanically dissect dead leaves and needles or partly digest them like the earthworm leaving a substrate ideal for bacteria and fungi. The release of water and CO_2 may be thought of minor importance in this respect; however, soils would be rather depleted of nutrients like calcium, magnesium, phosphorous and nitrogen compounds without this decomposition. Hence the cooperation of trees with the decomposers is the fundamental base of a long living forest. Tropical rain forests which grow in extraordinary diversity on extremely unfertile ground are the best examples. Modern mankind has apparently forgotten the old wisdom of the Chinese culture which practised such recycling from organic material in a perfect way. Our daily life is filled with waste production. Nobody can escape and what follows is the ugly part of the American way of life, which Vance Packard described in his book *The Waste Makers*. Municipal refuse is one of the greatest problems in modern cities, so that engineers build waste incinerators to reduce the quantity of refuse at the cost of the atmosphere. Again, there is no other way for long- term survival of mankind, except for us to learn what our ancestors already knew and practised, the careful recycling of limited resources.

6. Symbiosis Versus Chemical Warfare

Symbiosis is the term for a cooperation between trees and fungi. Symbiotic fungi build up a network around the fine roots of the trees and help them to get nitrogen compounds and other nutrients from the decaying humus, whereas the trees spend assimilated carbon hydrates, especially sugar compounds, built up in green leaves and translocated to roots. This 'mycorrhiza' as this special symbiosis is called forms a protecting mantle around the roots against the attacks of pathogenic fungi. Such cooperation is the secret of the good growth of pines, e.g. on poor sandy soils.

Cooperation is what we need at present in human society, too, instead of chemical warfare which is also practised by trees to prevent invading parasites which try to live off the host's tissue. The production of resins by pines and other conifers against the attack of bark beetles is a good example. A healthy tree can easily defend itself whereas a tree weakened by other stress factors can be successfully invaded by bark beetles and finally killed, thus making place for young seedlings already waiting for a chance to grow up. Trees use those chemicals only as defenders whereas fungi have a well developed chemical system to penetrate the skins of needles, leaves, twigs, or roots, which must be seen as an aggressive weapon they need for survival.

In most cases, however, there is an equilibrium, a stalemate between host species and attacking species so that both can live for centuries or millenia in the same region, which would not be the case with modern warfare by atomic, chemical or biological weapons.

7. Decentralized Economy

Forests are the best example of a decentralized economy combined with the greatest biodiversity. Every tree depends on the nutrients of the site. It cannot fly away like a bird or dive like a fish searching for its daily food. But the units are still smaller. A tree has thousands of leaves increasing its surface by a factor of 12 to 25 in comparison with the ground area it stands on. And these leaves again have thousands of cells containing various micro-generators of chemical energy, the chloroplasts with their specific light-trapping apparatus. Their main advantage: production takes place where it is needed or in very close surroundings. Our big electricity-generating plants appear crude and heavy in spite of their high technology. Their main disadvantage is that their waste heat cannot be used because heat does not allow long transport paths. Learning from trees would mean building up local production and restricting long-distance transport to a minimum.

8. Patience

Let me end with a quality which is rare among Western people — patience. A tree stands still at the same site for a hundred or many hundreds of years. It is waiting until its maturity when it begins to produce seed. And then it spreads its seed, every year like a birch or in periods of several years like a beech or Norway spruce, thus trying to reproduce the species. Shouldn't we Greens learn a bit from their patience?

When the German Greens lost their seats in the Bundestag in December 1990, deep frustration grew up among the candidates and staff. Shouldn't we try to spread our ideas into society from some other place? It is hard, I know, after more than forty years of struggle for the environment. But it is possible and it is needed. I am pretty convinced that the worldwide Green movement will continue to grow and thus strengthen the German Greens to regain the confidence of the public.

We need many people to join us. Hence let me end with some personal words:

> I was blown by the wind
> By forces stronger than me
> But I was swimming like a trout
> Against the current of the stream.
> I wish you, I hope
> You could do the same.

Teo Wams

The Deceptive Appearance of the Dutch Environment Plan

Travelling has become an embarrassing experience for Dutch environmentalists these days. In many countries we are received with jealous looks and remarks like 'Do you have any problems left in your country?' Many people expect the Dutch environmental movement to be very enthusiastic about government policy as it is described in the National Environment Policy Plan (NEPP). During a visit to Poland I even met people who were seriously annoyed by our criticism of Dutch environmental policy.

However, the fact that people in other countries have an impression of this policy as being very effective and far-reaching says more about the PR skills of the Dutch government than about the actual quality of its policies. It cannot be denied that the Netherlands is among the group of countries with the best environmental policies, but in the face of the challenges posed by the goal of sustainable development, the plan is no more than a first step. One of the most important criticisms brought forward by the environmental movement is that the government backs away every time the need for structural changes in production and consumption is mentioned.

Political History of the Plan

The first Dutch National Environment Policy Plan was published in late spring 1989. It immediately received severe criticism, not only from the environmental movement, but also from trade unions, consumers' organizations and political parties. At the time the plan was presented, the government consisted of the Christian-Democrat party (CDA) and the conservative Liberals (VVD). Ed Nijpels, the Minister of the Environment of the time, was a member of the latter party. A few months later this government fell, because the VVD did not agree with one of the elements of the plan. This was the proposal to cut tax benefits for people who commute by car. The election campaign that followed was the greenest in Dutch history. Every party promised the electorate to save the environment, once they got into power. The prime minister, Ruud Lubbers, even made a solemn vow to reduce carbon-dioxide emissions by 2 per cent annually once his new government was installed. In the elections the Liberals were badly punished for their political behaviour. The new government consists of the CDA and the Social-Democrat party (PvdA). Hans Alders, the new Minister of the Environment, is a member of the latter party. This coalition has rapidly become the government of broken promises. The first six months saw scarcely any developments in the field of environmental policy, as the new minister was preparing an improved policy plan. When this so-called NEPP-Plus was presented, it proved to be a bitter disappointment. There were very few concrete improvements in the policy goals and measures. The promise of Mr Lubbers to reduce CO_2 emissions by 20 per cent by the year 2000 had already been forgotten. Instead a meagre 3 to 5 per cent reduction was proposed.

Proposals with respect to product policy, financial policy instruments and acid rain were similarly disappointing. At present the environmental movement is pressing the government to focus all its attention on the realization of the plans. This is based on fear that prolonged debate about the objectives of environmental policy will not lead to improvements, but only cause further delay in the realization of those plans that have already been approved.

State of the Environment Report

In the autumn of 1988 the government's Institute for Public
Health and the Environment (RIVM) published a report on the
state of the Dutch environment. The report identifies and
analyses sixteen different environmental threats, divided into
five spatial levels of scale (summarized in Table 1). It describes
the present situation regarding all sixteen environmental problems and presents forecasts for the next twenty years, based on
in-depth analyses of trends.

Table 1. Environmental Threats Identified in
   'State of the Environment'

Level of Scale	Environmental Problem
Global	Climate change Ozone layer
Continental	Ozone in troposphere Acidification Dispersion of aerosols Nuclear accidents
Fluvial (Rhine and Meuse)	Eutrophication of surface waters Dispersion of toxic substances
Regional	Eutrophication of soil and ground water Dispersion of toxic substances in soil and ground water Dehydration of ecosystems Waste management
Local	Noise Stench Ambient air quality in cities Indoor air quality

The State of the Environment report caused a shock in politics, the media and public opinion. Its first conclusion, based on a broad overview of environmental problems, was that the environment in Holland is still degrading. Environment policy has up till now been ineffective in many respects. One of the few improvements is the fact that surface water has become somewhat cleaner as a result of intensive sewage treatment. The second conclusion was that in order to achieve a sustainable environmental situation, most types of pollution have to be reduced by 70 to 90 per cent (Table 2). In order to achieve this, the report stresses, technical measures are not sufficient. Structural changes in the economy of the country are indispensable. On the basis of this report the Minister of the Environment at the time, Ed Nijpels, had to admit that our country is probably the most polluted in the world. It is one of the most densely populated nations on the globe, with a very dense infrastructure, highly productive agriculture (despite its small surface Holland is the world's second agricultural exporter) and a large chemical and petrochemical industry. As a consequence the number of cars and cattle per square kilometre are both higher than anywhere else in the world and the use of fertilizer and pesticides has reached a world record. It is therefore not surprising that Holland's per capita contribution to the greenhouse effect is among the highest in the world.

All these activities in such a small area cause a terrifying degradation of the environment. The most pressing problems are acid rain, ground water pollution, incineration and landfilling of waste, soil pollution by old toxic waste dumps and the manure surplus. The report specifically mentions the environmental factors that pose the most serious threats to human health at present. These are: air pollution indoors and outdoors, radon, UV radiation, cadmium and noise.

Table 2: Necessary Emission Reductions in the Netherlands

Problem	Substance	Reduction
Greenhouse	CO_2	80-90%
Acidification	SO_2 NO_x NH_3	80-90% 80-90% 80-90%
Smog	hydrocarbons	80%
Ozone layer	CFC's	100%
Rhine/North Sea	several	75-90%

(figures from *State of the Environment* report)

No Structural Measures

Nearly half a year after the State of the Environment report was published, the government presented its National Environment Policy Plan. The plan is based on the findings in the report and makes the achievement of sustainable development within one generation the official target of government policy. In order to achieve this goal, an impressive number of 220 so-called actions are formulated, varying from taking the initiative towards a global treaty on climate change to introducing a deposit scheme for domestic appliances. Total costs of the plan are no less impressive, steadily increasing to an annual level of Nfl. 16 billion (c. £5 billion) in 1994. Of the extra costs created by the plan (Nfl. 8.5 billion, i.e. c. £2.5 billion), 15 per cent will be paid by the government, 55 per cent by the private sector and 30 per cent by consumers. With these facts the Dutch government has deeply impressed the media and politicians in other countries. The picture becomes less impressive, however, once the NEPP is judged on the basis of its effectiveness. For example, the forests will not stop dying if the plans concerning acidification are brought into practice. The plan states unashamedly that 'with the proposed policy 20 per cent of the Dutch forests can be protected'. This quotation has become a symbol of the lack of effectiveness of the whole NEPP. Table 3 compares some of the emission reductions that are expected if the NEPP is carried out, with reductions that are deemed necessary by the authors of the State of the Environment Report. As is shown here, the goals of the policy plan are not negligible, but further reductions in the order of 50 per cent are needed in order to achieve a sustainable situation. CO_2 emissions are a special case. Whereas reductions of at least 80 per cent are needed, the Dutch policy only achieves a 3 per cent cut in the year 2000.

Table 3. Policy Targets in Dutch Environmental Policy Plan*

Substance	Reduction	Necessary**
CO_2	3-5%	80-90%
SO_2	80%	80-90%
NO_X	50%	80-90%
NH_3	50-70%	80-90%
hydrocarbons	65%	80%
N, P	50%	75-90%
cadmium	60-70%	80-90%

* year 2000

** as mentioned in *State of the Environment* report

This clear-cut contrast between what is needed and what will be achieved caused the bitter reactions of the Dutch environmental movement to the NEPP. 'With this plan politicians prove that they are unable to stop the fundamental threats to the environment,' was the first sentence in a declaration issued by two major environmental organizations (Stichting Natuur en Milieu and Vereniging Milieudefensie). These harsh words were not only based on the cold figures as presented in Table 3. The political background to the plan was at least as disheartening.

The essence of this is that only *technical* measures were seriously considered during the preparation of the plan. Proposals for *structural* measures were excluded at a very early stage of the planning process. Such measures are: significantly reducing car traffic, cuts in the number of cattle, reducing the energy intensity of industry, shifts from the use of virgin raw materials towards recycled materials, and banning products that contribute to the waste stream. As the government has decided to approach the environmental problem by means of a consensus strategy, interest groups were given the opportunity to successfully prevent such structural measures from being included in the NEPP. This has not only made the plan less effective than it could be, it has also made it extremely expensive. As long as structural changes are a political taboo, technical measures are the only possibility. These demand large investments, but they do not reduce pollution sufficiently. Degradation of the environment is thus not brought to a halt despite these high costs. Future clean-up activities are made unavoidable, which will cost enormous sums of money. Because of this, the success of interest groups in preventing structural measures will prove quite harmful on a macroeconomic level.

Throwaway packaging materials may serve as an example of this. Banning a large part of these materials is no doubt harmful for the industry that produces them. On the other hand companies that produce refillable packagings will thrive by such a policy. Moreover, enormous costs in the field of waste collection and treatment can be prevented. Less incineration and landfilling capacity is needed, so leakage of toxic substances to the ground water and emission of dioxins are partly prevented. These threats to the environment caused by waste treatment represent unknown future costs for clean-up and rehabilitation. Technical measures like separate collection of plastics may reduce the latter problem, but will further increase the costs of waste collection and treatment. So, even though specific interests are harmed by structural measures (waste prevention), the economy as a whole will not suffer but will probably profit. The same is true for the economic effects of reducing car traffic, reducing the number of cattle and other structural measures.

This is not just 'Green theory'. In the National Environment Policy Plan three scenarios are compared for their economic consequences (Table 4). The first is a business-as-usual scenario, the second is a scenario based on drastic technical measures, the third includes structural as well as technical measures. From an environmental point of view, the third scenario is the better one. It reduces pollution most effectively, which is not surprising. More surprising, however, was the finding that the economic consequences of the third 'structural' scenario were no worse than those of the second 'technical' scenario. In fact, both scenarios have quite modest economic consequences as compared to business as usual: economic growth is reduced by zero to 4 per cent over a period of twenty years. This is a minor change, compared to total economic growth over the same period which is estimated to be almost 100 per cent. Assuming that other European countries will not be inactive, but will develop their own far-reaching environmental policies, the third scenario will even have positive economic consequences compared to the reference.

The environmental movement was shocked that even with the support of such reassuring findings the Dutch government did not have the courage to develop a pro-active environmental policy, including badly needed structural measures. As mentioned, the most important reason for this is that economic sectors which fear to suffer from such measures have been very successful in influencing the contents of the NEPP. Such sectors include agriculture, transport and the chemical industry.

Table 4. Scenarios for Environmental Policy and
Their Economic Effects (year 2010)

	scenario1[I]	scenario 2[II]	scenario 3[III]
CO_2	+35%	+35%	-20 to -30%
SO_2	-50%	-75%	-80 to -90%
CFC's	-20%	-50%	-70 to -80%
landfilling of waste	0	-50%	- 70 to -80%
GNP by volume#	-1.3%	-1.9% to -3.5%	-4.2% to +0.5%
consumption#	-1.0%	-1.2 to -2.4%	-2.1 to +1.2%
unemployed#	+18,000	-17,000 to +44,000	+18,000 to -58,000

[I] business-as-usual scenario
[II] scenario based only on technical measures
[III] structural as well as technical measures
compared to predicted development (1985-2010): GNP +99.4%,
consumption +120% and unemployment -400,000.

Mechanisms for Structural Change

To get a more concrete impression of how technical and
structural measures may contribute to the solution of environmental pollution, the University of Groningen developed a
scenario for the reduction of CO_2 emissions for Friends of the
Earth. The main question was whether and, if so, how a 60 per
cent reduction by 2010 could be realized. The final conclusion
of the report was that a 25 per cent reduction could be reached
with a maximum application of technical means for energy
conservation. In other words: a 25 per cent reduction of CO_2
emissions can be achieved without imposing any specific limits
on economic growth as foreseen. In order to reach the 60 per

cent target, a further 35 per cent reduction has to be realized by means of structural changes and reduced growth rates for specific sectors. The scenario mentions such sectors as the chemical industry, metals, packaging materials, greenhouse horticulture, traffic and fertilizer. The report furthermore stresses that structural changes in these sectors contribute at the same time to the solution of other problems, such as acidification, waste and ground water pollution.

Reduced growth in the sectors mentioned above will at least partially be compensated for by extra growth in other sectors, for instance public transport, recycling, maintenance, energy conservation and non-fossil energy sources. In other words: abatement of the greenhouse effect implies both selective reduction and growth of various sectors within the Dutch economy.

By giving in to pressure from interest groups representing the sectors that have to be reduced, time and resources are lost that are essential for a successful start to the complicated process towards structural change. In this way the situation becomes more difficult by the year. For instance, in the cattle breeding sector large investment in technical measures is envisaged in order to prevent compulsory reduction in the number of cattle. This weakens the economic position of the sector, but does not really solve the environmental problems that it causes. It can be expected that in a few years time reductions in cattle will have to be realized in great haste. This will cause much greater damage than it would have done originally, because the sector has been weakened by its investment in technical measures and due to loss of time the structural measures will have to be carried out in great haste.

Even though all relevant research proves otherwise, the government still clings to the dangerous myth that a sustainable society can be achieved without harming any sectoral interest group. Because of this attitude government policy is losing credibility. Precious time for the development of policy instruments and scenarios is lost. In certain cases proposals for structural changes have already been developed by the environmental movement. This is the case for transport and packaging.

In the spring of 1990 Friends of the Earth presented a

scenario aimed at reducing pollution from packaging materials by 70 to 90 per cent. This report concludes that such ambitious targets are achievable with a mix of several measures: introduction of deposit schemes and refillable packagings on a large scale, compelling the industry to produce only packaging materials that can be re-used and/or recycled, banning certain harmful materials like aluminium and PVC and, finally, encouraging the sale of unpacked products.

Earlier a group of environmental organisations had presented a plan for a national transport system, based on public transport. Compared with the continued growth of car traffic, as expected, this plan would reduce emissions by 80 to 90 per cent, produce the same amount of traveller kilometres and save the national economy billions of guilders.

Further development of policy instruments that can bring about such structural changes must have high priority. Financial instruments can play a central role in this respect. Whenever market forces can be used in favour of environmental ends instead of against them, this chance should be used. Levies and deposits in particular can be very effective. It is hard to imagine how the vast investment in energy conservation that is needed to fight the greenhouse effect can be initiated if energy from fossil fuels is not made more expensive. In agriculture the use of pesticides can be significantly reduced by imposing a levy on the price of these chemicals. This has been shown in practice in several Scandinavian countries. Deposits, for instance on packaging materials or domestic appliances, are powerful instruments in stimulating separate collection and re-use of materials.

Drastic structural changes in national economies take place all the time. Sometimes these changes are planned, more often they are brought about by influences from outside. In general one might say that those countries that are most stubborn in ignoring the necessity of adjustment to changing conditions, experience most harm in the end. In the Netherlands the environmental movement is building up pressure to convince the government, but also other parties involved such as trade unions, consumers' organisations, farmers and the industry, that they should no longer deny or resist the necessity of restructuring society towards sustainability. Only by starting today can we prevent painful experiences tomorrow.

Maria Guminska

Air Pollution and Health Consequences in Poland

During the Second World War, Polish industry was completely destroyed. After the war it was rebuilt — but under Soviet direction — with a one-sided emphasis on extremely intensive coal-mining, together with the steel and heavy industry sector.

To cover the constantly growing energy needs of heavy industry, almost 190 million tons of hard coal and 70 million tons of brown coal were used every year.[1] Part of the coal is converted into coke for the Cracow and Katowice steelworks. Since Polish coal contains a rather high content of sulphur, nitrogen and fluorine, c. 10.1 million tons of toxic gases were emitted in 1989,[2] including sulphur dioxide (3.9 million tons), carbon monoxide (3.0 million tons), nitrogen oxides (1.5 million tons), and volatile organic compounds (1.7 million tons).[3] The total amount of dust emitted to the air in Poland in 1988 was 3.4 million tons.[4]

Therefore, already in 1983, 27 areas of ecological hazard were recognized in Poland.[5] The danger zones include 11.3 per cent of the country's surface, with approximately 13 million people or 35 per cent of Poland's population. One in three Poles lives in an area designated as an 'ecological hazard', because of contaminated air or water. Five of these areas are already in the state of ecological disaster because of pollution-related losses in forests, crops, buildings and human health.

The most visible air pollution problem is the damage to the country's forests. A recent official survey confirmed that 50 per cent of the forests are badly damaged. An especially bad situation is in the region near the border with Czechoslovakia and East Germany, which is called 'the black triangle of pollution'. In that area large parts of forest are completely dead. Acid rain also has a negative effect on soil and water so that large parts of farmland are highly acidic. In addition to acid rain, the falling dust contaminates soil with heavy metals or other chemicals.

The problem is especially bad in the south of Poland, in the regions of Katowice (Upper Silesian Industrial District) and Cracow.[6] This part of the country is the subject of intensive studies.

Cracow is a magnificent medieval city, the previous capital of Poland, with many monuments and relics of history, architecture and art. It is on the UNESCO list of zero-class world heritage. However, after the Second World War, Cracow was changed into an industrial city.[6] In its neighbourhood in 1950 were located an aluminium smelter and the Lenin steelworks with more than 700 chimneys. Toxic compounds from the factories hang for days over the city in the Vistula river valley because of frequent temperature inversions. The lack of ventilation causes the worst ecological situation in the country. Toxic gases from the industry mix together with smoke from local coal-power plants or domestic stoves, mainly in winter. The most disturbing damage has been recorded in the central, ancient part of the city.[6] We can see destroyed monuments, ornaments, and stonework. Damage is spreading more quickly than repair efforts.

The environment of Cracow was studied by a special commission of the Polish Academy of Science. This commission completed a list of the most toxic compounds present in the environment of Cracow. The same pollutants that are toppling trees, soiling crops and eating away buildings are toxic for human health.[6]

The emitted pollutants are the major risk factor for public

health. Millions of people in Cracow and Upper Silesia live in conditions that are a daily hazard. In relation to health we usually know effects of particular pollutants, but the situation is more complicated if they are in a combination of compounds with synergistic action.

Simply breathing is the greatest hazard. In the ambient air, sulphur dioxide is over twice the annual maximum allowable concentration, hydrogen fluoride seven times (especially at the time when aluminium was produced from kryolite), nitrogen oxides six times, and suspended particles up to 20 or 30 times.[7] The noxious gas molecules attach themselves to tiny particles or soot and are carried to the lungs where they mix with water to form potent acids. All these irritant gases or air-borne particles from industry, as well as from car exhaust gases, enter deep into the lungs where they irritate epithelial cells of the airways leaving the lungs vulnerable to attack by viruses or bacteria, and also do their damage by impairing the body's immune system.

In the Cracow region it was possible to observe a direct reaction from the respiratory system one or two days after the peak of emission.[8] For smokers living in the polluted area, the problems can be even worse.[9] Their lungs are already damaged by tobacco smoke. During nine years' observation it was possible to see an evident increase in chronic bronchitis and asthmatic reactions. Especially sensitive are children from Cracow. They show four times more cold symptoms and chronic bronchitis, and three times more asthma, than children from non-polluted towns.[10]

The prolonged respiratory diseases lead to respiratory insufficiency and an increase in cardiovascular disease. One of the risk factors for the cardiovascular system is also the huge amount of carbon monoxide (about 1,000 tons per day) emitted from the steelworks.[7] It is difficult to evaluate how much it could be from all sources (including traffic and domestic heating). Carbon monoxide has a very negative effect on human health, contributing also to the greenhouse effect. In humans, it blocks oxygen transport by blood and causes tissue hypoxia. Hypoxia and various stresses cause in consequence a compensatory hypertension which was found in about 25 per cent of Cracow residents.[11]

This is related to increased frequency of myocardial infarcts, ishemic heart disease and stroke. Cardiovascular mortality represents around 50 per cent of total mortality.

Most typical, however, for the Cracow region are the consequences of prolonged exposure of residents to air contaminated by hydrogen fluoride from the aluminium plant.[12] The emissions were stopped after the electrolysis division was closed in 1982, but the negative health effects are still present. Independently of the local irritant effect of hydrogen fluoride on airways, fluorides penetrate easily to blood and to the cells, where they inhibit many cellular processes, especially those connected with cell energy formation in the form of ATP molecules, which are chemical energy carriers, converted in the organism into all other energies.[13] Fluorides thus diminish somatic strength and muscular activity as well as the formation of bioelectric energy, especially in the nervous cells.[14] Finally, fluorides accumulate in bones. Depending on the age, 60 to 90 per cent of residents in the vicinity of the aluminium plant suffered from bone pains and spine stiffness.[12] This was a sign of skeletal fluorosis. Fluoride made the bones more brittle, so that fractures take longer to heal. Although the emission of fluorides diminished after the most dangerous department of this factory was closed, the amount of degenerative diseases of the spine continued to increase as a late effect of exposure to fluorides.

Pollution also contributes to a range of mental illness, especially related to the negative effects of carbon monoxide, hydrogen fluoride, organic solvents and lead ions on nervous cells and the brain. Gasoline in Poland still contains a high concentration of lead, which is already forbidden in many countries, since many studies have shown that lead ions cause brain damage and mental retardation, especially in children. Lead salts present in polluted air and absorbed from the lungs to the blood stream reach the brain cells, where they damage many enzymatic reactions. Therefore, lead can impair learning in children and promotes hyperactivity. Children express more aggressiveness and irritability. A report of the Polish Academy of Sciences from 1985 pointed to increased indices of mental retardation among school children.[15]

All toxic compounds mentioned above can accumulate in the placenta of pregnant women, leading to a degeneration seen in morphological and histoenzymatic studies.[16,17] This has a negative influence on the development of the foetus. In addition to increased numbers of spontaneous abortions, 45 per cent of pregnant women develop complications and 30 per cent of children are born with health problems — prematurity or low birth-weight. Infant mortality at 18 per cent is still very high, four times higher than in the Western countries.[18] Many congenital malformations are also reported, especially heart defects which may be related to exposure to various genotoxic compounds.[19]

In the ambient air of Cracow there were also mutagenic compounds such as polycyclic hydrocarbons emitted during coke production and chlorinated hydrocarbons emitted from a chemical factory which caused mutations and malformations in plants.[20] Mutagenic compounds are also carcinogenic and increase cancer mortality.[21] Standardized indices of cancer mortality are still lower in Cracow or Silesia than in some Western countries, but they are increasing over time. Exposure to carcinogenic compounds from industry started later, and since several years are needed between exposure and appearance of tumour, an increase in cancer mortality can be expected in the future. Cancer statistics may also be modified by the reduction of six to eight years' life expectancy (68 for men and 75 for women), since cancer mortality rapidly increases with age.

In demographic studies a peculiar effect was also found in the countries of the eastern bloc — a surplus mortality of men of working age.[22] This was also found in Cracow, but not in small villages of the region, so it may be related to the polluted environment of the town.

The price paid by the society for air pollution and degradation of the natural environment is enormous. It covers not only economic losses but is an important factor in the radical worsening of people's health and quality of life. Independent of the threat to future generations, pollution reduces somatic stength and mental ability by diminishing biological energy.[23] Air pollution is one of the major risk factors producing tens of thousands of cases of respiration or heart ailments, birth defects, aborted pregnancies and mental retardation. All these effects can be seen in Poland because levels of air pollution are a hundred times higher than those experienced in Western Europe. Since they are great risk factors, there is every reason to blame pollution for the decline in public health.

The only solution is through preventive measures, of which the most important is the elimination of exposure to toxic compounds in the environment. It is a moral problem, because human beings have the right to safe conditions of life and development.

Great social and political changes in Poland have created the conditions for several new initiatives. Some groups of scientists would like to introduce nuclear energy as an alternative energy source, but another group points to the possibility of an increase in energy efficiency or energy conservation, which requires general economic reforms as well as the introduction of renewable energy sources such as water, wind, biogas and solar energy.

All these health consequences create reasons for such a reorganization of industry and energy supply, to make a safer environment. But this cannot be solved on the local scale as long as the problem is not solved on a global scale, in order to save 'our common future'. The new idea of 'sustainable development' requires a respect for many barriers and limitations which will join development with homeostasis. Its realization is one of the aims of the Polish Ecological Club, an independent, non-profit, non-governmental organization.

Notes

1. *Rocznik statystyczny*, GUS 1980-1989, Warszawa (*Statistical Yearbook*, Main Statistical Office, Warsaw, 1980-1989).
2. *Monitor Ochrony Srodowiska – Atmosfera*, IOS, Warszawa, listopad 1989 (*Monitoring Environmental Protection – Atmosphere*, Institute of Environmental Protection, Warsaw, November 1989).

3. Kacprzyk K., Zurek J., *Quality of the Environment in Poland,* Institute of Environmental Protection, Warsaw, 1990.

4. *Ochrona Srodowiska 1989,* GUS, Warszawa, 1989 (*Protection of Environment in 1989,* Main Statistical Office, Warsaw, 1989).

5. Kassenberg A., Rolewicz G., *Przestrzenna diagnosa ochrony Srodowiska w Polsce (Spatial Diagnosis of Environmental Protection in Poland),* Komitet Przestrzennego Zagospodarowania Kraju PAN, 89, PWE, Warszawa, 1985.

6. Guminska M., Delorme A. (eds), *Kleska Ekologiczna Krakowa, (Ecological Disaster of Cracow),* Polski Klub Ekologiczny, Krakow, 1990.

7. Wydzial Ochrony Srodowiska, Gospodarki Wodnej i Geologii Urzedu Miasta, *Ocena stanu srodowiska wojewodztwa krakowskiego i dzialania podejmowane dla jego poprawy (Evaluation of Environment Quality in District of Cracow and Actions Undertaken for its Improvement),* Krakow, 1988.

8. Powroznik M., Morawska-Horawska M., Rysz M., Tumdajski T., *Badania zwiazkow miedzy warunkami aerosanitarnymi a liczba zgonow w Krakowie lla wybranych jednostek i grup chorobowych (Correlation Between the Air Pollutions, Meteorological Conditions and Death Numbers from Selected Diseases in the region of Cracow),* I. Folia Med. Cracov. 23, 1982/83, 211-220; *Wplyw wybranych warunkow pogodowych i zwiazana z nimi wielkosci zanieczyszczen na zgony w Krakowie (Influence of Selected Weather Conditions and Associated Air Pollution on Death Rate in Cracow),* II Folia Med. Cracow. 26, 1985, 115-120.

9. Nikodemowicz E., *Wplyw zanieczyszczen srodowiskowych na uklad oddechowy czlowieka (The Influence of Environmental Pollution on the Respiratory System in Humans),* Folia Med. Cracov. 24, 1982/83, 173-180.

10. Rudnik J. (ed), *Epidemiologial Study of Long-Term Effects on Health of Air Pollution.* Problemy Medycyny Wieku Rozwojoweg v 7, PZWL, Warszawa 1977; II. Suppl. PZWL Warszawa, 1982.

11. Krol W., *Srodowisko Krakowa a choroby ukladu sercowo- naczyniowego (The Environment of Cracow and Incidences of Cardiac Diseases),* Folia Med. Cracov 24, 1982/83, 169-172.

12. Guminska M., Salwinska-Cieckiewicz B., *Magnez w moczu u ludzi narazonych na dzialanie zwiazkow fluoru z huty aluminium przed wylaczeniem i w rok po wylaczeniu emitorow (Urinary Magnesium Concentration in Humans Chronically Exposed to Fluorine Compounds, Emitted*

by the Aluminium Foundry Prior to and One Year After Closing Down the Source of Emission), Folia Med. Cracov/. 26, 1985, 49-57.

13. Guminska M., Kedryna T., Marchut E., Stachurska M.B., *ATP, glukoza i mleczan krwi u ludzi narazonych na dzialanie zwiazkow fluoru pred i po profilaktycznym stosowaniu soli magnezu (Blood ATP, Glucose and Lactate Levels in Individuals Chronically Exposed to Fluorine Compounds Prior to and After Prophylactic Supplementation of Magnesium Salts)*, Folia Med. Cracov. 26, 1985, 93-97.

14. Guminska M., *Biochemical Mechanisms of Environmental Fluoride Action, Archiwum Ochrony Srodowiska* 3-4 1990, 105-115.

15. Franiczek W., *Wplyw zatrucia olowiem na rozwoj umyslowy, percepcje wzrokowa i neurotycznosc u dzieci (Effect of Lead Poisoning of Children on Their Mental Development, Visual Perception and Neuroticism)*, Ped. Pol. 57, 1982, 405-410.

16. Niwelinski J., Zamorska L., *Morfochemia lozysk ludskich z okregu Skawiy (Morphochemistry of Human Placenta from the Region of Skawina)*, Folia Med, Cracov. 23, 1981, 347-354.

17. Zamorska L., *Niwelinski J., Niektore aspekty rozrodu u czlowieka w aktualnej sytuacji ekologicznej Krakowa (Some Aspects of Human Reproduction in the Contemporary Ecological Condition of Cracow)*, Folia Med. Cracov. 24, 1982/83, 203- 209.

18. Panstwowy Zaklad Higieny, *Sytuacja zdrowotna ludnosci Polski w roku 1987* (National Department of Hygiene, *Health Status of Polish Population in 1987*), Warszawa, October 1988.

19. Guminska M., Sterecki M., Wojcik Z., *Ocena stanu zdrowotnego mieszkancow wojewodztwa krakowskiego ze szczegolnym uwzglednieniem warunkow ekologicznych (Evaluation of Health Situation in Cracow Inhabitants with Consideration of Ecological Conditions)* W: 'Ekologoczne uwarunkowania zdrowia i zycia spoleczenstwa polskiego' (S. Godzik, P. Wojcik red) SGGW-AR, Warszawa, 1990, 251-301.

20. Cebulska-Wasilewska A., Guminska M.,*Zastosowanie pomiarow czestotliwosci mutacji somatyczych u Tradescantia do badan efektywnosci mutagennej zaniczyszczonego powietrza (The Application of Somatic Mutation Frequency in Tradescantia to Measurements of Mutagenic Activity of Polluted Air)*, Folia Med. Cracov, 28, 1987, 131-138.

21. Chorazy M., *Czyniki rakotworcze w otoczeniu czlowieka. W: Chemiczne substancje toksyczne w srodowisku i ich wplyw na zdrowie czlowieka (Carcinogenic Factors in the Human Environment)*, (Red. M. Gu-

minska), PAN, Ossolineum, Wroclaw, 1990, 177-196.
22. Okolski M., Pulaska B., *Umieralnosc w Polsce w okresie powojennym wedlug przyczyn zgonow, Studia Demogr,* 3, 73, 1983, 3-36.
23. Guminska M. (ed), *Chemiczne substancje toksyczne w srodowisku i ich wplyw na zdrowie czlowieka (Toxic Chemicals in the Environment and Their Impact on Human Health),* PAN, Ossolineum, Wroclaw, 1990.

Colin Tudge

Good Science, Good Zoos, Good Conservation

If the present Green movement has a conceptual fault, it is in seeming to reject, sometimes, the *means* by which Green ideals can be brought about. We are too far down the line of planetary destruction, and the human population is already too big, for us and the rest of the world to survive except by deployment of excellent science and technology. More specifically, we have already reduced the wilderness to such an extent, and brought so many species of animals and plants so close to extinction, that we cannot hope to save either except by astute and quantified ecology, and by good genetic theory rigorously applied. In general, it is wrong of Greens simply to blame science for our ills, and reject it, as so many seem to do; and it is wrong to suppose that we can save nature simply by adopting a 'hands-off' attitude. Specifically, if we seriously want to save a significant proportion of the world's remaining large animals from extinction, then we have to take their affairs in hand. For the time being at least we have to 'manage' them in the wild, and keep reserve populations in captivity. In particular, the world's zoos have acquired — suddenly, it seems — a serious and necessary role in conservation: to breed the necessary stand-by populations.

But zoos can succeed in this newly defined task only by cooperation, and the growth of cooperation within the zoos of Europe (including the United Kingdom) during the 1980s has been a very important conservational advance. The hope that there may soon be a pan-European association of zoos, including those of Eastern Europe, and indeed spreading beyond Europe, is cause for rejoicing. Zoos have not always been popular, or deserved popularity; but people who truly care about animals, and particularly the Greens, should put their weight behind this new zoo movement.

Why, though? And how come? After all, there are plenty of arguments *against* conservation by captive breeding. The general point is that the protection of habitat is more important and more efficient, and conservational effort should therefore focus upon that. The specific objections are that captivity is innately cruel, and that to impose it in order to 'save' animals is perverse. Besides, the critics say, animals bred in zoos are fit only for zoos. Whatever they may look like, they have lost their claim to be wild animals and might as well be dead.

At first glance, the exhortation to concentrate attention on habitat protection seems to make perfect sense. Arithmetic alone suggests that is worthwhile. After all, biologists now estimate that the world may contain 30 million different *species* of living creatures, most of which are animals. Some biologists (such as the leading ecologists Michael Soule and Jared Diamond) argue that about half of those could be faced with extinction within the next century. There are only about 1,000 zoos worldwide, and if they all did all the breeding they can, they could hardly contribute to the salvation of more than a fraction of the theoretically endangered 15 million. But most species, including most endangered species, live in tropical rainforests, and indeed, each one lives in only a small part of the rainforest. So if we 'saved' just a few million hectares from the chainsaw we could, it seems, save many more species, at much less cost, than we are now spending on zoos. Besides, *unless* we conserve habitat, there seems no point in conserving animals. Should they be saved just to spend the rest of time 'behind bars'?

These arguments are forceful, but incomplete. To begin with, no serious conservationist denies the necessity to save habitat. Every biologist stresses that this must be the priority. It quickly becomes apparent, however, that there are enormous difficulties, and that habitat protection alone, for many species, is not enough.

The difficulties are of several kinds. One is world politics. National parks are the most protected of wild places (with various kinds of 'reserve' enjoying lesser degrees of protection). Historically, these parks have come into being only after decades of wrangle, and usually only when many of the species they are destined to contain are already threatened. But even national parks are vulnerable. In some, local farmers are allowed to graze livestock; of course, for there is nowhere else for them to go. Governments create the parks; but governments come and go. Some of the world's most important parks are in places of political turbulence, and in times of war, wildlife goes by the board. Little seems to have been written about the effects of the Ugandan troubles or the Vietnam War on the local animals and plants; or indeed of the First World War on, for example, the antelope of the Middle East. The human suffering overshadows the loss of animals and plants. But the effect nonetheless can be devastating: and it is as well if as many as possible of the animals and plants can *also* be kept elsewhere.

But the arithmetic does seem overwhelming. Fifteen million species is far too many to save in captivity. And indeed, we have to admit that for most endangered animals, habitat protection *is* the only hope; for most animals are in fact insects, and most of those insects are tropical beetles, which means that most *endangered* animals are tropical beetles. Many of them are extremely specialized — for example, feeding on particular leaves of particular trees — and unless we conserve those trees, and the places where they grow, then the beetles seem doomed anyway.

Large animals need habitat protection too, of course. But for many of the larger species, even the best possible habitat protection may not be enough. Each individual large animal needs a lot of space, and as we will discuss below, populations of animals need to be surprisingly large (at least several hundred) if they are to be 'viable'. That is, if they are to survive indefinitely into the future. The single remaining preserve of the Javan rhinoceros, for example, contains only fifty individuals — and is not big enough to harbour more. There are plans to create more reserves, but in crowded South-East Asia this is far from easy. Besides, poaching still has not been brought entirely to a halt, and ecologists calculate that if only three Javan rhinos are poached per year, then that will bring the species to extinction. The same is true, in different ways, for most of the world's big cats, for many bears, for wild dogs, and so on. Carnivores in general are even more endangered than herbivores, for large carnivores need so much space that even Yellowstone, in North America, may not be big enough for its grizzly bears. Such species as these need the best possible habitat protection but they will also need reserve populations elsewhere.

In general, then, we have to admit that captive breeding is a sensible strategy only for a minority of the world's endangered animals. Yet for large animals in particular it is *necessary*.

If we concentrate our captive breeding efforts on the large animals, then the arithmetic does begin to make sense. For the large animals are the vertebrates: mammals, birds, reptiles, amphibians and fish. The world contains only 4,000 mammal species, 8,000 birds, 5,000 reptiles and about 2,000 amphibians. Of these — the land vertebrates — about 2,000 are thought to be in perceptible danger. Dr William Conway, director of the Bronx Zoo in New York, has estimated that if all the zoos in the world devoted half their space specifically to breeding endangered animals, then they could at present save about 800 species. That is less than 2,000, but it is not ludicrously less. With a reasonable effort, the world's zoos could save all the world's endangered large vertebrates by captive breeding. That surely is worth doing. It really does not make sense to argue that we should not try to save the Javan rhinoceros and the Persian leopard by captive breeding, simply because we cannot save every Amazonian leaf beetle by captive breeding. We can see how absurd that argument is if we turn it round. After all we might as well argue that it is not worth trying to save beetles by habitat protection because it is not possible to save Javan rhinos by habitat protection.

What of the other criticisms, that zoos are innately cruel and that animals bred in them are no good for the wild? Well, on the first point, it is all too clear that many zoos in the past *were* cruel, and that the world still contains a great many zoos that are as awful as ever. They do not have to be, however. Animals can be captive, and yet be able to carry out virtually all of the activities they would in the wild. Go to Apeldoorn, in Holland, where monkeys roam free over many hectares, mixing with the visitors as and when they (the monkeys) choose; and where the gorillas, though not quite so free, live in one of two large, neighbouring groups in interesting terrain. Try Arnhem, also in Holland, where birds at least fly and nest free in a tropical rainforest within a plastic bubble. Try the Monkey Sanctuary in Looe, Cornwall, where the woolly monkeys spend their days among their own kind, behaving among the trees as they would do in the wild, and are into their fourth generation. Try Glasgow, where the bears have a couple of hectares, trees and hills, and again spend their days (as they would in the wild) searching for food, making nests, and interacting with their own kind. Some large animals may indeed be unsuitable for captivity; notably the cetaceans, the whales and porpoises. But even elephants can do well if given the space (as Chester, in the north of England, is contriving to show); and polar bears, albeit blanched *bêtes noires* of the anti-zoo lobby, do well if treated not as if they were sealions but as if they are, indeed, *bears* — with grass and trees, as well as water and cold rocks.

Neither is it true that zoo-bred creatures cannot return to the wild. Indeed the modern philosophy is that in the fulness of time — when wild habitats can again be made safe for them — they *should* return to the wild. Some creatures of course are more difficult to rehabilitate than others. Those that live in complicated habitats such as forest are harder to put back than those who live in simple places, such as desert. Thus orangutans are harder to reintroduce than, say, Arabian or Scimitar-horned oryx.

Nevertheless, reintroduction is *already* a proven technique. So far, the reintroduction of the Arabian oryx to Oman is the most convincing example. But 100 other such reintroductions (including the Bearded vulture in Austria) are now in train worldwide. *If* the human population ever begins to go down again (and we will all be in enormous trouble if it does not) then reintroduction will become commonplace. Already Britain is taking land out of agricultural production (in the policy of 'set-aside'), not because the population is going down but because productivity is going up; and mainland Europe will soon follow suit. Already it is sensible to consider reintroducing the wolf and the boar to Britain. Such reintroductions need not be started with captive-bred animals, but they could be, if required. In the USA, captive-bred red wolves are even now being reintroduced in Carolina.

If we concede, though, that captive breeding does have a part to play in the conservation of land vertebrates (and to a limited extent of other creatures) we may still ask, what is so special about Europe? And why should we enthuse so much about the new wave of cooperation?

To take the second question first: the main reason for cooperating is again one of arithmetic. Genetic theory, computer modelling, and field studies have shown over the past twenty years that if a population of animals contains fewer than about fifty individuals, then it is more or less bound to go extinct within a few decades. The reasons for this include natural disaster — such as epidemic. But the reasons are also 'stochastic', i.e. statistical. Thus most animals tend to give birth to male and female offspring in equal numbers — at least if this is averaged over a long time, and if the population is large. In the short term, however, a mother may have three or more sons in a row, or three or four daughters. For such reasons, small populations sometimes find themselves with an entire generation who are all of one sex. This happens often enough (statistically) to produce a significant likelihood of extinction.

Fifty individuals is far too few for comfort, however. The largest, long-term problem is that of inbreeding: too well known among the aristocratic houses of Europe to require explanation. In general, if animal populations contain fewer than about 500 individuals, they are liable to go extinct within a few generations because of inbreeding.

But what individual zoo can afford to keep 500 tigers, or even 500 antelope? Neither would it make sense to do so, for if all the

500 individuals that were left of an endangered species were in one place, they could all succumb to the same natural disaster. It is safer to spread them out.

The theory on which these ideas were based was developed in the 1970s. It was then that the world's most advanced zoos began to realize that they should cooperate with each other — instead of competing for custom, and competing to buy animals from the wild, as they had done hitherto. But for cooperative breeding programmes to work, the zoos have to be sophisticated — aware of modern conservation theory; they have to be reasonably wealthy, so they can afford to keep animals well and exchange them for breeding purposes; they need to be reasonably close geographically, so that transport is not too expensive and the animals are not traumatized by excessive journeys; and — preferably — there need to be a lot of zoos in the cooperative, to ensure that the total populations really are large.

The Americans led the way in cooperative breeding. Britain followed suit, with its own Joint Management Breeding Programmes, in the early 1980s. Mainland Europe came on board in 1985, with its 'EEPs', where EEP stands for Europäisches Erhaltungszucht Programm. The EEPs began with 19 species; and five years on, as EEP chairman Gunther Nogge (director of Cologne Zoo) told the Seventh Conference at Cologne in June 1990, there were EEPs for 58 species. The numbers still fall far short of the 2,000 that might theoretically benefit, but they are rising exponentially. North America alone expects to have 200 cooperative breeding programmes by the end of the century.

Europe came relatively late to the cooperative breeding scene (albeit by just a few years!), but it has particular advantages. First, Europe (including Britain and Eastern Europe) covers a huge area, has a huge population, and is rich; ideally suited to maintain scores of well-appointed zoos, far enough apart to avoid disease problems, but close enough to work together. Britain's zoos, though traditionaly separated, are already joining EEPs (albeit inhibited for some species by quarantine laws). Europe is able, too, to spread beyond Europe without raising too many transport problems; and indeed EEPs are already cooperating with Israel, Delhi, and some African countries. Before long, indeed, Afro-Eurasia could become one large cooperative group.

Secondly, captive breeding programmes that will truly avoid inbreeding depend upon sophisticated genetic theory — albeit theory that can boil down to rules of thumb. Thus, it is important that each individual in the 'founding' population breeds equally, otherwise some genes will be too well represented among the descendants, while others will be lost. But if animals are left to themselves, then some individuals *do* breed far more prolifically than others. Secondly, it is best to regulate family sizes; to breed from all three offspring of an individual who has triplets, and from only three among a litter of sextuplets. To keep track of which animal in which zoo is having which babies, and who is the father of whom, would be impossible, were it not for computer technology and accompanying software — plus techniques such as 'genetic fingerprinting' to assess paternity.

Increasingly, too, it will be necessary to employ 'high tech' methods for 'rescuing' species whose numbers are already so low that recovery cannot be guaranteed by conventional methods. Some of those techniques will be used, too, simply to facilitate the flow of genes between the different zoo populations, without having to shift the entire animal: an exercise that can be traumatic both for the animal itself and for the companions it leaves behind, and which is inevitably expensive. Artificial insemination is the most versatile of these techniques, especially if combined with freezing of sperm. AI and freezing are already widely applied in human medicine and in agriculture, especially for cattle and increasingly for sheep breeding. But for many other animals freezing of sperm has so far proved more difficult. Thus pig sperm is not routinely frozen, even though pigs are big business and attract a great deal of research; and for most 'exotic' species, AI and freezing have not even been attempted. However, scientists at the Institute of Zoology, sited at London Zoo, are confident that within ten years they will frame general principles which will enable them to devise appropriate techniques for virtually all species (or at least all mammals), more or less to order.

Equally promising is the technique of 'oocyte maturation'. When a female mammal is born — or even before birth — her ovaries already contain all the eggs she will ever produce; perhaps 100,000 or more. In the course of her life, during her oestrus cycles, she matures and releases only a fraction of those eggs. When she dies, the majority (and all the genes they contain) die with her. Now, for a few species at least, it is becoming possible to take immature eggs and culture them to the point where they can be fertilized in a petri dish. Again, general principles are needed to make this available to all animals. When the techniques are developed, however, it will be possible simply to take a biopsy of an ovary from a living animal, involving a small operation under anaesthetic, and rescue many hundreds of its eggs. This might be done not only in zoos, but also in the wild, bringing genes from the wild into captive populations without taking animals from the wild, or even disturbing them for more than a few hours. In vitro fertilization, already well developed for humans and cattle, should prove relatively simple, once oocyte maturation and sperm preservation have been perfected.

All the scientists involved with these techniques stress, however, that they are 'back-ups'. The genetic principles are more important, knowing which animal to cross with which. More important too is the logistic and financial framework that alone can make it possible to carry out proper breeding programmes. The overall aim, though, as everyone agrees, is to strive to maintain or re-create large and viable populations in the wild. The high tech is a step on the way to achieving this; and if the high tech succeeds, then it will render itself unnecessary. In the short term, however, species such as the Javan rhino may well have cause to be grateful for it.

Thus, the whole enterprise of captive breeding needs good science and technology; and this again is something Europe can provide. The Institute of Zoology sited at London Zoo is one of the world's principal centres both of the necessary genetic theory, and of advances in reproductive biology. At Amsterdam Zoo, biologists with Holland's National Foundation for Research in Zoological Gardens are advancing theory and providing practical back-up for EEP programmes. Germany, too, has fine zoo science, and is in general the most advanced among European countries in making zoo curatorship a specific profession.

In short, captive breeding has become necessary, and Europe's zoos seem poised to become the world's principal focus of activity (although North America is not liable to give up its claim lightly!). About 200 zoos from 25 countries are already taking part in EEPs. If they are fully to succeed, they need the backing of governments and (preferably) of industry; and they need to be supported by the conservation community as a whole. True Greens must perceive the necessity of captive breeding and of good zoos, and contribute by helping to ensure that every individual enterprise comes up to scratch.

Nick Robins

Europe in the World Economy

Following the Euro-phoria of the late 1990s — spurred by the European Community's single market programme and the collapse of communism in central and eastern Europe — the European economy is entering a period of uncertainty and doubt. Recession in the West and restructuring in the East have had a sobering impact. However, beyond these problems lies the more serious issue of European integration itself. Indeed, it is becoming increasingly clear that the traditional market-led model of economic integration in Western Europe cannot continue in light of either the events of 1989 and 1990, or the ecological prospect of 2000.

The revolutions of 1989 have made a Europe of 24 (the EC Twelve, the EFTA Six and the Comecon Six — excluding the USSR), with a variety of economic styles and potentialities, a distinct possibility during the coming decade, making a mockery of a 'single market'. The turmoil in the Middle East and North Africa following the invasion of Kuwait by Iraq in 1990 has exposed the multiple dependencies that bind the two halves of the Mediterranean together: not only is Europe reliant on external oil supplies, but in economic and demographic terms, North Africa is already a part of the Community. Both situations require the Community to take an explicitly political instead of a laissez-faire economic approach to integration, adopting regional reconstruction plans on a scale not seen since the 1940s. Finally, the continuing likelihood — if current trends continue —

of a world more divided, environmentally degraded, less secure and poorer by 2000 has revealed the ultimate bankruptcy of the current disintegrative model of integration. By contrast, a new economics of integration would be driven by the need to nurture human and natural capital, in place of the current market logic of breaking open human solidarities and natural cycles. In this sense, the integration of economies would be replaced by the goal of integrating financial, human and environmental factors into economic decision-making.

However, this will call into question the very purpose of 'Europe': the hyperbole of 1992 had allowed policymakers to view the Community as the core of a new superpower, alongside the USA and Japan in a post-Cold War 'triad'. The economic strength generated by market integration was central to Europe's membership of this club. Yet the 'Europe' of this vision threatens to ressemble Narcissus, obsessed by its own image, and ignorant of either the environment or the rest of humanity. But in the emerging 'multi-level, one world economy'[1] Europe can only be seen as a regional intermediary between global and local economies. Rather than striving for a 'single' market, the European Community, together with its partners in Eastern and Central Europe, should aim to implement a programme of economic subsidiarity, so that production is organized at the lowest appropriate level.

While the EC has adopted the principle of subsidiarity within the context of political union as a way of avoiding the term federalism, it has shied away from examining the radical decentralist implications for the economic sphere. Within a programme of economic subsidiarity, the role of supranational organizations such as the Community should be to incorporate ecological criteria into all areas of decision-making. It should also facilitate the process of decentralization, and undertake tasks (such as Europe-wide environmental planning and energy pricing) that cannot be made at lower levels. In place of self-congratulatory narcissism, this dual strategy of environmental integration and economic subsidiarity could place Europe in the vanguard of a global effort to achieve ecologically sustainable development.

Integration or Disintegration?

Traditional 'European' responses to external challenges have revolved around two polar opposites. The first is one of retreat into fragmentation and national certainties. This is what characterized the reaction of Western European countries to the economic crisis of the early 1970s, bringing to naught the plans for economic and monetary union conceived in the Werner Plan. By contrast, the second approach calls for an intensification of the existing European Community's integration process, and its extension to the rest of the continent through full or quasi-membership of both EFTA and Comecon countries. In this scenario, the internal market would stretch from the Atlantic to the Urals, and a single currency would be valid from Limerick to Lvov.

Both options are, however, flawed. The escalating globalization of economic activity has made a return to national strategies of growth in one country impossible, as the Mitterrand experiment of the early 1980s showed; the social and ecological costs make it both unpalatable and unsustainable. Nevertheless, the appeals to nationalist fundamentalism, whether from right or left — witness the similarity of approaches to the EC's 1992 programme taken in France by the Communist party and the Front National — are unlikely to diminish in coming years. Although these forces will thrive on the systemic instability of the international economy, they will hopefully remain at the periphery of political and economic debate.

In this context, a programme of seeking greater economic security through European integration appears attractive; already trade between the 18 nations of the proposed European Economic Area (EC and EFTA) far outweighs external trade. Even by the time of the EC Hamburg summit of 1988 the completion of the internal market was deemed 'irreversible' by the assembled heads of state of the Twelve. Certainly, the market-led integration pursued by the EC with such vigour over the past five years appears to go with the grain of international competition. Yet by seeming to fight the economic battles of today, Europe could lose tomorrow's ecological war. Although the 1992 process is nothing new — merely a delayed implementation of the Community's initial dreams of a Common Market — it has accelerated and served to legitimize a capital- and environment-intensive model of development that is no longer sustainable.

One response to this criticism of market-led integration would be that Europe is not alone in this; '1992' is only part of a wider process of globalization. This much is true. However, the European dimension is important because the final shape of the integrated Europe has not yet been set. The situation is sufficiently plastic, both politically and economically — particularly following the events of 1989 and 1990 — to enable 'Europe' to break the international log-jam that has held back structural reform since the collapse of the post-war economic order over 20 years ago.

The Costs of Interdependence

Since the early 1970s, the world economy has been in a state of dynamic disarray: increasingly destabilizing interdependencies have developed between different regions of the world. The 25 'golden' years of growth following the Second World War ended as the US economic engine ran out of steam and the cheap energy which had fuelled the boom quadrupled in price. The link betweeen the dollar and gold was broken, ushering in the current situation of gyrating exchange rates. Instability has become a systemic feature of an increasingly borderless world, where financial flows now outpace trade in material goods many times over.

An increasingly zero-sum relationship has developed between the affluent and poor regions of the world. In particular, while the deflationary monetarist purge of the early 1980s shook the North, it ravaged the South; commodity prices collapsed and debt surged on the back of high interest rates. While the North, Europe included, entered a period of expansion in the mid-1980s, many countries of the South were driven further into poverty. Earlier hopes of a 'trickle down' in wealth were exposed as the debt crisis grew, with a net transfer of $50 billion from

South to North in 1989. As the South Commission noted, 'a large part of the cost of controlling inflation and introducing structural changes in the North was borne by the South.'[2]

Much has been made of the parallel shift from a industrial to a service economy in the North, and to its relative 'dematerialization'. Heavy industries have declined in favour of information-intensive sectors; new synthetic materials have replaced natural commodities. The combination of high oil prices and government energy conservation strategies has helped weaken the link between economic growth and energy consumption. In the OECD region, energy intensity — the amount of energy needed to produce a unit of Gross Domestic Product — fell by 20 per cent between 1973 and 1985. However, the removal of the twin pressures for conservation — high prices and government intervention — reversed the improvement during the late 1980s. In addition, this relative improvement conceals heavy absolute use of energy consumption, with all the attendant pollution implications in terms of acid rain and global warming. Furthermore, while the economies of the North were becoming increasingly 'immaterial', imports of resource- intensive products are filling the gap in domestic production, so that the global balance sheet looks less impressive.

Whilst in environmental terms the process of 'dematerialization' has only slowed the rate of environmental degradation, in economic terms the consequences have been immense: commodity-based economies have been hard hit as relative prices for their products — expressed as terms of trade — plummetted. As a result, 'Europe, as the single market is put in place, is less dependent on the underdeveloped world than at any time in the last century'.[3] Essentially, the shift to a knowledge- and information- intensive economy has undermined the value of the South's two main areas of comparative advantage, cheap unskilled labour and raw materials. These developments raise the prospect of a hyper-efficient, capital-intensive North, increasingly floating free — in relative terms — of economic and resource ties with the South. A simplistic 'greening' of Europe could intensify this trend. Conservation strategies would further weaken prices for basic commodities, increasing the pressure to exploit nature more aggressively to maintain income levels. True conservation can therefore come only as part of a coordinated programme of resource transfer to support the diversification of developing country economies away from export-led commodity extraction.

It is in this context of an increasingly divided and unstable world that the EC's internal market programme, launched in 1985, can best be located. By removing the remaining barriers to trade, the Community hoped to propel itself onto 'an upward trajectory of economic growth lasting into the next century'.[4] The goal was to create an economic powerhouse to match, and hopefully surpass its two rivals, the US and Japan; the impact of the South was ignored. To achieve this goal, the Commission saw the concentration of production in the name of economies of scale as a key goal. A new breed of Euro-champions has been created in an unprecedented wave of takeovers and mergers: according to the Commission, no less than 1,300 transborder acquisitions, worth an estimated 30 billion ECU, took place in 1989 alone. Regardless of the economic consequences of concentration — such as dulled competitive pressures — the social and environmental implications are considerable.

In the absence of measures to fully integrate environmental costs, the encouragement given to the increasing concentration of production could lead to a substantial misallocation of resources, as well as to growing pollution. In particular, cheap transport costs have become the sinews of integration, facilitating the establishment of single factories to serve the entire European market. The EC's Task Force report into the environmental implications of the single market programme, published in 1989, gave a snapshot of the forces at work in the integration process. Even the relatively minor stimulus to growth projected by the Commission — 4.5 to 7 per cent over the medium term — would lead to substantially greater proportional increases in environmental damage, it said; road haulage alone was projected to increase by 30 to 50 per cent.

More worrying, perhaps, has been the realization that the compensatory structural fund payments made to the regions as part of the internal market deal 'will be one of the most important environmental issues arising from 1992'.[5] Thus the very measures designed to improve the prospects for the regions look set to erode their basis for sustainability. The Commission has recognized that indiscriminate growth is a problem that requires a corresponding acceleration of environmental protection. The corollary that market-led integration is simply unsustainable has not been accepted, however. Nor is this surprising when EC Commission president Jacques Delors' vision of a New Europe rests on the back of a successfully completed internal market.

Furthermore, the market-led model of integration continues to fail to provide adequate livelihoods for the people of Europe, where unemployment remains proportionately higher than in the US or Japan, despite demographic stagnation. Indeed, much of the Commission's projections of job creation through the internal market were based on governments taking accompanying measures; these have not materialized. While many during the 1980s noted the end of the era of full employment (see particularly James Robertson's *Future Work* and André Gorz's *Metamorphoses du travail*), proposals for 'ownwork' or 'work for oneself' fell on deaf ears. Even strategies for local economic development, named by Delors himself as 'une réponse européene au défi de la mondialisation'[6] have thrived only in adversity. The regional peripheralization that many fear will be exacerbated by the internal market is matched by increasing social peripheralization between an inner core of workers with stable employment prospects and a growing outer mass with temporary or no employment.

Meanwhile, on a global scale, the implications of an economics of exclusion are even more pronounced in terms of widespread under- and unemployment in developing countries. Here, the situation looks set to worsen with a labour force expected to grow by at least a quarter by 2000, against a background of the mounting substitution of cheap labour and raw materials by capital. In this context, it would be naive to expect the transition to a market economy will bring adequate employment prospects for the countries of Central and Eastern Europe. The rapid creation of sustainable community economies is an essential counterpart to the process of marketization (see Guy Dauncey's essay in this volume).

Integration and the Remedial Economy

Currently, 'Europe' stands ill-placed psychologically and institutionally to tackle these challenges. Partly this is linked to a belief in the EC myth that it can ride the tiger of corporate restructuring and produce an integrated and harmonious society. Partly, it is linked to the Community's obsession with singularity, despite protestations about subsidiarity. The vision is of a single market served by a single currency, rather than an economy organized from the bottom up. A sustainable Europe will be a Europe of many markets (and none) and of many currencies. However, the decentralist institutional ramifications of this defy the singularizing logic of 1992. By giving priority to the free trade in goods, services, people and capital over the ability of member states and localities to develop integrated environmental programmes, the Community is in fact pulling the ecological rug from under its own feet.

The main obstacle to change, however, remains the lingering belief in 'remedial' social and environmental policy. The justification for market integration — as for economic growth, more generally — is that only through creating an ever-larger market can the wealth be generated to pay for policies to remedy 'externalities' such as regional peripheralization or escalating transportation pollution. There are two problems with this argument. First, it is simply wrong: the process of uncontrolled integration creates more problems than can be remedied after the event. Second, it is politically and financially naive: there is no guarantee that the payments will be made in sufficient quantities. Furthermore, it could be impossible, since the sums involved could be insupportable, for the reason that remedial work invariably costs more than prevention. It is thus not surprising that so many problems remain unsolved. From welfare policy to pollution control, only the symptoms and not the sources of the problems are tackled. But to the tendency to peripheralize human and natural capital is marked by designating them as mere social and environmental 'dimensions' of the internal market rather than core concerns.

An Alternative Approach

The conventional logic of European integration needs to be replaced by one that integrates economic efficiency with equity and environmental sustainability. As natural capital — comprising the environment's capacity to supply raw materials and absorb wastes — is increasingly becoming the scarce factor of production, efforts must be made to reverse the current process whereby 'the market actually forces large-scale substitution of labour by the environment.'[7] This process of labour displacement and environmental extraction is now happening on a global scale and at an accelerating pace.

A minimal policy response to this problem would be to make producers pay the full cost of maintaining environmental capital through direct charges or indirect standard setting, carbon taxes or emission controls. However, because much of the current debate about the rights and wrongs of enviromental taxation has occurred in isolation from the wider economic picture, the radical implications have been obscured. Essentially, the full integration of environmental costs would transform the nature of work, by increasing the total amount of labour required. It appears that not only can full environmental pricing drive a wedge between the economy and environmental destruction, as Professor David Pearce has suggested, but also between the economy and unemployment. The challenge for Europe is thus not only how to implement such a environmental pricing programme, but how to link it to the inevitable process of labour extensification, and in particular, how to generate opportunities for employment in developing countries.

An ecological pricing policy should be seen as merely one part of a broader process of economic transformation. The democratization of industrial development is another aspect: citizens and employees should have formal, legal rights to information on corporate environmental impacts and participation in major industrial decisions. In addition, funds should be established on a 'polluter pays' basis to retrain the workers displaced by the process of increased ecological costs, along the lines of the

'Superfund for Workers' proposed by labour and environmental activists in the USA.

The events of 1989 and 1990 provide the opportunity for this integration process to be truly European. Until the events of 1989, 'Europe' was seen as almost synonymous with the EC. But confining any strategy to the Twelve is no longer possible. The development prospects for Central and Eastern Europe clearly depend on membership of a wider, multi-level European economic region. But the Gulf War also exposed the equal if not greater dependence of much of Africa and the Middle East. In both cases, potential political and demographic instability on the borders of the prosperous west demands a collective programme to promote long-term sustainability.

The starting point would be a phased introduction of a Europe-wide programme of energy taxation: since high energy use is so fundamental to current production and consumption patterns, the European level would be the most appropriate. Revenues could be distributed between conservation programmes, income tax reductions and a fund to finance low energy paths in oil-importing developing countries. Here, an energy strategy based on solar power — in the widest sense — would cut capital intensity, reduce dependence on imported oil, create jobs and reduce environmental impacts. According to the principle of economic subsidiarity, however, many other environmental factors such as water could be priced at much lower levels, according to local needs. The impact of the progressive extension of full environmental pricing, within the framework of an overall strategy promoting economic subsidiarity, would be to decentralize the production of goods and services. This would be further enhanced by measures to close material cycles through more stringent recycling requirements.

The process of decentralization would not happen either automatically or smoothly. Considerable investment — particularly since the 1992 inspired capital concentrations — has been sunk into highly interdependent trading patterns that ignore environmental costs. Unfortunately, much of this could prove to be wasted as the full costs of transportation are paid. As a result, a conscious policy of political, economic, financial and institu-

tional decentralization would be needed, in anticipation of the
re-fragmentation of the economy. Considerable government
intervention would be necessary to assist regions particularly
dependent on unsustainable trade, and to build up local capacities for autonomous development.

On an international level, Europe, as by far the largest trading
bloc, could make an important start to improving the conditions
for many developing countries reliant on commodity exports by
introducing stabilization programmes. A programme of environmental integration would require the progressive reduction
in raw material use. However, this would need to be implemented in a way that liberated developing countries from the
constraints of commodity dependence. One method would be
to transform the current system of tariff barriers to tropical
produce, for instance, into raw material charges, the proceeds of
which would be returned to the exporting nations to finance
diversification projects. Furthermore, moves toward economic
and monetary union (EMU) could be restructured as the first
part of a much-needed redisciplining of the world's financial
markets. Under an 'EMU-plus' programme, the ECU would be
used to smoothe international currency fluctuations, while
traded and non-traded currencies at the local and regional levels
would be encouraged as buffers against the fragilities of interdependence.[8]

Beyond the Economics of Narcissism

The age of 'European' integration pursued by the European
Community through the removal of barriers and the concentration of production is at a turning point. The argument that the
market must pay its way, that environmental and human capital
must be nurtured and enhanced in light of the growing world
population, has won increasing acceptance. The question is now
one of implementation. But to do this effectively will take a
broader appreciation of the development possibilities for Europe than one linked merely to the mechanistic use of Pigovian
eco-taxes. Thus there will need to be the realization that real
development in the South will only occur through trade rela-

tions built on positive discrimination and paying for long-term commodity stability. In the place of the current economics of narcissism will come the first truly European pattern of integration, based upon the coordinated management of shared resources for long-term sustainability. The imperialistic vision of a single market supplanting all others would then be consigned to history.

Notes

1. Robertson, James, *Future Wealth* (Cassells, 1990).
2. *The Challenge to the South* (Oxford University Press, 1990), p.56.
3. Mayo, Ed, *Beyond 1992* (World Development Movement, 1990), p.4.
4. Cecchini, Paolo, *1992 – The European Challenge*, 1988, p.xvii.
5. *The EC Structural Funds*, WWF/IEEP, 1990.
6. *Initiatives et Solidarités* (Syros, 1987), p.8.
7. Hueting, Roefie, and Leipert, Christian, *The Environmentalists*, 1990, p. 29.
8. Weston, David, and Kemball-Cook, David, *New Economics*, no. 16.

Philippe Van Parijs

Basic Income: A Green Strategy for the New Europe*

Poverty, Emancipation, Unemployment

I am strongly in favour of the introduction — at the European level, as soon as possible and at as high a level as possible — of what is now generally called a basic income, i.e. an income granted to every citizen or permanent resident on an unconditional basis. To obtain such an income, it would not be necessary to have worked or contributed previously, or to be registered as unemployed. And everyone (of the same age) would be entitled to the same amount, regardless of the level of income received from other sources and whether the recipient lives alone or is cohabiting.[1]

My reasons for favouring this approach have mainly to do with the need to eradicate *poverty*, to promote *emancipation* in general and the emancipation of women in particular, and to combat *unemployment*. The first two points I shall consider only very briefly; my main aim here is rather to explain the fundamental issues at stake in the choice we must make between a basic income and other possible measures to combat unemployment.

It would be ludicrous to maintain that poverty is simply a question of monetary income. Yet it is even more ludicrous to claim that poverty can be overcome without some form of guaranteed minimum income. If I am firmly in favour of the totally unconditional form of guaranteed minimum income represented by a basic income, it is because any form of conditional guaranteed income presents in a high degree one at least of the following three drawbacks (and often all three at once): 1) Because of the intrusions into an individual's private life which it legitimizes and the social stigma that attaches to it, conditional assistance is humiliating for those receiving it; 2) Since conditional assistance is restricted to those in need of it, it is withdrawn as soon as anyone starts to manage on her/his own and therefore has the effect of catching recipients in the unemployment trap; 3) Such assistance allows many of the most deprived to slip through the safety net which it claims to provide, because ignorance or intimidation prevents them from claiming their entitlement. A basic income, on the other hand, would give rise to no humiliation, it would eliminate the unemployment trap and tighten as far as possible the mesh of the net. Moreover, at any given level of minimum income it would be more expensive than conditional forms of benefit only if the 'cost' were naively measured by the volume of financial flows to be handled by the state. If instead the cost were measured by the real resources (in working time, paperwork, etc.) which a community needs to devote to managing its transfer system, the opposite would be the case.

Emancipation is not a pure question of income either. But it is not possible without a minimum of financial autonomy. The problem is how we can ensure that every person — and particularly those millions of women in Europe who have no income of their own and live in total economic dependence on their spouse — will enjoy that autonomy, while avoiding both of the following pitfalls: either urging all women to retreat into the home, which traps them in the family cell; or obliging all women to take up work outside the home, which is tantamount to forced labour. In order to achieve financial autonomy for every individual, male and female, and avoid the first pitfall, one might consider implementing what in Eastern Europe used to be known as the 'anti-parasite' law: making gainful employment both a legal obligation and a legal right of every citizen, to be supplied by the public authorities if the private sector fails to provide it. This avoids the first pitfall, but clearly not the second. To ensure financial autonomy without recourse to forced labour, one solution would be what is sometimes called a 'housewife's wage'. This avoids the second pitfall, but evidently not the first; such a payment would be analogous in principle to the repatriation allowance which some wish to see paid to migrant workers, nappies and pots and pans here being the equivalent of the country of origin. To achieve financial autonomy for everyone and steer a course between both pitfalls is not, however, impossible. *That is precisely what is achieved by a basic income.*

The End of Full Employment?

Those who advocate a basic income as a way of fighting poverty or promoting emancipation were as justified in their views two decades ago as they are now. However, a further reason has been apparent for some years now; and it is the logic of this reason which explains why the idea of a basic income has suddenly aroused such renewed interest.

For nearly two decades most West European countries have been experiencing a situation of massive unemployment. Millions of Europeans are vainly seeking work. There are not enough jobs to go round which are both *economically viable* (their cost does not exceed what demand is able to pay) and *socially adequate* (the earnings from them are not less than the minimum necessary to meet the needs of a household). What initially seemed the most obvious way to put an end to this massive unemployment was to seek to speed up the rate of growth. But in view of the speed with which technical progress was eliminating jobs, it rapidly became apparent that a fantastic rate of growth would be necessary even to keep employment stable, let alone to reduce the number of unemployed — a rate of growth, indeed, which even if it were possible, would hardly be desirable. Alternatively, one might then want to consider a substantial reduction in workers' earnings, the idea being that by reducing the relative cost of labour, technology could be redirected in such a way that fewer jobs were sacrificed. Even a relatively modest rate would then be able to stabilize and, gradually, reduce present levels of unemployment. However, such a policy would not only hamper productivity growth and run the risk of upsetting demand stability. Above all, it would impose an unacceptable standard of living on a large part of the population — all the more so in that a reduction in wages would involve a parallel reduction in unemployment benefit and other replacement incomes, so as to preserve work incentives.

If we cannot or will not rely on either an acceleration in growth or a reduction in earnings, do we then have no option but to regard full employment as an impossible target? We are, indeed, condemned to this view if by full employment we mean a situation in which virtually everyone who wants a *full-time* job can obtain one which is both *economically viable* (without any subsidy) and *socially adequate* (without any additional allowance). But we are not so condemned if we are willing to redefine full employment by leaving out one, at least, of the three conditions underlined in the foregoing sentence. To each of those conditions there is a corresponding possible strategy for reducing unemployment which involves neither an increase in the rate of growth nor a reduction in the level of earnings.

The Dilemmas of Working-time Reduction

The first strategy is the social redefinition of 'full-time', i.e. a reduction in maximum working time whether by a reduction in the maximum number of years worked (extension of compulsory school attendance, lowering of the retirement age, sabbatical years, etc.) or by a reduction in the maximum number of hours worked per year (longer holidays, the 30-hour week, etc.). Since there are not enough jobs for everyone who would like one, let us not allow a small number of people to appropriate them: they must be rationed. If this strategy is to be seriously considered as a way of solving the unemployment problem, the reduction must be both dramatic in its extent (unemployment in Europe is still running at about 10 per cent) and neutral in its effects on wages (otherwise the dynamic impact is likely to cancel out the direct impact of job-sharing). Working time must therefore be reduced by some 10 per cent on average with a corresponding (average) reduction in gross earnings levels.

However, such a strategy at once comes up against three unavoidable dilemmas. Firstly, either the across-the-board percentage reduction in gross earnings is not differentiated according to pay levels (hourly wage levels are simply retained unchanged), in which case the lowest wages will fall below the social minimum; or a greater reduction in the highest gross earnings is introduced, thus protecting those with the lowest incomes and maintaining the overall wage bill at the present level, in which case the relative cost of the least skilled jobs increases considerably, stepping up the pressure for their elimination through mechanization. In other words, a dramatic and financially neutral reduction in working time is necessarily detrimental to the least qualified jobs — either because it kills the supply (they pay less than replacement incomes) or because it kills the demand (they cost firms a lot more per hour than they used to).

That is not all. As everyone knows, unemployment is very unevenly distributed, both according to regions and to skills. This generates a second dilemma: either the reduction in working time is undifferentiated across the board, which would lead to massive inefficiencies (bottlenecks for certain skilled jobs and in certain regions, high cost of retraining in new skills, and of moving either the workforce or the means of production); or it is so devised as to affect the various categories of workers only in so far as there are job seekers with the required skills, which ensures that the system is not plagued with the inefficiencies just mentioned but imposes unacceptable inequalities — surgeons and executives, for example, being allowed to continue to work sixty hours a week, whereas primary school teachers and seamstresses might not be allowed to work more than ten.

Finally, when we think of reductions in working time, we are mainly thinking of salary- and wage-earners. But what of the self-employed? Here again, a hard choice has to be made: either they are to be treated in the same way as employees and their work shared, which would entail intractable problems in enforcement (an inspector would have to be able to check exactly how many hours a butcher puts in in her/his own backyard) without any guarantee that the extra efforts exerted would lead to any increase in recruitment except to the labour inspectorate; or no reduction is imposed on the working hours of the self-employed, in which case the enforced reduction in salaried employees' hours would mostly serve to increase the numbers of 'falsely self-employed', i.e. employees artificially detached from the salaried staff of a firm so as to allow them to work 'for themselves' for as many hours as they want. It would, furthermore, constitute a flagrant injustice, victimizing those who have no option but to be and remain salaried employees.

Subsidize the Employer or Liberate the Employee?

Awareness of these dilemmas help us to understand why the campaign to reduce working time, even in those countries where the trade-union movement has been sympathetic, is moving at a pace which is insufficient even to make up for the new rationalizations. This forces us to take another possibility into account. While it is not possible to provide everyone seeking employment with a job which is sufficiently productive, without external intervention, to be both economically viable and socially adequate, it is, however, possible to use those activities which are sufficiently productive to 'subsidize' others, rather than (vainly) trying to share out 'productive' jobs amongst all.

Two options, widely different in their consequences, are available. One consists, in its pure form, of *flat-rate employment subsidies*: a sum of money approximately sufficient to cover the basic needs of workers and their families is paid to the employer in accordance with the number of persons (s)he employs. The other option, in its purest form, is the introduction of a *basic income*: a similar sum is paid directly to every citizen (or permanent resident), and hence to every actual or potential worker, male and female, without any conditions being imposed.[2]

In many ways a general flat-rate subsidy and a universal basic income are similar. In particular, they both address head on the

first dilemma mentioned in connection with working-time reduction: the least skilled can be employed at a lower cost to their
employer without this needing to take them below the 'social
minimum', because of the wedge between labour cost and
standard of living generated by the subsidy or the grant. There
is, however, one fundamental difference between the two approaches. In the first, the pressure to take up employment is kept
intact, in the second it is removed. As a result, less productive
jobs made viable by the first approach are likely to be just as
unattractive as those which existed previously, whereas those
made viable by the second approach can only exist if workers
with the right skills find them sufficiently attractive. If the motive
in combating unemployment is not some sort of work fetishism
or a fear of leaving part of the population without a job to keep
them busy, but rather a concern to give every person the
possibility of taking up gainful employment in which (s)he can
find some accomplishment, then there is no doubt that the basic
income approach is to be preferred. If, moreover, for the
reasons outlined earlier, we cannot hope to eliminate unemployment either by accelerating growth rates or by lowering earnings
levels or by imposing a reduction in working time, then basic
income provides the only viable strategy for effectively fighting
unemployment in the sense in which it is essential that the latter
should be fought.

The Relevance of Basic Income Today

Why should basic income be made particularly relevant by the
changes that are now occurring, East and West, and giving
Europe a new shape? The 'democratic revolutions' in Eastern
Europe have most probably sealed the fate of the socialist dream
— the idea that state control over the means of production could
provide the core of a desirable society. But it does not follow that
there is no major breakthrough ahead, that we are stuck — at best
— with roughly the sort of capitalism we have got, and that the
main battles left are essentially of a defensive nature: to protect
civil liberties, the welfare state and our ecosystem against the

powerful pressures deriving, directly or indirectly, from capitalist competition. The potential breakthrough that is worth fighting for is precisely the introduction of a basic income, which
builds on the conquests of the welfare state in order to achieve
for people's *real* freedom what the abolition of serfdom and
slavery did for their formal freedom. This breakthrough is fully
consistent with a market society. It provides a sort of 'capitalist
road to communism', a way of remaining true to the valuable
emancipatory ideal incorporated in the communist 'realm of
freedom', while dismissing the institutional framework of so-
called 'communist' regimes as an inappropriate way of pursuing
it. The collapse of these regimes makes basic income capitalism
more relevant than ever as an attractive horizon for European
societies.[3]

With the establishment of the single European market in
1993, the introduction of at least a partial basic income is
becoming far more than a sheer horizon. Increased mobility of
both people and capital, increased competition in all areas make
it imperative and urgent to set up at least elementary social
protection on a European scale. How could this be done? Social
insurance systems are structured in such complex ways, and in
ways that differ so much from one country to another, that trying
to harmonize them to any significant extent looks a hopeless
task. One might then think of trying, more modestly, to introduce a European guaranteed minimum income scheme — on the
model of the British 'supplemenatary benefits', the Dutch
'bijstand', the Belgian *'minimex'*, the German *'Sozialhilfe'*, the
French *'revenu minimum d'insertion'*, etc. But if this scheme is to
be uniform across the European Community, it will either (if
low) badly damage the situation of the worst off in the more
affluent countries of the Community, whose current minimum
income level is higher than the European one would be; or (if
high) create a disastrous unemployment trap in the less affluent
countries, whose current median wage is close to what the
European minimum income would be. And if it is not uniform
across countries, it can be safely expected to generate all sorts of
unfortunate consequences, whether of a pragmatic or a sym-
bolic nature (selective migration to high-benefit countries, feel-

ing that there is a hierarchy of 'castes' of European citizens, whose membership is determined by nationality, etc.).

The roads thus sketched can and will be tried — at least as thought experiments. But my forecast is that, as a result of this process, more and more people will start thinking about a very simple alternative option. Why not introduce, say at the same time as the European currency, what could be called a Euro-grant: a basic income at a comparatively low level (say, £150 a month) paid unconditionally to every permanent resident of the EEC, and financed directly by a European tax, say a uniform taxation on private and corporate energy consumption. This Eurogrant would of course not replace all welfare state provi-sions (old age pensions, unemployment benefits, student grants, disability allowances, means-tested minimum income guaran-tees, etc.); these would only be reduced by an amount equal to the grant, and abolished only if they did not exceed this amount.[4]

In low-wage countries without a guaranteed minimum in-come, this would amount to introducing a form of income guarantee that does not create an unemployment trap. It would also provide those countries (and particularly their poorer regions), which tend to consume far less energy per capita than others, with a large, stable and non-stigmatizing net transfer of resources that reaches their citizens directly, instead of having to pass — with a heavy 'leaky bucket' toll — through a maze of programmes and organizations. In high-wage countries with a guaranteed minimum income, on the other hand, the introduc-tion of a non-means-tested Eurogrant is more like the introduc-tion of a right to work than like the introduction of a right to an income. For contrary to what happens under means-tested income maintenance systems, no one would have to give up her/his Eurogrant when finding a job. Hence, though the proposed package would not suppress the unemployment trap — because of residual income supplements provided nationally — it would significantly reduce its depth. Such a scheme, moreover, could serve as a partial substitute for European agricultural policies. It would help to guarantee small farmers a regular income, and would constitute overall a large net transfer from the cities to the countryside.

For many, including myself, this partial basic income would only count as a first step. But it is now high time to focus on it and look closely at the legal, economic, political and sociological problems its implementation would raise. This is the way forward for this — radical but realistic — Green strategy for today's Europe.[5]

Notes

1. The European literature on basic income has grown very quickly in the last few years. Tony Walter's *Basic Income, Freedom From Poverty, Freedom to Work* (London: Marion Boyars, 1989) provides an excellent general introduction, while *Arguing for Basic Income. Ethical foundations for a radical reform* (P. Van Parijs ed., Verso, 1992) provides a comprehensive critical discussion of competing justifications. The Newsletter of the Basic Income European Network (c/o Walter Van Trier, BIEN's secretary, 21 Bosduifstraat, 2018 Antwerp, Belgium), published three times a year, contains announcements of, and reports on, many relevant events, as well as short reviews of all types of relevant publications (from pamphlets to working papers) in several European languages.

2. An intermediate option would consist of paying the allowance directly to each (actual or potential) worker, but only on condition that (s)he actually works or makes her/himself available for suitable full-time work.

3. Basic income is presented and discussed in this perspective in a special issue of *Theory & Society* (Dordrecht: Reidel) vol. 15, no. 5 (1986), also available in Spanish translation as a special issue of *Zona Abierta* (Madrid: Fundacion Pablo Iglesias) no. 46/47 (1988). The relevance of a basic income to the future of Eastern Europe is discussed by Gérard Roland in the last chapter of his *Economie politique du système soviétique* (Paris: L'Harmattan, 1989).

4. A similar scheme has been proposed on a national scale by the Dutch Scientific Council for Government Policy (WRR) in an important report (*Safeguarding Social Security*, report 26, abridged English version, The Hague, 1985) and extended to the EEC by the report's senior author, Prof. Nic Douben, in 'Partial Basic Income in the Eu-

ropean Community', paper presented at the Third European Conference on Basic Income, Florence, September 1990.

5. I scrutinize at some length the nature of the connection between the demand for a basic income and Green concerns in 'Impasses et promesses de l'écologie politique' (*Esprit* 171, May 1991, pp.54-70).

* This chapter draws on the author's contribution to the hearing on 'The guaranteed basic income and the future of social security' held at the European Parliament at the initiative of its Green-Alternative group (Brussels, November 1986) and on his address to the Third European Green Congress (Stockholm, August 1987). An earlier French version has been published in *L'Europe en Formation* (Nice) summer-autumn 1989, pages 47-57.

Amory B. Lovins

Making Markets in Resource Efficiency

Most economists view the economic process as a closed loop of production and consumption — an endless, circular, disembodied flow of exchange value. In fact, however, that loop is embedded in the physical reality of a negentropic flux from resource depletion to pollution. Yet today, both these thefts from the future are not priced, so they bear little or no penalty. Resources are conventionally valued at only their cost of extraction, not their long-run replacement; pollution, at zero.

As economics professor Herman Daly notes,[1] ignoring the throughput of matter-energy

> ...is as if biology tried to understand animals only in terms of their circulatory system, with no recognition of the fact that they also have digestive tracts. The metabolic flow is not circular. The digestive tract firmly ties the animal to its environment at both ends. Without digestive tracts animals would be self-contained perpetual motion machines. Likewise for an economy without an entropic throughput.

By ignoring throughput, most economic policymakers can

'treat the world as a business in liquidation,'[2] counting depletion of capital as income — notwithstanding the late J. R. Hicks' classic definition of income as 'the maximum amount that a person or community [can] consume over some time period and still be as well off at the end of the period as at the beginning.' Depleting or polluting natural capital stocks that yield flows of resources and services, whether priced or 'free', undermines the ability to produce artificial capital — including the artificial capital meant to substitute (supposedly reversibly) for losses of natural capital.

Most successful economies use market mechanisms to pursue this self-deception more efficiently — and thereby add dangerous new layers of confusion. Optimal allocation of resources, as Daly points out, has nothing to do with optimal scale of operations, and 'a boat that tries to carry too much weight will still sink even if that weight is optimally allocated.' Nor does optimal allocation embody any feedback about when to stop: it does not reveal when growth becomes 'anti-economic', the National Product becomes too gross, and basic needs become sacrificed to extravagant wants. Nor, finally, are markets meant to address such central needs as community, beauty, integrity, or justice. Markets are meant to be *ef*ficient, not *suf*ficient; greedy, not fair. If they benefit whales, wilderness, God, or grandchildren, that is purely coincidental. Markets are very good at what they do, but their purpose is far from the whole purpose of a human being.

Nonetheless, a partial substitute for ethics in guiding economic activity can be to price depletion and pollution at considerably more than zero. This is a desirable, though perhaps not a necessary and certainly far from a sufficient, condition for morally acceptable economic behaviour: certainly it is much better than treating depletion and pollution as free goods, because if people don't pay what a thing really costs, they'll never know how much is enough. Pricing depletion and pollution encourages doing more with less, substituting resource efficiency for throughput, and thereby abating depletion and pollution simultaneously. This often saves money too, so one can do well by doing good.

Prices Without Markets

That much is now widely accepted. The 'polluter pays principle' (if not also its essential counterpart, the 'depleter disburses doctrine') is already reflected in some nations' law and custom, at least partly, and is gaining further force as rising concern over *Waldsterben* and global warning favours serious consideration of carbon and sulphur taxes.

Much less attention, however, has been given to helping people respond to those corrected price signals by using market mechanisms *to make a market in saved resources* (or in abated pollution). Merely pricing depletion or pollution does not bring together buyers with sellers; it does not take advantage of the power of market mechanisms fully exploited by many dispersed actors. Prices without markets are as if shares had quoted values but no bourse; or as if commodity prices could be negotiated only face-to-face between single dealers in small transactions in the bazaar but not acted upon by diverse parties elsewhere. This narrow vision of prices' potential pauperizes what could and should be a rich field for creative action. It imposes a penalty for, say, pollution *without providing a corresponding opportunity to escape that penalty by translating one person's potential loss into another's profit* — thereby eliciting actors who can achieve important economies of scale in supplying 'hassle-free' packaged responses to the price signal.

Making markets in saved resources and in avoided pollution holds much practical promise as a complement to, and in many cases a substitute for, regulatory intervention to mandate or prohibit particular behaviour. My colleagues and I have for some years been developing ways to supply this market approach to the efficient use of energy and water. This idea is now rapidly starting to catch on: many concepts which, a year ago, were only a gleam in the eye are now entering successful use by conservative, hard-headed, profit-making, and far from altruistic corporations.

The Efficiency Revolution

The underlying premise of this discussion is that efficient technology which wrings more work out of resources is generally cheaper, even in private internal cost, than making or mining more of them. (This is empirically true virtually everywhere for marginal electricity, fuels, and water, and probably applies to many other resources too.) Producers thus have an economic incentive to sell less of the resource and more efficiency in using it — before someone else does. This changed mix of factor inputs to produce a desired service — less of the costly intermediate good (the resource) and more of the cheap one (the resource productivity) — reduces the total factor cost of providing the service. The producer then saves operating costs or capacity costs or both,[3] reduces financial and political risks (including those arising from externalities), manages uncertainty so as to minimize regret, and can sell cheap efficiency more profitably than costly resource. Often the producer's business opportunity can be said to be arbitrage on the difference between the producer's and the customer's discount rate: a difference which, in the case of energy, is typically about tenfold.

The opportunity to profit from selling efficiency is real, pervasive, and arrestingly large. Our research has shown in detail a full practical potential, by equipping today's US factories and buildings with the best equipment now on the market, to save about three-fourths of all electricity now used, at an average cost (c.0.6 cents/kW-h) far below the cost of just operating a coal or nuclear station, even if building it costs nothing.[4] The potential is probably rather similar in western Europe, and even larger and cheaper in most east European and developing countries. Similarly, full use of the best technologies already demonstrated, but not yet all on the market, could save nearly four-fifths of US oil at an average cost (c.$3/bbl) well below that of simply *finding* new domestic oil.[5]

Most of the best of these efficiency technologies are less than a year old; their cost-effectiveness has improved, in the case of electricity, by roughly sixfold in the past five years and by nearly thirtyfold in the past ten years. And thanks to a corresponding *cultural* revolution within the US utility industry, many electric companies *are in fact* making more money at less risk — and, importantly, are also having more fun and hence attracting more talented people — by selling less electricity and more efficiency. These ideas are still quite new in Europe, but fortunately seem to be falling on fertile ground, as they hold enormous potential for restructuring east European economies.

Negawatt Markets

How can one harness the business incentive to save a resource more cheaply than it can be produced? The United States electric utility industry provides an illuminating example.

Since the mid-1970s, many US providers of electricity or natural gas have realised that a saved watt (which we may call a 'negawatt') is just like a generated watt, only cheaper, cleaner, safer, and faster to produce. Such utilities have therefore helped their customers to save electricity (or gas) through such specific programmes as information, technical design support, concessionary loans, leases, gifts, and rebates for buying efficient equipment. Such programmes are widely used, well understood, and highly successful; they can and do actually yield large, fast, cheap savings with high confidence.

Today, however, a complementary set of more market-oriented approaches is emerging from work at Rocky Mountain Institute and elsewhere. In essence, these techniques make saved electricity (or other saved resources) *into a commodity* subject to all the features of modern markets in wheat, copper, and sowbellies. Applied to saving electricity, for example, this can mean:

- **Local fungibility.** Saved electricity can be traded between *customers*: customer A, wanting cheap electricity, can privately arrange to invest on customer B's premises to save electricity there. The utility, acting as a negawatt broker, can then resell to A the amount of electricity just saved at B's facility, but at a discount, so that the utility's saved operating costs (because the saving generally costs less than short-run marginal generating cost) is split between A and other customers.

- **National fungibility.** Saved electricity can be traded between *utilities*: utility A can pay utility B to save electricity in B's territory and then sell it back to A at a mutually advantageous price. The first such contracts were recently signed.[6]
- **International fungibility.** Saved electricity can even be traded between *countries*. For example, Hydro-Québec's proposal to build a very costly hydroelectric dam and sell to Vermont 450 megawatts of its output, at a price which over time works out to about 9 cents/kW-h, is unattractively expensive. But Vermont's suggested counteroffer is to go to Montreal, fix up buildings there to save 450 MW, and then buy it back for (say) 3 cents/kW-h. The total cost to Vermont — perhaps 1 cent/kW-h to save the electricity, then 3 cents/kW-h to buy it back — will be far below Hydro-Québec's 9 cents/kW-h asking price. But Hydro-Québec would make more money by accepting the counteroffer, because the 3 cents/kW-h power is from an old dam amortized decades ago, so that price is almost pure profit, and comes without the financial and environmental risks of the new dam. If 3 cents/kW-h isn't the right price, there is plenty of room to negotiate.

   This is pure arbitrage on the difference between the cost of making and the cost of saving electricity. The scope for such profitable arbitrage is very large, especially within the logic of the post-1992 internal market in west Europe and the opening up of east European economies. Competition between megawatts and negawatts will soon teach utilities and nations that electricity is almost always worth more saved and resold than wasted at home.

- **Derivative instruments.** Markets in saved electricity can be not only spot markets but also futures and options markets — an ideal way to hedge planning risks. A 'negawatt future' would be an underwritten promise to deliver a certain amount of saved electricity at a certain time, place, and price. That contract would have a market value. This concept is now under serious discussion.

- **Peak-load covenants and secondary markets.** Another marketable instrument could be a binding covenant that a given factory or facility will never use electricity at more than a certain peak rate, so the utility needn't go on planning as if it were going to, and can avoid costly capacity. This 'capped demand covenant' would have a value in a secondary market. It is like the US Environmental Protection Agency's present practice of regulating air pollution under the 'bubble concept': someone wanting to open a polluting factory in a place with dirty air must first abate that much pollution somewhere else in the same airshed. In practice this is done, not by physically finding and cleaning up another plant, but by buying from a broker, at market price, a previously earned certificate of decreased air pollution. Buying stabilized or reduced electrical demand should be no different.

  A special case, already widely practised, is the 'curtail to threshold tariff': a customer expresses willingness, in rare power emergencies, to receive less electricity than usual, down to a certain 'threshold' mutually chosen in advance. The utility then pays the customer monthly for each peak kilowatt by which such curtailment is available, whether it is actually exercised or not.

- **Auctions.** Saved electricity can be bought by competitive bid to minimize its cost. A utility (or an independent broker) wanting a certain number of megawatts can simply solicit bids for that much electricity, or less, to be made *or saved or displaced* by anyone, by any means, at a series of increasing prices, until the target is reached; or the auctioneer can simply ask for bids and choose the lowest ones. Such 'all-source bidding' is now required in eight of the United States and is spreading rapidly. Efficiency bids generally undercut power plants, beating even industrial cogeneration and otherwise competitive renewable energy sources.

  As a special case, one US utility offered industrial modernization grants — cash given to help adopt more efficient processes or equipment which would save electricity more cheaply than the utility could make it. The grants simply went to those firms which bid to save the most electricity per dollar of grant.

- **Cross-marketing.** Electricity is usually suplied by monopolists operating in a specifically franchised territory. But there is no monopoly on electric *efficiency*; it may be freely sold anywhere.[7] Thus about a dozen investor-owned utilities already sell efficiency, for fun and profit, in the territory of other utilities less alert to their opportunities. One US utility sells electricity in a single state but efficiency in six states. (Before long, I dare say, German utilities will be investing to save electricity in France, Greece, and the Soviet Union as routinely as in the Federal Republic itself.) It is even possible for a natural-gas utility to make a large profit selling *electric* efficiency — and thereby change the behaviour of buildings in ways which open up new gas markets.

- **Sliding-scale hookup fees.** A useful adjunct to these market-making methods is to internalize some of the social costs of inefficient buildings by charging, before connecting any substantial new building to the grid, a fee which is positive *or negative* depending on the efficiency of the building. This has major advantages for all parties—builders, financiers, buyer/occupants, utilities, and other customers. Such a scheme is halfway through being passed into law in one state, and half of it is in use (with the other half proposed shortly) in four others.

One state is seeking to apply a similar concept to new automobiles by adjusting its normal 5 per cent sales tax upward or downwards, over a range of 0-10 per cent, depending on efficiency. It would be even better to have a *negative* tax for the most efficient cars — the more efficient, the bigger the rebate — for buyers who scrap their old, inefficient cars so nobody will ever drive them again. (Bring in a death certificate — or two bumpers and a fender? — and get your rebate. Or scrap your old car, *don't* replace it, and collect a bounty.)

Such methods can make negawatt markets in which everyone can play, promoting bounty-hunters who go looking for opportunities to invest in correcting inefficiency wherever they find it. That is surely a faster — and, thanks to the resulting competition, a cheaper — way to wring out inefficiencies than relying on a few large institutions alone.

Other Resources

Similar methods are already being applied to saving water in dry parts of the United States and in places facing costly expansions of wastewater-treatment capacity to abate pollution. Sliding-scale hookup fees, giveaways, mass retrofits, rebates, arbitrage, inter-utility trades of saved water — all are rapidly entering standard practice. In fact, one water-short town has invented a new method: any builder wanting to construct a new house must first install water- saving equipment (or fix leaky water mains) to save that much water elsewhere. The result: builders equipped a third of all the houses in town with efficient fixtures in the first two years.

Could not similar methods apply also to other scarce resources? Could not the social value of not burning oil, for example, be reflected in prices signalled by spot, futures, and options markets in *saved* oil, so that arbitrageurs can exploit the spread between barrels and negabarrels? Could not 'negatons' of saved or recycled metals be traded alongside tons of virgin metals? Might not one firm or country use brokers to find others with whom resource efficiency improvements and pollution abatements could be profitably traded? Why not acquire resources by auctions which establish the functional equivalence of new with saved resources, of pollution with abatement? How much is it worth paying people to stay *off* the roads so we needn't build and mend them so much? As with subatomic particles, for every resource there is an equal and opposite 'anti-resource', for every activity an abatement, each arguably meriting a value and a market.

Making markets in resource efficiency and environmental protection has even wider implications. Consider, for example, the analogy between energy and security. People don't want kilowatt-hours; they want energy services such as comfort, light, mobility, and torque. But if the only way they know to get the services is by buying elecricity, then a choice to use less electricity and more efficiency cannot be expressed in the market; utilities will therefore have an effective monopoly in providing the final services; and price elasticity of demand for electricity will appear to be very small. The solution is to articulate, make available, and make markets in the efficient use of electricity, so that electricity must openly compete with electrical productivity.

Analogously, people don't want weapons; they want to be safe and feel safe. But if the only way they know to get security is through weapons, then the weapons vendors will have an effective monopoly in providing security services, and price elasticity of demand for weapons will appear to be very small (reinforced by the monopoly, monopsony, and often corrupt political process through which the weapons are bought). That is why Rocky Mountain Institute is trying to articulate and bring to market the specific, practical elements of an alternative concept of security — so that other ways to achieve freedom of fear from privation or attack will become more available as alternative intermediate goods with which weapons must compete in the political marketplace.

Putting a proper price on depletion and pollution cannot replace a proper regard for our moral obligations to beings in other places, forms, and times. But prices *imaginatively combined with flexible, accessible markets* can at least apply to corrective mechanisms the same vigour and ingenuity — the same genius of the market, the same diversity and adaptability — that have got us into this mess. Markets that *apply* the new price signals, and focus them into action, will at least help make the struggle between destroying the future and creating it a more nearly equal contest whose issue is less in doubt.

Notes

1. H.E. Daly (World Bank), 'Steady-State versus Growth Economics: Issues for the Next Century', Hoover Institution Conference on

Population, Resources and Environment, Stanford University, 1-3 February 1989.

2. H.E. Daly, 'Sustainable Development: Some Basic Principles', keynote address, ibid. The present paper's opening section is much indebted to Daly's many seminal writings.

3. In US regulatory practice, however, the normal process of price formation unfortunately rewards utilities for selling more electricity and penalizes them for selling less. This perverse incentive has been successfully corrected by a simple balancing-account mechanism in California. In July 1988, the Conservation Committee of the National Association of Regulatory Utility Commissioners unanimously endorsed two new regulatory principles now starting to enter state practice: that by this or other means, utilities' profits should be decoupled from their sales, so they become indifferent to whether they sell more or less electricity; and that any utility which reduces customers' energy-service bills should be allowed to keep part of that saving as extra profit.

4. This potential is documented in encyclopaedic detail by Rocky Mountain Institute's Competitek update service, currently provided to approximately 80 utilities and other organizations in 18 countries.

5. A. B. Lovins, 'Drill Rigs and Battleships Are the Answer! (But What Was the Question?)', in R. Reed & F. Fesharaki, eds, *The Petroleum Market in the 1990s* (Westview, Boulder, Colorado), 1989, or Rocky Mountain Institute Publication no. S88-6.

6. Electricity saved at the point of use requires no transmission, but rather *frees up* transmission capacity to 'wheel' the cheapest power around the grid; so negawatts, rather than paying a wheeling fee, deserve a wheeling *credit*.

7. 'Selling efficiency' means selling any required mix of advice, design services, project management, financing (usually the most important part), equipment, installation, commissioning, operation, maintenance, and monitoring. It is essentially an information/financial product.

Guy Dauncey

The Fourth Way: Building a Sustainable Community Economy

There is another way. In between the rocks of a communist state-controlled economy and the whirlpools of a capitalist free-market economy, there is another way.

There is a way which encourages business, creates jobs, preserves the environment, develops community, meets people's needs, and fosters both wealth and wellbeing, which is neither capitalist nor socialist, which avoids both the social and environmental abuses that accompany free-market capitalism and the rigid hand of state planning that crushes initiative and enterprise, and yet which retains the best qualities of both systems.

It is the Third Way. As a path of economic development, it is scarcely 30 years old, compared to the 150 years of socialism and the 300 years of capitalism. It is a path of practice, not of theory. Its principles and values have been developed on the ground in the villages, towns and cities around the world where it is being developed, not in books or papers. This is why you will not find much written about it in print.[1]

As a method of economic development, it does not produce millionaires, or expensive cars and luxury homes, but it does create meaningful jobs for local people within their own communities, and it does create stable communities, in harmony with their cultures and in command of their own destinies.

The Third Way is the path of *community-based economic development*. It is founded on four values and four principles.
The four values are:

1) care for the individual members of the community;
2) care for the local community as a whole;
3) care for the community's culture; and
4) care for the community's economy.

The four principles are:

1) the practice of community resourcefulness and empowerment, as well as individual resourcefulness and empowerment;
2) the pursuit of community profit, as well as individual profit;
3) the build-up of community ownership, as well as individual ownership;
4) the importance of cooperation, sharing and mutual support, as means to these ends.

These are the cornerstones of health, wealth, wellbeing and prosperity in a community economy.

The emphasis on community provides the essential middle ground that is missing from both communist and capitalist economies, with their emphasis either on the collective (communism) or the individual (capitalism). The emphasis in community economic development is on the actual community where people live, be it a village, town, region or neighbourhood, and on the individuals for whom that community is home.

The Third Way is young, but it is not young enough to have incorporated the principles and values of environmental sustainability into its practices. When the communities described below started along the community economic path, the environmental movement was still too young for people to appreciate its importance. So while the community economic path can bring prosperity and wellbeing to a community, and enable a community to establish control over its own destiny, and avoid the constant social and environmental abuses that accompany free-market capitalism, it does not yet address the practical issue of ecological sustainability in the way it operates.

For this reason, I have entitled this essay 'The Fourth Way: Building a Sustainable Community Economy'. The more we learn about sustaining the environment, the more we realize that decisions affecting a local ecosystem are best made by those who know that ecosystem best and who have lived there the longest. A forest is best protected by those who have learnt to dwell in it. A river is best protected by those who live on its banks and fish from its waters. An ecosystem is a community of species, which includes its human inhabitants. Only when those inhabitants make collective decisions about their relationship to the local ecosystem can we have development that is ecologically sustainable. The processes of community economic development lend themselves perfectly to the needs of ecological sustainability, which is not true of capitalist or communist development. In a community economy, economic development decisions are made by the community as a whole, not by individual businessmen, developers or state planners. A community which plans its economic future can also plan its ecological future. *Community decision-making and ecological decision-making are inseparable.* This is why ecological sustainability must be underpinned by a community economy.

Before considering how to build a sustainable community economy, we must first consider how to build a community economy. This is best done by example.

In the tiny villages of Ballinakill, in Connemara, on the west coast of Ireland, a community of just 1,700 people is building itself a new future.

Connemara has been poor for as long as anyone can remember. Most farms are less than 15 acres, the soil is poor, and the young traditionally leave to seek a better future in Dublin, London or America. In 1970, the villagers formed a Community Council, and then established a Credit Union, or community-owned bank, to establish control over their own financial savings. In 1971, they formed a community-owned development company (Connemara West) to explore new ways of developing their community and its economy. They raised £13,000 from 500 local people and built nine thatched cottages for holiday-makers. Holiday cottages are usually owned by someone from the city, so the rent leaves the local economy and contributes no further value. In Connemara, the villagers themselves own the cottages, so the rent remains within the village, where it contributes to the community economy and is used for community purposes.

When the cost of the cottages had been paid off, the villagers used the income to build a centre for traditional Irish music, song and dance. In 1978 they bought an old school for £21,000, and used it to house a Farmers Coop, a Fish Farming Coop, a sports centre, five local crafts businesses, a shop, a cafe and the development company. They established a three-year craft training programme for young people, followed by a permanent two-year course in fine woodwork and furniture-making, in partnership with the regional technical college, which led to young people starting their own woodworking company. They are now developing their own radio station.

The people of Connemara have discovered how to become resourceful, as a community. Before 1970, there were just six organizations in the community. There are now 31, including nine which have economic goals such as the Sheepbreeders Association and the Craft Cooperative, four sporting groups, and an active environmental society. All this from a population of only 1,700 people.

> 'Things don't fail because of money. They fail without commitment. What is needed is fantastic commitment, dedication, and a belief in what a community is doing. There *is* goodwill and potential, but governments can't seem to harness it. For some reason, it seems to be the government in conflict with the people' (Michael O'Neill, Teach Ceoil).[2]

The town of Esperance, 750 km from Perth on the southwest coast of Australia, has 10,000 inhabitants. In the mid-1980s, land prices began to fall, there was a bad drought, and the local farming economy began to decline. Left to free-market capitalism, the town would have simply faded away, and the farms would have returned to the wild.

That was not to be. In 1985, Ernesto Sirolli was asked by the Minister for Regional Development to see what could be done. Ernesto is a community facilitator, not a businessman or a developer. He believes in people's dreams, and he helps make them happen.

> 'Human nature is like a plant: if you give it sun and water the human being will grow. You have to have faith, faith in people. There's nothing I can do in Esperance if no one in Esperance wants to do anything. I'm a midwife; if nobody's pregnant, well, forget it' (Ernesto Sirolli).[3]

Sirolli spent several months in the community, listening, learning, and encouraging people in their own resourcefulness. When there were obstacles, he helped find ways through them. He helped an unemployed fish-cannery manager to launch his own fish-smoking plant. Word got around. The farmers came to him to ask for help in exploring ideas such as developing a sheepskin products business, and local sausage production. (The town was importing all its sausages, costing the community $10,000 a week. A local producer set up shop, and soon took 10 per cent of the market, adding $1,000 a week to the local economy.) A committee was set up, and a full-time development worker was hired. Two months later he had 45 projects on the go, plus an aboriginal subcommittee which led to 15 new jobs in aboriginal businesses. After ten months, Esperance had 35 new businesses and 58 new full-time jobs, for an outlay of $32,000, which saved $377,000 in unemployment benefits — a 1,000 per cent return on the investment. An additional $4,900,000 was flowing around Esperance each year through the new activities.

The first principle of community economic development is community resourcefulness. Instead of complaining about the government and waiting for someone to provide you with jobs, you start thinking about ways in which you can help yourselves, such as how you can help people start their own businesses, and how you can raise your own capital, or start your own community bank. You get together, and you get on with it. You seek community profit, not individual profit.

The best-known example of a successful community economy has been built in Mondragon, in Northern Spain. The story begins in the 1940s, in the wake of Franco's fascist onslaught against the Basque country. A Jesuit priest, Jose Maria Arizmendi-arrietta, held discussions with local people about the economic implications of Jesuit Catholic theology. They found answers in the work of Robert Owen, who emphasized the importance of working cooperatively as a community.

> 'Salvation is achieved through community action, and involves the development of the capacity to think, to invent, and to serve' (Don José Maria).[4]

In the 1950s, the people of Mondragon started developing their own worker-owned cooperatives. A cooperative bank (the Caja Laboral Popular), a college, a technical research centre, several schools and their own social welfare fund soon followed. By 1990, 20,000 people were working in a network of 180 linked cooperatives.

One of the most remarkable things about Mondragon has been its success. In the recession of the early 1980s, when the surrounding region of Spain was experiencing 30 per cent unemployment, the Mondragon coops had just 37 people on welfare — an unemployment rate of 0.18 per cent. At the same time, they experienced a zero per cent business failure rate. They chose to close three coops, but not one failed, even though the market for goods fell by 10 per cent all over Europe.

How did they achieve this? By mutual support — the fourth principle of community economic development. The Mondragon cooperatives have detailed cooperative agreements through which they help each other. As well as owning their own cooperatives, the workers also own the bank, the Caja Laboral. They hire the managers, and decide on policies and priorities.

Through the Caja, they have put in place a system of mutual support which may be one of the most significant economic breakthroughs of the century. The bank helps every cooperative to think and plan ahead. If a coop's yearly future survey shows trouble looming, appropriate changes are made, with the bank's help. If need be, the cooperative is closed down. The workers move to other cooperatives or join training courses, and steps are taken to begin creating a new cooperative to take its place. The processes of birth and growth are nourished by the bank. The rewards of this collective intelligence are demonstrated in the results: zero business failures, and zero unemployment. Mutuality goes a step further at Mondragon: when demand fell by 10 per cent in the early 1980s, and companies across Europe were firing 10 per cent of their workers, the workers at Mondragon simply took a 10 per cent wage cut. They care about each other, and they share both the good times and the bad.

There are many other examples which show how a community economy develops. In Bangla Desh, the Grameen Bank is lending money to landless villagers on a system of 'peer group collateral', with great success. In Chicago, a privately owned bank operating on community economic principles is the only one out of 14,500 American banks to put more money into a low-income neighbourhood than it takes out. In British Columbia, Canada, a community currency has been pioneered which enables local people to trade among themselves without need for normal money. In Britain, business development agencies are helping local people, including unemployed teenagers, to start their own businesses, with considerable success, and minimal cost. In Modena, Italy, small businesses have established their own loan guarantee fund to ensure that they can meet their capital needs. There are at least 30 practical processes which a community can use to develop its economy. Together, they form the toolkit of community economic development.[5]

Those who are involved in the development of the Third Way around the world have seen from their own experience that it can bring solid results of a lasting nature. Once the dimension of ecological sustainability is added, a developmental path emerges which is sorely needed all around the world, wherever there is poverty, need, hunger, environmental abuse, frustrated hope or unliberated dreams. It allows people to have a vision they can truly believe in, in the communities where they live.

> 'Where there is no vision, people perish'
> — prophet Isaiah.

> 'There is something fundamentally wrong in treating the Earth as if it were a business in liquidation'
> — Herman Daly, economist, World Bank.

> 'We need to build a wholly new global economic system' — Vaclev Havel, president of Czechoslovakia.

The newly democratic countries of Eastern Europe have a particularly urgent need both for vision and for change. They have the option to embrace the Fourth Way as their chosen path of development, and move directly to an economy, a set of values, a social order and a way of life that are ecologically sustainable, economically successful, community-oriented, personally fulfilling and globally equitable, without having to learn from painful experience that the free-market capitalist path *does not have the ability* to deliver these particular goals.

If a country decided to choose the Fourth Way as a path of development, how should it begin? Two routes are possible: The first involves establishing pilot community economic initiatives in chosen communities, so that people can learn by example. This is the route that the West European countries are taking by default, in the absence of any national vision or leadership. The leadership is coming from creative individuals who press ahead on their own initiative in the communities where they live. It is an effective method, for people do learn by experience — but it is slow. It takes up to 30 years for a community to establish a new economy, however you go about it. After 30 years of adopting this approach, you would have a few successful examples of a community economy, while the rest of the economy would have developed along traditional capitalist lines, with all the disadvantages this brings. For this reason, this approach is not recommended. There is simply not the time, either ecologically, politically, socially or globally.

The second route involves a deliberate choice of the Fourth Way as your country's developmental path, be it Latvia, Poland, Slovenia, Brittany or Ireland. The knowledge and experience already exists in communities around the world. What is needed is a developmental framework which will enable the bottom-up processes of community development to take off, facilitated by a top-down process of training and support.

There are four core institutions which must be established in a community which is seeking to develop a sustainable community economy. These are:

1) a Community Government;
2) a Community Development Agency;
3) a Community Bank;
4) an Environmental Stewardship Council.

The *Community Government* is the democratically elected government of the local community, with the powers and responsibilities to raise taxes, pass by-laws, take initiatives, and draw up community plans. Most countries in Western Europe are far too centralized, and do not give sufficient powers to the local community level to allow for an effective developmental process. A community as small as 1,000 people needs its own local government, so that its people can express their will and take responsibility for developing their future.

The *Community Development Agency* enables a community to assess its problems and needs, articulate its vision of a desirable future, and take practical steps to realise that future. This takes a lot of learning, and patient listening. It takes the skill of facilitation, which is the art of assisting a community, group or individual to realize, express and act upon its deepest problems, feelings, hopes and wishes. It requires training in new skills, such as management, planning, envisioning and community development.[6]

The Community Development Agency can help people start business initiatives. If there is need for housing, it can help people form a housing company. If there is high unemployment, it can establish support systems for unemployed people. If there is need for special skills, it can set up training programmes. It can purchase property in the name of its shareholders. In Eastern Europe, a Community Development Agency could purchase state-owned factories and farms, if members of the local community thought it appropriate. It can issue shares to local people, who become co-owners of any business or property owned by the people.

The *Community Bank* collects the savings of local people and lends them out to finance initiatives which are socially, ecologically and economically sound. It takes steps to ensure the health of any business that it lends money to, and plays an active role in guaranteeing the long-term economic development of the community.

The *Environmental Stewardship Council* has the responsibility to ensure that all economic development is ecologically sustainable, and to shift the local economy onto a long-term sustainable basis. The Council can use a wide range of tools to achieve its goals, including developing an inventory of the local ecosystem, establishing local ecological stewardship groups, starting restoration projects, setting up educational programmes, launching 'greening of business' programmes, establishing guidelines to govern the use of natural resources, conducting environmental impact assessments on new developments, etc.[7]

The Fourth Way does require a free-market economy which allows prices and wages to find their own level, to allow initiative and reflect natural demand, so reforms to that end are still needed in Eastern Europe. It also requires an open trading system — but one that includes the full environmental cost of produce in its price system, and discourages unnecessary trade and transportation. The development of local currencies may be one way in which regions can encourage greater local self-reliance, and lessen unnecessary trade.[8] It requires national and regional frameworks of policy and legislation which encourage environmentally sustainable forms of transport, energy, farming and resource extraction. These, and many other national policy initiatives, are unfortunately outside the scope of this essay, which is limited to the local level.

At this stage I will take off the hat of writer and put on the hat of policy consultant, to address the question Ministers of Economic Development will face if they want to launch their countries on the path of sustainable community economic development: *'How do we start on this path?'*

The need for action is now. The development will be bottom-up — but the beginning can be facilitated in a top- down way. I suggest a four-state process:

YEAR 1
Stage 1: Form national committees for each of the four core community institutions, and give them six months to consult the best practitioners globally and come up with recommendations on what shape those institutions should take.

Stage 2: Form four separate teams, and give them six months to develop a one-year training programme for each core institution, to train teams of community facilitators who would go into communities to help them establish the core institutions.

YEAR 2
Stage 3: Run the training programmes in regional centres all over the country, accompanied by educational radio and television programmes, to allow others to share in the learning process. Use an action-learning approach so that trainees begin the process of community discussion and involvement during their training. Establish regional associations to provide ongoing training and support to the facilitators once they are at work. Pass legislation to provide the core community institutions with the necessary operating frameworks.

YEAR 3
Stage 4: Hold elections for local community governments, and empower the community facilitators to help the community governments to establish community development agencies,

community banks and ecological stewardship councils in each community. Begin work on the various processes of sustainable community economic development, as defined by the various problems, needs, dreams and goals of each community.

This has been a necessarily brief and incomplete outline of the steps which could be taken to begin to build a sustainable community-based economy. More detail could be provided, but space prohibits. Much has been written about the need for 'sustainable development', but up until now, very little has been offered in practical terms. This essay makes a concrete start in that direction. The practice is based on the concrete experience of community economic and environmental initiatives from around the world. The philosophy is based on a host of thinkers who have been an inspiration to the green movement for more than 30 years.[9]

This is not a pipe-dream, it is something solid and achievable. Ministers of Economic Development: please take note.

The different countries and regions of Eastern (and Western) Europe will need support as they embark on the task of building sustainable community economies. There is need for a major international programme to provide the necessary education, training and support. *We cannot go on pretending that the two separate processes of capitalist economic progress and environmentally sustainable development will somehow 'magically' become one*. We *must* address the fact that if the countries of Eastern Europe pursue the traditional path of free-market capitalist development, the effect will be a social and environmental disaster. This is already true for many countries of the South.

Practitioners of sustainable community economic development around the world should meet together, perhaps at the regular TOES meeting (The Other Economic Summit) which happens every July in parallel with the G7 superpower economic summit, and make plans to approach the United Nations, the World Bank and the various development banks with proposals for such a programme.[10] The whole structure of international assistance needs to be reshaped to reflect the goals and priorities of sustainable community economic development. There is need for a new global Marshall Aid programme to kick-start the process, and turn the ideals of 'sustainable development' into realistic and realisable programmes which countries can draw upon. It is a big thought — but we have to think big.

There is simply no time to do otherwise.

Notes

1. A good understanding of the processes of community economic development can be gained from the following books:
   Dauncey, Guy, *After the Crash: The Emergence of the Rainbow Economy*, Greenprint, London, 1988 (includes a detailed reference list and addresses);
   Meeker-Lowry, Susan, *Economics as if the Earth Really Mattered*, New Society Publishers, Philadelphia, 1988;
   Strandberg, Coro, *Nine Case Studies of Community Economic Development in British Columbia*, SPARC, Vancouver, 1985;
   MacLeod, Greg, *New Age Business: Community Corporations That Work*, CCSD, Ottawa, 1986;
   Benello, George, et al, *Building Sustainable Communities: Tools and Concepts for Self-Reliant Economic Change*, Bootstrap Press, New York, 1988.

2. Dauncey, *After the Crash: The Emergence of the Rainbow Economy*, see above.

3. Originally quoted in the Australian magazine *Work Matters* (date unknown).

4. MacLeod, *New Age Business*, see above.

5. Dauncey, *After the Crash: The Emergence of the Rainbow Economy*.

6. Bryan, Frank, & McClaughry, John, *The Vermont Papers: Recreating Democracy on a Human Scale*, Schumacher Society, Barrington, MA, USA, 1989;
   McClaughry, John, *Bringing Power Back Home — Recreating Democracy on a Human Scale*, Schumacher Society Lecture, Barrington, MA 01230, USA, 1987.

7. Todd, John, *Towards an Ecological Economic Order*, Schumacher Society Lecture, Great Barrington, MA 01230, USA, 1988.

8. Swann, Robert, *The Need for Local Currencies*, Schumacher Society Lecture, Barrington, MA 01230, USA, 1989;
Kennedy, Margrit, *Interest and Inflation-Free Money*, Schumacher Society, Barrington, MA 01230, USA, 1990.

9. This way of thinking has been expressed most clearly by the economist and philosopher, E. F. Schumacher.

10. The Other Economic Summit, New Economics Foundation, 88-94 Wentworth St., London E1 7SE, UK.

Fred Harrison

Geonomics: The Making of a Post-Socialist Society

The ideological distress of the former Marxist societies offers a unique dialectical opportunity to participate in the transformation of society. The experiment under way in Eastern Europe stems from the recognition that not only was there a fundamental flaw in the economic foundations of the old economic order, but also that the ecological crisis could not be resolved by the existing system of values and institutions. Mikhail Gorbachev, in acknowledging the need for perestroika, built into his last rites the admission that the environmental crisis was an inextricable part of the decision to end one social system and begin the search for a new approach. Here, then, was the first systemic confession that social behaviour and industrial processes were unsustainable.

The assault on nature had been as vicious as the denial of civil liberty. The reason is not difficult to fathom. According to Marxist economics, land (defined to encompass all of nature's resources) is a free input in the productive process. The labour theory of value provided the rationalization for what was to become the ritual sacrifice of nature on the altar of a social system that venerated labour power and set the value of the power of nature at zero. The result was tragically visible. Anyone watching could see the evolution of a lunar landscape in which rivers were polluted, resources exhausted, fertile soil impoverished and landscape wreathed in vapours of death.

This process of despoliation was a rational one, within the

terms of the Marxist theoretical framework. As the productivity of labour and capital diminished, so apparent 'value' was raised by the expedient of increasing the inputs of raw materials (Gorbachev 1988: 18-21). The extensive exploitation of the 'free' resources of nature were not reckoned in nation's balance sheet, so the real costs in terms of the waste of labour, capital and land were concealed. This process could continue for as long as the resources were there to be used and abused. But it was only a matter of time before the system broke down; nature, if not society, would fight back, providing the logic for what, in Marxist terms, could only be characterized as a counter-revolution. If ever there was a holistic challenge, this was it!

Eastern Europe needs a qualitative change that simultaneously satisfies the demand both for economic development and the restoration of the integrity of the natural foundation on which society is built. Yet some of the leading market economists have confessed, in print, that they were unable to articulate a formula for smoothly engineering one component of the problem — the transformation towards a market — let alone simultaneously address the ecological imperatives. The best they have offered is a sledge hammer, and the advise that the former socialists should buy carbon copies of the western blueprint. The sledgehammer was appropriate for knocking down the Berlin Wall, but it is not the sophisticated instrument that is needed to effect change with the minimum of hardship and the maximum prospect of goal achievement. The demise of socialism has exposed the vortex in the philosophical system that underpins the market economy of the West.

Social science is not really an impoverished tool. By returning to the philosophical roots, we can assemble a set of principles that identify the wrong turning points in history and derive lessons that enable us to prescribe remedial measures. In their essential nature, varying only in degree, the problems in the former socialist countries are also embedded in both the industrially developed economies and the Third World. The lessons of history can be generalized to meet the socio-economic and environmental challenges elsewhere in the world.

Economics is rooted in the classical theories that were developed two centuries ago. That the fundamental hypotheses of Adam Smith[1] and David Ricardo are still regarded as fruitful suggests that current problems may not be with economics as a social science, but in the ideological application of the theories. For example, is there not something offensive about the lingering belief that economics is the 'dismal science', which enables people to libel nature as 'niggardly'? Nature is bountiful, and economics opens one of the gates (that marked 'Materialism') to at least partial happiness. The 'dismal' tag is an ideological device to distract people from the causes of poverty and the abuse of nature.

Modern political philosophers, starting with John Locke, misdirected the evolution of culture by failing to resolve what was to become an inescapable problem: the limits to private rights in property. They had no difficulty in demonstrating that, for the sake of liberty, no individual could be owned by another. Similarly, theprivate ownership of man-made artifacts (whether as consumable goods or in the form of labour-saving/wealth-producing capital equipment) was self-evident. These goods are infinitely reproducible, but they come into existence only if we mix our labour with the materials of nature. So, providing he was armed with the right of access to nature, no able-bodied person need want for the material goods required by himself and his family.

That was the key problem: regulating access rights to land, to ensure that everyone had a share. The philosophers ducked it. Locke, in *The Second Treatise on Civil Government*, argued that while land was given by God to mankind in general, it was necessary to accord the individual the right of access to the fruits of nature, if he was to sustain his life. And to protect the right of the individual to his labour, it was necessary to grant exclusive rights to the property in which he mixed that labour. The ownership of land, however, was not so easily resolved.

'God gave the world to men in common, but since he gave it them for their benefit and the greatest conveniences of life they were capable to draw from it, it cannot be supposed he meant it should always remain

common and uncultivated. He gave it to the use of the
industrious and rational (and labour was to be his title
to it); not to the fancy or covetousness of the quarrel-
some and contentious. He that had as good left for his
improvement as was already taken up needed not
complain...' (Locke 1690: 29).

Locke — who did not defend the waste of natural resources —
defended the private ownership of land because there was 'as
good left for....improvement as was already taken up.' But what
happened once society was confronted with what we can call the
Demographic Imperative? Sooner or later, the virgin lands were
going to run out, and there would not be enough of the earth to
directly accommodate everyone's needs. When the last frontier
was closed, what then? Locke did not offer a solution, and by the
time it happened, the rules of the property game were set in
cement — a social contract, Locke called it. Those who did not
already own land were literally held to ransom (economists call
it paying rent) by those who controlled the life-support system:
earth.

This tradition of private property in land was taken for
granted by the classical economists, which meant that they were
not psychologically equipped to deal with the social problems
that flowed from the simple arithmetical logic of the Demographic Imperative. For the same reason, there was insufficient
communal interest — expressed in terms of property rights — to
protest when the landowners abused nature. In the 19th century, society simply had no right to interfere with the way a man
used his landed property. And as for the property that was held
in common — notably the rivers, oceans and the skies — there was
no organized social expression of proprietorial rights to protect
them: hence (shades of what was to happen in Eastern Europe)
the wilful use of these last 'commons' as dumping grounds for
waste, at no economic cost to the user.

Here, then, we have our first lesson from history. By failing to
exact rents from those who wished to use the common property
as a sink for their waste, the cost structure of the industrial
revolution was seriously distorted. The profits of capital were

higher than they ought to have been, which encouraged the invention of technological processes that favoured the destruction of the environment. Another consequence was the bias in favour of capital-intensive methods, which skewed the system of production against labour. The former socialists, then, if they wish to avoid the mistakes of the past, ought to be cautious about importing the technology and managerial practices that are the offspring of the inappropriate technology of the 19th century.

The next major error also sprang from the ideology of property rights. This found its damaging expression in economics. Smith, and then Ricardo (who gave his name to the theory of rent), recognised the unique characteristics of land — broadly defined to include all of nature's resources. Early in the 20th century, however, economists banished 'land' by subsuming it under the concept 'capital'. The essence of land as a unique factor of production was conceptually destroyed. Today, so far as economists are concerned, land is simply not important, and is accorded derisory treatment in the major university textbooks.[2]

The conscious decision to define away the unique characteristics of land — finite, freely given by nature, and fragile (at any rate, in her subsystems) — was ideologically motivated. It was accomplished by economists who opposed the views of Henry George, the one economist and social reformer in the past 200 years who sought recognition for land as of primary importance to society (Gaffney 1982).[3] Because Henry George was pro-market and pro-nature, we would expect to find in his philosophy a model on which to build the post-socialist society.

The Georgist Model

In terms of the Lockian problem — how can we ensure there is enough land available for everyone? — Henry George provided a solution in terms of fiscal policy. Alternative approaches were not satisfactory (the socialist preference for land nationalization he dismissed as unworkable: who would deny that, now?).

George noted that it was impossible for literally everyone to have a piece of land: the fragmentation of holdings to uneconomic units (as has happened in France) renders this an unacceptable solution. But, said George, why not simply guarantee to the user the secure possession of land, in viable units, while capturing rents for the general benefit of the community? This insight enabled George, in *Progress and Poverty* (1879), to argue that the rental value of natural resources would be sufficient to finance socially-necessary expenditure. Furthermore, the individual was freed to deploy his creative energies in a market that was no longer encumbered by the exercise of monopoly power which sprang from the existing tax-and-tenure arrangements.

These insights provide the former socialists with another lesson: it is possible to develop a practical formula for retaining a key feature of socialist philosophy — the community spirit, the dimension to life that was seriously underplayed by the Individualism that sprang from the Age of Reason. By renting land to users, all the benefits of free enterprise (based on the private ownership of man-made capital and the market system) could be enjoyed without alienating the community's ownership rights to its life-support system: earth. At the same time, the post-socialists would be stealing a march on their western competitors, whose economies are cyclically afflicted by the recessions that follow bouts of land speculation (Harrison 1983).

This Georgist model appears to fulfil some of the conditions for economic development, but does it also address the need to restore the integrity of the environment?

On matters ecological, Henry George was ahead of his time by a century. In *Social Problems* (1883: 41) he warned:

> 'We do not return to the earth what we take from it; each crop that is harvested leaves the soil the poorer. We are cutting down forests which we do not replant; we are shipping abroad, in wheat and cotton and tobacco and meat, or flushing into the sea through the sewers of our great cities, the elements of fertility that have been embedded in the soil by the slow processes of nature, acting for long ages.'

If Henry George were alive today, there is no doubt about where he would stand on the problems of the Amazon; on the intensive exploitation of the soil by agribusiness; and so on. But his would not have been a helpless cry of despair; he would have stepped up his advocacy of the fiscal philosophy that insists every user should pay the full rent to the community for the privilege of monopolizing the finite wealth of nature.

Here, then, we have the third lesson for the former socialists. By charging the full rent for using land, they conserve nature. The beneficial impact of this fiscal discipline can easily be related to the urban sector of western society. Leaving land idle, or under-using sites for the sake of a large capital gain in the future, would no longer be economically viable, for the speculative under-use of land (foregoing income today for the capital gain tomorrow) would be penalized. Owners would be fiscally coerced into husbanding the resources of nature. Urban communities would be more compact, today, if — over the past two centuries — they had not been encouraged to sprawl by speculators who happily leapfrogged vacant sites and extended the boundaries of towns and cities onto prime agricultural land.[4]

The socio-ecological benefits of land value taxation, in the rural context, will be elaborated below. Here, we note that the environmental benefits of Henry George's economics — Geonomics — have been examined in the context of developed western economies (Backhaus and Krabbe 1991), but not for post-socialist societies.

One final point needs to be made about Geonomics, before addressing the immediate needs of society in the post- perestroika era. It casts an astonishing new light on the way the history of industrial society might have evolved if the politicians of the early 19th century had acted rationally in the interests of social development.

The evolution of the factory-based mode of production, originating with the industrial revolution in Britain at about the time Adam Smith was writing his magnum opus, need not have been associated with the wasteful plunder of natural resources and the destruction of the living environment. The theoretical insights and fiscal instruments for developing an efficient economy that respected nature were available to the policy- makers at the outset, for Adam Smith drew their attention to the following:

> 'Both ground-rents and the ordinary rent of land are a species of revenue which the owner, in many cases, enjoys without any care or attention of his own. Though a part of this revenue should be taken from him in order to defray the expences of the state, no discouragement will thereby be given to any sort of industry. The annual produce of the land and labour of society, the real wealth and revenue of the great body of the people, might be the same after such a tax as before. Ground-rents, and the ordinary rent of land, are, therefore, perhaps, the species of revenue which can best bear to have a peculiar tax imposed upon them' (Smith 1776: Bk II, Ch. 2, Article 1, p.370).

To this day, the principle of fiscal efficiency defined by Adam Smith, which he elaborated with a full analysis of the impact of the land value tax on the economy, remains one of the uncontroversial theories of economics.

Thus, while Smith was not tuned into the needs of the environment in the way that Henry George was, he was nevertheless led to define the tax policy which, had it been implemented, would have enabled the free market to protect nature. All that was required was the political determination to make users pay society — through the tax system — an annual rent for using natural resources. This would have been consistent with the pricing principles of capitalism; and tenants, of course, were paying that tax to private landlords. Furthermore, a land tax had been a principal method of raising government revenue since the Middle Ages. So by opting for a tax structure that favoured the most efficient approach to producing wealth, society would have automatically undermined the growing power exercised by land monopolists who, freed of the land tax, were not penalised for abusing nature in the pursuit of unearned income.

Even Karl Marx might have evolved such a system, for the first of his ten demands in *The Communist Manifesto* (1888: 104) was this: 'Abolition of property in land and application of all rents of land to public purposes.' But whereas Smith favoured private property in land, Marx reacted to the abuses that he witnessed in the dark, satanic mills by opting for the social ownership of all property and the elimination of the market (for which, read: the freedom of individuals to exchange the products of their labours).

The unique aspect of Henry George's philosophy was that it comprehensively articulated the rights of the individual, the community and of nature in a single system. That is why Richard Noyes (1991) has characterized Geonomics as the dialectical 'synthesis' — the uniting of what is best in the western market tradition (the freedom of the individual) with what is best in socialism (the spirit of the community), to produce a *Weltanschauung* that is sui generis.

Land as a Fulcrum

The process of transforming society has to start somewhere, and the ideal starting point is the land market. Welded into the framework of the free market — which cannot function properly without the simultaneous development of democratic processes — the rational land market becomes the focus for a boot-strap operation that unleashes the power of the individual. This prospectus is fleshed out, and defended, as we review the creation of markets for each of the three factors of production.

Labour. East European workers are highly educated and skilled, and will quickly match the West Europeans and North Americans in their productivity, when they are armed with capital. The principle that wages have to reflect the true worth of labour inputs is conceded by the former socialists. The major learning problem, however, especially for the USSR, is the development of entrepreneurial expertise. At least some people have to acquire the habit of taking risks, and working for themselves, if the supply side is to match the desires expressed by consumers on the demand side of the economy.

Capital. Extensive investment — retooling — is required, to establish a competitive private manufacturing industry and service sector. This is not a major problem. Ironically, one of the Soviet Union's anxieties, during the early debates on perestroika, was that people had accumulated 200 billion roubles and did not know what to do with it! This encouraged the anxiety that people might be tempted into becoming speculators. Providing the most harmful form of speculation (in land) can be neutralized (which it can, as we shall see), this surplus cash could constitute the financial foundation for renewal. In addition, foreign investors expressed enthusiasm for pumping capital into the former socialist countries, once the rights of property were established.

The public sector also needs to invest, and this raises a special problem. Since a government does not directly create wealth, it must obtain its money from other people. How it does so has crucial implications for the process of reindustrialization. Infrastructural investment is crucial, to enable the wealth producers to transport their goods to market. What is the appropriate tax system for a post-socialist society? Western advisers have sidestepped this question, but it is at the heart of the challenge.

Land. In the USSR, all land is held in common. In other East European countries, especially in Poland, a significant proportion of land remained in private ownership after the Communist party took control. For the present discussion, I shall focus on the Soviet case: this enables us to draw in broadbrush strokes and lay bare the essentials of the picture. The conclusions, however, are equally applicable to the other former socialist countries.

The land market and the appropriate fiscal policy provide the dynamic for an accelerated development towards a market-based society where the rights of nature are on an equal standing with the rights of people. The essential principles of this model are as follows.

First, public land has to be placed in private hands, if individuals are to invest their labour and capital in new enterprises. Land should remain in social ownership, however, and users should pay the full annual rental value to the community for the privilege of exclusive possession. This is no more than a generalization of what happens in the West, where tenants pay rent for holding secure title to land for a given period of years. The essential difference, of course, is that the rent, instead of flowing into the community chest, goes into the pockets of private landowners. The Western tenanted sector works as efficiently as the owner-occupied sector, so private ownership is not a precondition for kick- starting the economy in the direction of the free market.[5]

Second, the tax regime should be one that both maximises the incentive to generate the goods and services demanded by consumers, while recognising the unique characteristics of nature — finite in supply, life-giving in importance.

Third, an institution has to be created to facilitate the reallocation of land in the absence of selling prices. For if the full market rent is paid as a tax to the community, landholders have no rental income to capitalise into selling prices. How, then, is land to be allocated, in the first place, and then reallocated once prospective second-generation users express their need for land? This can be achieved by auctions. The person who offers the highest rent for the factory or shop site, gets the land. But how, in the Soviet Union, is it possible to create a market if there are no 'market rents'? Land owner and potential users are already striking bargains, agreeing rental payments, and reassigning possessory rights to property:

> 'In Transcaucasia, the Baltic republics and later on in Moscow too it has become common for state-owned service establishments — coffee shops, cafes, small restaurants, hairdressers, beauty parlours, etc. — to be leased by co- operatives. The rent is agreed with the local authorities and is fixed for a period of five years. At the end of this term the contract is renewed and the rent may be raised' (Zaslavskaya 1990: 85).

The missing element is the market mechanism for bringing together those who would wish to enter into a competitive process for the right to occupy these properties. Initially, this is not a problem: any movement in the direction of creating new jobs in a privatized sector is welcome. At some point, however, given the finite supply of the choice locations, two or more people or companies will want to possess a particular site. That is when the property owner — the community — should maximize its returns by demanding the market price. And the market price can only be established on the basis of competitive bidding.

Rekindling Freedom

How, in the absence of a risk-taking tradition, can we expect people to participate in auctions? Stalin killed the kulaks, but all that is needed for the re-creation of the spirit of individuality is the vital sense of freedom. That quality is now awakened. Many people have already taken the first step by resigning their membership of the Communist Party, or by staging protest marches in Red Square. Material necessity will compel some of them to enter the village hall on the appointed day and make an offer for however many acres they need to feed their families. At first, caution will no doubt dictate low levels of rent. With those first bids, the market has come into existence.

Consider the psychological implications of that first nod of the head in the crowd, as the auctioneer waits to bring down his gavel. What we see is the nurturing of the spirit of enterprise: of the individual expressing a willingness to take risks and go-it-alone on his own farm, secure in the knowledge that he can invest his labour and savings in the land, because he has security of tenure — just like tenant farmers and shopkeepers today, in the West.

The auction room would confront land users with the elementary disciplines of entrepreneurship. The first risk-takers would have to calculate the prices they could expect to receive for their produce, how much they wanted to keep of that income as their wages and how much they needed to purchase or hire their tools. That brings them to the bottom line: the surplus income that is called rent. That is the amount they can bid for the use rights to land. Ricardo rides again on Soviet soil!

Observers reported that employees on the great state farms were holding back from taking the first step into private farming (Steele 1990; Meyendorff 1990). The unsatisfactory state of the social infrastructure was a key factor. The absence of roads to transport produce to market before it perishes on the back of the waggon does not encourage risk- taking. The USSR will have to embark on a massive programme of public investment in roads, electricity, water, and so on. Where is the money to come from? A tax on people's wages? That would be self-defeating. The whole object is to provide the maximum incentive for people to work more productively. To tax their incomes is to deter them from earning that extra slice of income. A tax on the interest (confusingly called 'profits,' which includes land rents) that they generate with their capital? But that encourages people not to save; or to put their money under the mattress, which dampens the rate of economic growth.

A tax on land rents, then? Why, that is exactly where the community's money is coming from, under the Geonomic model! Recall Adam Smith's point that a tax on the rental income of land does nothing to deter the production of wealth. But the tax on land values is even more beautiful than that: it triggers a virtuous circle. As it benignly nudges the economy forward, so the value of land increases. In other words, land value taxation expands its base. Other taxes tend to contract their bases, by introducing distortions to incentives and the wealth-creating process. So where the challenge is to simultaneously encourage private investment and generate funds for social infrastructure fast, the rational tax policy is the one that flows from the retention of land in social ownership.

But would land value taxation yield sufficient income to meet the pressing needs of the public sector? Western economists would say no; but their views are to be disregarded. They lack both an understanding of the macro-economic importance of the land market, and as yet they have no sense of how much land is worth on the nation's balance sheet (Gaffney 1970).[6]

What are the alternatives to the Geonomic model? There are two. One is to sell land, the approach favoured by Boris Yeltsin, the president of the Russian Federation. The other, advocated in what became known as the Shatalin 500-day plan, after one of its authors, is to give it away.

The sale option threatens serious social and economic disruption. Only those who can muster a capital sum can gain access to the land. That obstacle, as we know in the West, discriminates against prospective farmers who do not have the collateral with which to borrow enough money to become landowners.[7] As tenants with security of possession, however, they can raise the price of land — the first year's rent — out of the income they generate by their labour.

By adopting the western model of property rights in land, the Soviets would re-create the social divisions, anchored in the power of land ownership, which caused the revolution in 1917! They would be engaged in a reactionary process: no lessons would have been learnt to compensate for the slaughter of the millions of citizens who died in the gulags. Hardly a propitious return to 'freedom'.

What about giving land away — dividing up a collective farm among existing employees, for example? This is not an efficient approach, nor does it deal with the problem of reallocating land to second-generation users. An employee of a collective farm is not necessarily the right person to hold land, to the exclusion of others who may be more productive. The appropriate measure of efficiency is the ability to generate surplus income — rent.

Giving away the land also offends the sense of justice. Land, today, is owned equally by every member of the community: why hand it over — for nothing — to a minority of citizens, who would then be free to exercise the power that flows from land ownership? They would differentiate themselves through the process of accumulating unearned income. Society would be divided into a class structure on the basis of the exploitative power that attaches to the monopoly control of land. The new aristocracy would enjoy the absolute right to use and abuse land (such as: withholding it from those who wish to make good use of it), and levy an exaction from those who work (by renting out the land for private gain). This solution would be the swiftest way to reproduce the injustices of western culture! This divisive outcome quickly manifested itself in China during the 1980s, because the Chinese Communists failed to set the rents of tenanted land at competitive levels and they granted leases in perpetuity.

Ecology and the Land Tax

Assuming the Geonomic model were adopted, what would be the implications for the environment?

By linking the allocation of land to a land value tax set at the rate of 100% (= market rent) — yielding a revenue that should offset income from existing forms of taxation — the community would not only be developing the most efficient fiscal system; it would also be destroying the basis of land speculation. Speculation in land is motivated by the desire for a large, unearned capital gain in the future. Gain in this form is one expression of the social and environmental costs of abusing land. It can be more financially rewarding, for the individual, to leave valuable land idle, foregoing today's stream of income while awaiting the most propitious time to sell it. In western society, millions of acres of farmland on the urban fringe have fallen victim to this propensity: scrubland, used as a dumping ground for urban waste. Sometimes, a horse might be kept on a patch of land, but this is usually the rural equivalent of secondhand car dealerships or car parks on derelict urban sites. Eventually, the land is sold for fortunes.

What would happen if land holders were required to pay the community the full current cost of their sites (its rental value, as determined by the expression of alternative users' wishes in the marketplace)? There would be no stream of income to capitalise, so the financial incentive to under-use the land would be absent.

Parallel influences would be at work in the rural sector. Farmers, operating family-sized farms, would adopt ecologically sound methods. In the West, the excesses of agribusiness — extensive holdings, intensive cultivation — are an expression of the distortions arising from the economic pressure to justify the purchase price of land. That price is actually a measure of the value of the vast subsidies that are paid by taxpayers, and the deep protectionism that is accorded to agriculture. As a result, explains Sir Richard Body, a British parliamentarian and farmer, the fertility of the land has to be mined to make it pay for the exorbitant purchase price of land (Body 1991).[8]

But in advocating the social ownership of land, it is important to stress that this, by itself, is not sufficient to ensure environmentally sympathetic methods of cultivation. Over-pricing land is bad, but so is under-pricing. By not charging the full competitive rent, users are encouraged to abuse land: the fate of anything that is 'cheap'. An illustration is the over-grazing of publicly-owned range land in the United States, where ranchers have consistently paid less than the true market rent.[9] Another example is the wasteful cutting of timber on publicly-owned land in western Canada, where corporations are allowed to pay rents that are well below the competitive market value.

But it would be wrong to limit our analysis to the economic and ecological benefits of land value taxation. This one fiscal policy, if treated as a fulcrum for reform, would integrate those two dimensions into a new cultural matrix. The Geonomic model enhances the individual's access rights to land, so he can feed his family; the lowest incomes would be raised in a manner that has been concealed by economic analysts who have fallen for Malthusian perspectives (Harrison 1991), but which Henry George fully appreciated. And the political implications are enormous. Decision-making would be retained at the level of the local community, for Geonomics is a strategy for a bottom-up development: of self-help and local action, rather than down from the centre. Soviet farmers would not need to mortgage themselves to the big banks, just to gain access to land: in fact, by not having to purchase land, they would very quickly be depositing savings in the local bank, money that would then be available to finance other local businesses, contributing to a spirit of community based on that close interaction of people that is now largely lost in the West.

The legal framework for our model is already in place, in the USSR. The Property Law which came into effect in July 1990 instructs state agencies to lease land, which was to remain the inalienable property of the state. During the summer of 1990, when Gorbachev's authority was weakened in the face of mounting economic distress, there was the risk that a competing approach — the sale of land — would be institutionalized, as frustrated politicians flirted with the Shatalin 500-day plan.

Gorbachev, in seeking a compromise, drew a line on the land question: he suggested that, before selling land, the people ought to be given the opportunity to express their view in a referendum.

There was no doubt where Gorbachev stood on the land question; and, without (I presume) being aware of his philosophical antecedents (Leo Tolstoy advocated Geonomics for Russia as an alternative to the Marxist revolution [Redfearn book, forthcoming]), he was pushing the Soviet Union in the direction that would have been favoured by Henry George. By early 1991, however, his presidential authority was weakened further by the tensions that threatened the USSR itself. If but he knew it, a socially just solution to the distribution of rental income offered the best prospect for reconstituting the union. It is to this question that we now offer some final observations, since they further illuminate the equity and efficiency benefits of land value taxation.

Federation and Natural Resources

As social stresses threatened the unity of the Soviet empire in 1990, one rallying call of the nationalist movements was the demand that they should be allowed to retain exclusive possession of the natural resources in their territories. Russia declared her desire to retain the value of her mineral deposits, and Azerbaijan wanted her petroleum. This tendency to separatism could lead to civil war, warned Gorbachev. These claims focus the debate on reform in a useful way.

The federalists spent the winter of 1990 studying western constitutional models. The problems with these cases highlight the political tensions that exist as a result of the maldistribution of income generated by natural resources. In the USA, for example, people have wondered why Alaskans were allowed to retain the $100 billion oil-rent windfall. In Canada, where the debate has been explored explicitly in terms of the generation and distribution of rent, the dilemmas have been summarized in these terms:

> 'The missing link is supplied by the argument that society raises the demand for the services of land, and, land's supply being fixed, its value or rent. Thus the rent of land is not an exogenous windfall from society's point of view, but is a consequence of social actions and decisions. Henry George's rather loose application of this argument was that "the rent of land belongs to the people." In this case, it was not the government, but society as a whole, that created land value and so was entitled to it. Government's role was simply to capture the annual surplus from the land-owners' (Scott 1976: 9; see also McLure and Mieszkowski 1983).

A federal budget based on the rental value of natural resources has much to commend it. We have seen that the arguments that favour land value taxation for the individual land user also apply at the village, town and national levels. At the federal level, the principle of social justice assumes special importance for the disparate groups in multi-ethnic unions. They would be bound into a political system that recognized both the richness of cultural diversity and the need for the mutual support that is necessary for social harmony.

The USSR could quickly institute a rudimentary system of land value taxation (Gwartney 1990).[10] Then a formula to share out the value of natural resources would have to be developed. The criteria present little difficulty for people of goodwill. As a priority, money is needed to clear up the ecological disasters of the communist experiment — disasters which are transnational. What better than to pay for making good the damage to nature out of the rental value generated by nature? Then, there is the need to help the disadvantaged regions in their efforts to develop.

Our fiscal strategy does not entail a one-way flow of income, however, so the resource-rich areas need not feel deprived. For as the under-developed regions raised their incomes, so the value of their land would also rise — and, through land value taxation, their contributions to the federal budget would consequently increase. Here, then, at work, is the virtuous fiscal circle operating at the federal level, serving to bind nations into a union on the basis of mutual support and the recognition that the obligations of stewardship to nature fall on everyone, who are therefore entitled to an equal share of the benefits bestowed by nature.

We see, now, the outlines of a social and political structure bedrocked on an economic ethic that stems from a unique philosophy towards the social ownership and private use of the resources of nature. Geonomics unites the best elements of the two warring systems — capitalism and socialism — to produce the most practical blueprint for a post-socialist society. Ironically, this policy has escaped the attention of those in the West who retain a lingering affiliation towards socialism (as in Ryle, 1988). Even ecologists — with the notable exception of the British Green Party (Richards 1991) — have failed to articulate this philosophy for the social and ecological benefits that it yields.

Notes

1. Adam Smith received acclaim in Russia even before the publication of *The Wealth of Nations* (1776). Andrei Anikin reports that the first mention of Smith in Moscow was in 1768. He also notes that 'some Smithian concepts are entering, if only implicitly, official high level statements on economic policy.' The statements to which he refers are by Mikhail Gorbachev and prime minister Nicolai Ryzhkov. 'Gorbachev said in fact that humanity has not invented a more efficient and more democratic instrument of economic management than the market. Ryzhkov echoed him by saying that a most important condition for the efficient development of the market is "overcoming monopolism". Adam Smith would have readily underwritten both these statements' (Anikin 1990: 47- 48).

2. An explicit expression of this view, by Theodore Schultz, a Nobel Prizewinner in Economics, was justified on the basis that farmers had increased their use of chemicals relative to land (Schultz 1951).

3. That Marx was closer to the neo-classical economists than his American contemporary, is indicated by the name he gave to his magnum opus: the three-volume *Das Kapital*. No love was lost between George and Marx (Harrison 1979).

4. Economists have yet to recognise, let alone compute, the massive historic waste of labour and natural resources that went into the investment of social infrastructure in response to the motive of land speculation (with the notable exception of Mason Gaffney, professor of economics at the University of California, Riverside). Consider the roads that were laid, to link communities that came into being through the artificial displacment of people from the core of society by the exercise of the exclusionary power of private property rights in land. And then add in all the other services – schools, health clinics, recreation centres, etc. – which had to be provided for these displaced peoples. When we add on the wasteful use of resources in the core locations (under-used schools in some of Britain's inner cities today, for example), we begin to glean a picture of the prudence towards nature that would have prevailed in the past 200 years, if the opportunity to speculate in land had been neutralized.

5. In fact, on the whole, the tenanted sector must be more efficient than the owner-occupied sector. This is because tenants have to put to good use the property for which they are paying rent. If they did not do so, they would not generate sufficient income to pay the rent to their landlords, as well as wages to employees and interest to the investors of the capital that is being used. In the owner-occupied sector, however, proprietors are free to choose not to use their land. The speculative capital gain in the future more than makes up for the loss of current income. The vast quantities of derelict land that blot part of many city landscapes are not under the control of rent-paying tenants.

6. Robertson (1989: 106) argues that, for the tax on land values to be accepted as a practical proposition, it is necessary to first establish how much government revenue it could raise. This consideration has some relevance in an existing system where reform of the tax structure is being considered: the government needs to estimate the size of the base before implementing a new tax. It is a different matter, however, where a new system is being started from scratch; in this case, the macro-economic impact of the tax is also important.

On rental revenue, Backhaus and Krabbe (1991) point out that, in a modern economy, it is not enough to add up urban and farm rents. 'Land' in Henry George's definition embraces all natural resources, including minerals, landing time slots at airports, the radio spectrum, and so on; aggregating these rents yields an income of enormous proportions. Much of it is currently given away to a fortunate few corporations, which disguise the rental value of these natural resources as 'profits' in the balance sheets.

When economists finally return to their classical roots, and disaggregate land from capital — and therefore separate 'profits' into (i) interest on capital, and (ii) rent of land — the proportion of national income attributable to land under the current fiscal system will be found to be equivalent to at least half of the revenue spent by western governments. In the UK, land rents were conservatively estimated at 25% of national income in 1988 (Banks 1989). Orthodox economists say that 'rents' are around 2-5% of national income.

But even if we could not initially establish the yield of a land value tax, there are compelling social and environmental reasons why a government ought to introduce this tax forthwith. Governments that are starting again, as is the case in Eastern Europe, have to start somewhere; and they have the word of Adam Smith and every major economist since his time that, when it comes to fiscal policy, they could not find a more efficient point of departure into the future.

7. The implications of not providing everyone with an equal starting point were recognized in Czechoslovakia. In formulating their programme to privatize state-owned assets, politicians accepted that the winners were likely to be those who had accumulated 'dirty money'. They included 'the directors of the former state companies, the "Communist mafia", along with illegal currency dealers,' reported Colitt (1990). He quoted Dusan Triska, the deputy finance minister responsible for privatization, as insisting: 'We have to be blind to this injustice.' In other words, they were accepting the institutionalization of injustice in the foundations of the new social system; hardly an auspicious start.

8. A full discussion of the conditions that would optimize the circumstances under which sound farming practices would be adopted is beyond the scope of this chapter; the present author is in no doubt, however, that the bureaucratic model favoured by the so-called

advocates of the free market in the West is not the solution. Rather, a policy of free world trade, in which Third World farmers were allowed to compete on equal terms in the markets of Europe and North America, linked to a shift in the tax system outlined above, provides the best prospects for the harmonious use and conservation of the rural environment.

9. The degree of under-pricing in the past can be gauged by the decision of the US Senate, on 15 October 1990, to approve a five-fold increase in the fees paid by cattle and sheep ranchers over the years 1991-94.

10. Soviet officials, like those in Leningrad who have considered the reintroduction of a property tax, have sought guidance on the assessment of rents by literally dusting off the land-value maps that pre-dated the 1917 revolution (Parker 1990: 5). Once a rudimentary system was up and running, which with the aid of computer technology would not take long, it would be possible to institute a market-based system that was even more sophisticated than the one now employed in the West (Tideman 1990).

Bibliography

Anikin, Andrei (1990), 'Adam Smith, Russia and Soviet Economics', *Royal Bank of Scotland Review*, no. 166, June 1990.

Backhaus, Jurgen, and Jacob Jan Krabb (1991), 'Incentive Taxation and the Environment: Complex — Yet Feasible', in Noyes (1991).

Banks, Ron (1989), *Costing the Earth*, London: Shepheard Walwyn.

Body, Richard (1991), 'Protectionism, Rent and the Dynamics of Agricultural Degradation', in Noyes (1991).

Colitt, Leslie (1990), 'Czechs prepare to bid in the state sell-off', *Financial Times*, London, 12 November 1990.

Gaffney, Mason (1970), 'Adequacy of Land as a Tax Base', in Daniel M. Holland, editor, *The Assessment of Land Value*, Madison: University of Wisconsin Press, 1970.

Gaffney, Mason (1982), 'Two Centuries of Economic Thought on Taxation of Land Rents', in Richard W. Lindholm and Arthur D. Lynn, Jr., *Land Value Taxation*, Madison: University of Wisconsin Press, 1982.

George, Henry (1979), *Progress and Poverty* (1879), New York: Robert Schalkenbach Foundation, 1979.

George, Henry (1883), *Social Problems*, centenary edition, New York: Robert Schalkenbach Foundation, 1981.

Gorbachev, Mikhail (1988), *Perestroika*, London: Fontana.

Gwartney, Ted (1990), 'A Simple, Practical Protocol for Assigning Rental Value to Land', paper presented at conference on Concepts and Procedures for the Social Collection of Rent in the Soviet Union, New York, 22-24 August 1990.

Harrison, Fred (1979), 'Gronlund and Other Marxists', in R. V. Andelson, *Critics of Henry George*, Rutherford: Fairleigh Dickinson UP.

Harrison, Fred (1983), *The Power in the Land*, London: Shepheard Walwyn.

Harrison, Fred (1991), 'The Crisis of Transition from the Commons: Population Explosions, their cause and cure', in R. V. Andelson (editor), *Commons without Tragedy*, London: Shepheard Walwyn, 1991.

Locke, John (1690), *Second Treatise on Civil Government*; page reference is to *Social Contract*, London: Oxford University Press, 1947.

Marx, Karl (1872), *The Communist Manifesto*; page reference is to the 1967 Penguin (Harmondsworth) edition, with introduction by A. J. P. Taylor.

McLure, Charles E., and Peter Mieszkowski (1983), *Fiscal Federalism and the Taxation of Natural Resources*, Lexington, Mass: Lexington Books.

Meyendorff, A. (1990), 'Some Aspects of Leaseholding in the Soviet Union', paper presented to conference on Concepts and Procedures for the Social Collection of Rent in the Soviet Union, New York, 22-24 August 1990.

Noyes, Richard (1991), *Now the Synthesis*, London: Shepheard Walwyn.

Parker, John (1990), 'Current Institutions for Collecting Rent from Land in the Soviet Union: with suggestions for a more democratic system', paper presented to the conference on Concepts and Procedures for the Social Collection of Rent in the Soviet Union, as above.

Robertson, James (1989), *Future Wealth: A New Economics for the 21st Century*, London; Cassell.

Ryle, Martin (1988), *Ecology and Socialism*, London: Radius.

Parks, Michael (1990), 'Separatism Could Lead to Civil War, Gorbachev Says', *Los Angeles Times*, 9 October 1990.

Redfearn, David (forthcoming), *Resurrecting Tolstoy*, London: Shepheard
    Walwyn.

Richards, David (1991), 'The Greens and the Tax on Rent', in Noyes
    (1991).

Schultz, Theodore W. (1951), 'The Declining Economic Importance of
    Agricultural Land', *The Economic Journal*, vol. LXI, no. 244, Decem-
    ber 1951.

Scott, Anthony (1976), *Natural Resource Revenues: A Test of Federalism*,
    Vancouver: University of BC Press.

Smith, Adam (1776), *The Wealth of Nations*; page reference is to the
    edition by Edwin Cannan, Chicago: Univ. of Chicago Press (1976).

Steele, Jonathan (1990), 'Soviet hero declares war on the party', *Guard-
    ian*, London, 13 November 1990.

Tideman, T. Nicolaus (1990), 'Market-Based Systems for Assigning
    Rental Value to Land', paper presented to conference on Concepts
    for the Social Collection of Rent in the Soviet Union, as above.

Zaslavskaya, Tatyana (1990), *The Second Socialist Revolution: An Alterna-
    tive Soviet Strategy*, London: I.B. Tauris.

Sergio Andreis

A New Foreign Policy

Premise

'The question is, I think, the need to recognize the originality of the moral choice in the various situations, by overcoming the illusion of much modern scientism, according to which it is possible to extend science and technique to all fields of existence. What has happened in the world in the last years witnesses how irreducible history is to the perspectives of scientism: no science had foreseen the political changes which have taken place, nor the new social, economic and above all the ecological problems we are now facing. We are in a condition of deep ignorance vis-a-vis these enormous challenges, we don't know how to act, we don't have, at least for the time being, a science to guide us.'

In this way Hans-Georg Gadamer explained, in a recent interview, the role of philosophers in understanding the sense and direction of the events ahead of us. And asked whether the concept of dialogue can be of any help, he replied: 'Sure, "dialogue" is a concept of the European tradition; it is, however, only one manifestation of something more universal: the recognition of "the other" as rights holder. And then we cannot but realize that the ideal of dialogue is imperative in an era in which cooperation among all cultures seems necessary and inevitable because of the ecological threat that life on our planet is facing. It is the ecological problematic, and not only, or not mainly, the abstract ideal of communication and dialogue, which will push mankind on the road to solidarity. Within this framework the idea of "nationality", perhaps also that of a European national- ity, is bound to lose its meaning.'

Conflict Resolution?

In order to be able to influence conflict resolution, one has to be part of the conflict. To paraphrase an old slogan, if you are not part of the conflict, you cannot be part of the solution. Greens seem to have lost their ability to be part of the conflicts they themselves have contributed to creating. This has meant a tremendous loss of relevance in the political life of large parts of our continent.

But apart from this more subjective aspect, there are other more objective points I would like to raise. They indicate a drastic change in the nature of conflicts political and social forces are facing: powerlessness we have to come to grips with — Gadamer's 'deep ignorance'.

The resolution of conflicts implies: 1) the possibility to govern the variables at stake, the dynamics at work and the various parts at play; 2) 'having time' to bring about the changes needed. Both these elements are less and less present in the conflicts this continent and this planet are going through. Our societies are increasingly determined by processes out of control, so that the roles of the various components — the political and the eco- nomic ones alike — tend to become ever more reactive, rather than pro-active in shaping their own future. This seems to happen already at the 'easiest' level of the various kinds of conflicts, those involving human counterparts, i.e. relatively known sets of groups, acting according to relatively well-known rules.

The situation is still more complicated in the 'new' kinds of conflicts which tend to assume top priority for humanity as a whole, those in which survival itself comes into question: con- flicts in which at least one of the protagonists, nature, is turning out to be fairly unpredictable, to use a euphemism. Human beings — a tremendously conformist kind of social animal — keep making decisions as if they know what the consequences of those choices are; yet more and more what turns out is different from what had been expected. Technology places on the market, then, its own inertial developments, apparently increasing the unexpectedness of the results. The impression is that we are all travelling in the direction of that 'world governed by chaos' Gorbachev warned against in his book *Perestroika*.

To this one must add a question: how much time do we have to solve the conflicts facing us? The time dimension seems to become more and more uncertain and this is crucial when what's at stake are matters concerning survival and/or a very high price to be paid in terms of lives, or 'simply' in terms of social welfare and democratic standards in case adjustment strategies are not soon put into practice.

Robert Jungk elaborated the concept of an 'era of irreversible effects' to describe the times we have entered. He has argued that it is less and less possible to modify the effects of 'wrong' choices. Conflicts, like all other aspects of our lives, have been going through radical changes. To talk today of conflict resolution sounds to me almost arrogant, because, as I tried to outline, we are not even able to grasp in their manifold dimensions the conflicts we are living through. I wonder whether instead we should concentrate our attention to work on adjustment. Adjustment to the new conflict situations we create in spite of ourselves, so to speak, without the awareness we uncritically tend to ascribe to the species we belong to. Isn't it a consequence of developments at this end of the second millenium in the West that we should give up pretending to solve conflicts and substitute this with the attempt to adjust to conflict? Solving conflicts is, today, a hallucination of omnipotence, behind which impotence is to be found. Adjustment rather than resolution seems a more reasonable, in the sense of more ecological, approach: because it stresses the awareness of limits and emphasizes the search for survival strategies within, rather than outside, humankind.

The Crisis of the Greens

First a note, together with a warning. Note: I am referring here to the Greens as institutional experience, and not as a cultural phenomenon of which Green political forces are only one specific aspect. One could even argue that at the same time as Green parties are going through a visible crisis in large parts of Europe, the Green culture is constantly expanding. Warning: living in the country of Machiavelli — and of the Vatican — I think it obvious that environmental issues have been booming also because Green parties have been created, i.e. they have competed on the electoral level. Unlike other movements before — students, women, civil rights, peace, etc. — we have talked to parties in their own language and Europe-wide. This has stimulated them to pay attention to Green themes. The fear of losing votes has been, in this respect, the best way to teach environmental priorities. It would be naive to think that we would have been able to reach the same results without the electoral tool. Environmental NGOs, lobbies and pressure groups on the one side and the Green parties on the other are communicating vessels or Siamese twins. To think that one of the two can develop without the other is a suicidal illusion for both.

Greens are going through a crisis. In Chinese, the word *wei chi*, crisis, is formed by two ideograms. The first means danger and the second 'occasion for change'. A crisis is not necessarily something negative and the growth of individuals as well as of groups is possible only through crises. The main cause of the present crisis of the Greens has been a scissors-like development: between the institutional and the movement experiences, between the slogans and the practices, between the themes we have imposed on the attention of the political forces and our lack of elaboration as our intuitions were becoming common sense.

Greens have given political dignity to some of the themes and conflicts which will be crucial for the future of this planet. By doing this we have been given a sign of hope. A hope which risks fading away if we are not able to reconcile the various gaps which have grown between our intuitions and our political practice. 'Think globally and act locally' has become in our day-to-day work 'think locally and act locally'. Ideological disputes have often taken over environmental involvement, to the point where we are sometimes prompted by gut reactions rather than reality. Media, big business and political parties have stolen our language, mostly in a cosmetic attempt to hide their usual plundering of the environment.

The international politics of the Greens in Europe could be a metaphor for the obstacles we have been unable to overcome. Each of our parties has in the best of cases developed lines of international politics only from its own national perspective, and in the relations among us each of the parties we belong to has argued for an international politics based on the mere extrapolation of its own national context on the continental one. The worse thing is that we hardly developed any international campaign, as if Chernobyl, the destruction of the Mediterranean, the safeguard of the Alps or the death of the great European rivers could all be solved nationally.

And why haven't we been able to develop continental campaigning? One cultural element has already been mentioned, the think-locally/act-locally attitude. But there is also another one I would like to point out. We have tried the traditional parties' game and our actions have been paralysed by endless discussions on whether we should set up a network or a Green international, on which parties should be part of it, on whether more than one part from each country should be allowed. The result has been inactivity.

The almost fanatical search for orthodoxy and the mistake of having given priority to being exclusive, rather than inclusive as one would expect from ecological parties, give a very alarming impression as if we were doing everything in our power, using all our veto possibilities, to play our counterparts' game. Not just imitating the traditional parties — it matters little if this has been done by denying it: being desperately alternative sometimes means being desperately straight — even getting the results desired by the traditional parties.

It is no exaggeration to say that often the worst enemies of the

Greens have been the Greens themselves. It would be foolish to underestimate the signs of the crisis: the results of the elections in the central and eastern European countries, as well as in Germany and Denmark, the results of the Big Green referendum in California as well as of the two Italian referenda to drastically reduce hunting and the abuse of chemical pesticides in agriculture, are alarming.

To see our responsibility, our complicity in our defeat, is a task we cannot avoid, because if it is true that crisis is not necessarily something negative, it is also true that not facing crises may bring you into the situation of the person who committed suicide because he did not want to die.

If Greens are not able to handle the situation they find themselves in, it will be another sign of the underestimation of ourselves which has characterized our experience within the institutions: Greens in the first place seem not to have realized the enormous impact they have had on life in the industrialized countries.

Some Proposals

The following thoughts came out during a trip on the Trans-Siberian Railway. It was the summer of 1988 and Johan Galtung was among the people I was travelling with. I am very grateful to Johan for having materialized the proposals, which are still of interest for the growth of the Greens. The concept of a 'Green international' is of course to be understood as linking/networking and nothing like the centralized structures of past experiences of international party structures.

A Green International? Some Reflections
by Johan Galtung and Sergio Andreis

1. A Green wave is sweeping over Europe and the world in general, a wave of ideas and values, people, action, initiatives, movements, parties. The wave should not be confused with the political parties and their ups and downs alone. The wave is here

to stay and grow for the simple reason that this is where the major problems of our times are not only discussed, but responded to in ways that do not aggravate the problems even further.

2. The Green movement can be discussed in terms of five spaces and five major values:

Space   *Values*

NATURE   ECOLOGICAL BALANCE

HUMAN   HUMAN NEEDS
  somatic, mental, spiritual

SOCIAL   DEVELOPMENT
• equity/equality between genders, age groups,
  races, ethnic groups, classes
• participation, democracy
• human/animal needs and rights
• decentralization
• self-reliance

WORLD   PEACE
• development among nations
• trans/disarmament

CULTURE   ADEQUACY TO
• ecological balance
• health, enlightenment
• development
• peace

3. A number of movements, new, old and both, have grown up around these values and problems, such as the ecological movement; health, lifestyle and human growth movements in general; feminist groups; groups for children and retired people;

groups for racial equality; animal liberation; for religious/linguistic freedom; cooperative movements, trade unions and labour/socialist parties; human rights movements; movements for local autonomy; movements for self-reliance; peace movements; Third World liberation and solidarity movements; and movements for cultural conservation and renewal.

4. The basic political source for these movements around the world are the daily insults (often under such banners as economic growth, modernization and security) to precisely these basic values of ecological balance, human needs, development in the sense of equity/equality, participation, human rights, decentralization and self-reliance and peace all over the world.

5. The basic cultural sources of inspiration for alternatives are oriental cultures (particularly in a Buddhist or Daoist direction), native cultures, earlier phases in western history and new culture (including science) to be created every day as a response to the problems and to celebrate the solutions.

6. The Green Movement comprises all of this. It is a 'federation' of movements fighting, nonviolently, against violence and the threats of violence, against repression and exploitation, against economic and cultural misery and alienation. Our broadened world consciousness makes us more sensitive to the simultaneity of all these problems, and to their interrelations. The Green Movement is sceptical of efforts to trace all these problems back to one common social ill, and rather than sectarian efforts to solve one problem with the hope that the resolution of the rest will follow in the wake of that one, tries to respond to all of them.

7. Time now seems ripe for this movement to do what other political movements have done: go international. Because our planet has entered the 'era of irreversible effects' and this makes, even more than before, national approaches obsolete. Going international by founding a Green International. Among the

tasks of a Green International would be the following:

• serve as a clearing-house for Green movements and parties all over the world;

• in some cases coordinate initiatives by issuing declarations on burning issues, stimulating joint initiatives;

• stimulate and assist the growth of Green movements/parties all over the world, particularly in socialist and Third World countries;

• establish commissions for the study of major world problems and their solutions;

• organise a Green University;

• promote alternative cultures;

• promote alternative lifestyles;

• promote alternative sports;

• organise Green festivals;

• set up a Green publishing house;

• set up a Green World Newspaper (why only the *International Herald-Tribune*?)

8. to do these things, all of them of primary significance, the Green International would need some kind of centre. Later on, in line with Green preferences for networking, a network of centres would be preferable, or a moving centre; but a start has to be made somewhere.

9. At present that would probably have to be in Europe where movements explicitly identifying themselves as Green at the

moment are strongest. But it should be geographically close both to the socialist and the Third World while at the same time having a strong Green movement to draw upon as much work is needed.

10. Within Europe these criteria would point to Italy. The work and general orientation would, however, have to be global, including culturally/linguistically.

11. The Centre could in the first instance grow out of the Italian Green movement as a resource put at the disposal of the international Green movements, with a set of by-laws giving major power to an internationally composed board.

12. The Centre could serve as secretariat for the Green International which would in general meet anywhere in the world, but also might have some of its meetings at the Centre.

13. The Centre could be responsible for the elaboration of major reports on major world problems. The Socialist International has done important work for the Nature (Brundtland), Social (Brandt) and World (Palme) spaces, although its documentation is far better than its analysis and its remedies. On the general human and cultural predicaments it has remained silent, in line with the general socialist inability to create alternative culture. Thus, the Centre could function as think-tank, and not only for the Green movements and the Green International, in particular, but for the world as a whole, fearing dialogue with nobody. A place to start would be reports on the five spaces.

14. The Centre could take the initiative of founding a Green University, not to teach dogma of any kind, but to ensure that the themes underlying our current predicaments are adequately elucidated. Ultimately a network of Green universities might be established around the world, with degrees, comparable diplomas, etc.

15. The Centre should stimulate Green culture, here seen not only as culture that permits us to explore with all our faculties the deeper dimensions of our problems, but that is also participatory, drawing no sharp wedges between producers and consumers. The reconquest of cultural, including scientific, creativity would be a major focus.

16. The Centre should establish a Council of Insight, for instance drawn from and among the laureates of the Right Livelihood Award and exponents of Green thought and action. For communication among them electronic networks might serve. Their moral authority would be needed to underpin the type of statements that might be issued on special occasions. Great efforts should be exercised to have the green movement as a part of general socio-political life rather than as outsiders looking in, critically, pronouncing themselves on the rest of the world.

17. The Centre should stimulate Green lifestyles at the micro level, in terms of food habits, use of resources, including energy, and accountability with participatory, non-hierarchical structure.

18. The Centre could organize Green festivals every two years or so, bringing together politics and culture, including non-competitive sports.

19. The Centre should function as the nucleus of a network of Green publishing houses, ensuring rapid translation around the world of key documents and books.

20. The Centre should take some initiative in the direction of Green newspapers around the world, in the first instance seeing to it that Green perspectives and material reach the established press.

21. Financially such elements as donation of a building with access to camping ground and inexpensive accommodation

nearby; municipal funds for some of the administrative costs (electricity, telephone); individual donations; foundation support for specific projects would all have to enter the picture; a Green International having neither the automatic support of big business, nor of big labour.

Per Gahrton

Environmental Diplomacy: The United Regions of Europe

Internationalization, globalization, Europeanization are slogans of the day. Communications technology and global trends have made even the most isolated village part of a worldwide economic network. Modern production pollutes the environment of people thousands of miles away. It would be very easy, but superficial, to look upon the ongoing development as a single coherent trend of globalization. As a matter of fact the general globalization contains at least two contradictory undercurrents, one economic-integrative and one ecological-cooperative.

The economic-integrative globalization has its roots in the search for power and larger markets. Historically, this trend has taken the shape of classical colonialism, military conquests, trade wars and — in our times — the establishment of multinational corporations and harmonized large markets. Politicians of most blue and red shades have surrendered to the 'logic' of large-scale production and global market economy. The nation state is outdated, according to most opinion makers in the world (i.e. the US and Western European) media. The fact that most people in Eastern Europe and the Third World seem rather keen to keep and enlarge their national and even regional autonomy, is usually explained away as a temporary emotional sign of backwardness which will disappear as soon as market economics have saved their bankrupt economies and linked them into stable dependence on free trade and the world market.

The ecological-cooperative globalization has its roots in the search for peace and security. Historically, this trend did not become an important factor until wars began, through military technology, to directly involve and hurt non-combatant civilians more than soldiers while, almost concomitantly, democracy grew strong enough in some parts of the world to allow popular peace initiatives to form. Later, starting in the 1970s, transboundary environmental pollution evolved as a reason equally important to the threat of nuclear war for the need to deepen and strengthen international cooperation.

A major problem in the public debate is that many people and opinion makers are unaware of the double, and even contradictory, character of the globalization process. Thus those who oppose one aspect of it are considered to be narrow-minded nationalists and old-fashioned romantics.

In a major debate on Sweden and Europe in the Swedish parliament in October 1990, I was asked by the representatives of the extremely pro-EC Conservatives: 'Mr Gahrton seems to like all other European organizations except the EC. Why, what is special about the EC?'

The answer is rather simple. The European Community is a brainchild of the economic-integrative globalization, while the organizations that I favored, such as the Council of Europe, the UN Economic Commission for Europe, the European Conference on Security and Cooperation and the UN Environmental Programme, are all expressions of the environmental-cooperative globalization process.

On a global level, the United Nations has been an organizational forum for international collaboration since the end of World War II. Through its affiliated organs, WHO, FAO, UNDP, UNEF and others, the UN provides an existing basis for a more extensive international collaborative effort between sovereign nations.

In some parts of the world, continental organizations similar to the UN in nature have been developed alongside the UN itself. In the Americas, the Organization of American States has been formed, and in Africa there is the Organization of African States. Other types of regional collaborative organization are the League of Arab States and the Nordic Council.

Nine Basics for European Cooperation

It is my conviction that the organizational framework for the effort of European collaboration needs to meet certain basic demands when it comes to peace and environmental conditions:

1. *A European organization for collaboration must be open to all of Europe.*

   The fall of the Berlin Wall and the democratic changes in the Eastern European countries removed all reasons for limiting European cooperation to only parts of the continent. Pollution has no respect for political borders.

2. *Collaboration between the European countries has to be built on the principle of equality, regardless of size, population or power.*

   Every nation or ecological region has the right to maintain a certain self-rule. Therefore, every such basic entity of European cooperation should be represented at the European level equally. It's not acceptable that large populations, like the Russians, the Germans or the French, should be able to impose their will upon tens or even hundreds of small peoples just because of their size and number.

3. *A European collaborative organization has to be open towards the rest of the world.*

   Europe must not cooperate in ways that revive memories of its colonialist past. Europe should open up its borders and receive refugees from political oppression and poverty. It would be catastrophic if Europe developed as a major part of the North with hostility towards the South. That's why European cooperation should take place as far as possible within global frameworks like the UN.

4. *European collaboration should strengthen democracy.*

   A basic urge in Eastern Europe now is democracy. Any kind

of cooperation that does not correspond to high expectations for democracy might endanger the democracy achieved in some countries. Non-democratic structures created on the European level because of expedience, might endanger internal democracy in countries where democracy is in an infant stage and give legitimacy to those who demand 'forceful men' to cope with the present turmoil in the aftermath of dictatorship.

5. *European collaboration should encourage decentralization and regional self-determination.*

For many years demands for more local and regional power have been strong all over Western Europe. Most parties have promised 'decentralization'. Now such trends have priority in Eastern Europe. The Baltic states are planning local currencies and try to build border posts with Russia in order to demonstrate independence. Slovenia and Croatia have declared themselves sovereign states. European cooperation should not interfere with regional and local autonomy.

6. *European collaboration must not prevent individual countries from keeping achieved reforms and continuing the independent reform process at a faster pace than the average.*

There is a need for pluralism concerning political and administrative steering mechanisms. Centrally planned economy has failed, but liberal capitalism is a complete disaster as well if social and ecological considerations are taken into account. There is therefore an urgent need to test many measures in different political entities. The 'Californian regulations' on car exhaust emissions, which have been used extensively by European environmentalists to prove that very high demands are possible in a car-dependent society, would not have been possible if the United States had been as centralized as most European countries.

7. *European collaboration must be beneficial to the environment.*

To save the environment must be a primary goal of all European cooperation. Thus forms of cooperation that promote polluting activities and simplify the transfer of hazardous goods are totally unacceptable. If there is contradiction between economic and ecological aspects of cooperation the ecological (and social aspects) should prevail.

8. *A European collaborative effort must encourage interaction between people in all of Europe.*

Eastern and Western Europe have been cut off from each other for fifty years. Now the Iron Curtain has gone. In Western Europe people are free to travel. This right must be extended to all of Europe. It would be disastrous for the credibility of so-called Western freedom if the Iron Curtain that the East has now dismantled were to be re-erected by the West towards any European nationality.

9. *The all-European organizations should have supreme decision-making power in clearly defined, common questions, such as human rights and environmental destruction overlapping international borders.*

In order to make binding decisions at the European level respected, controllable and compatible with maximum local and regional autonomy, these must be very few. A European or International Court should deal with the most important and urgent matters only, not with masses of legislative details. If the supranational level is allowed to expand, it will soon suffer from the same bureaucratism and red tape as all other giant administrations.

Is the European Community an Appropriate Basis for All-European Cooperation?

According to many observers, the European Community is the 'only efficient' foundation for the cooperation of Europe. Is that so? Well, it depends what criteria for cooperation one favours. Let's check how the EC corresponds to the nine Green basics above:

1. *The EC is not open to all of Europe.*

The EC only includes around a third of all European countries. According to the EC's own views, it will expand to include only a few more countries within the foreseeable future. The reason for this is that the EC's economic-integrative model makes it necessary for new member states to have reached a certain level of development before they can join. Because of this, EC spokespeople have made it quite clear that it will be decades before several Eastern and Central European countries can become members. Turkey's application has been rejected and it is totally unclear how the USSR or the different Soviet republics will be treated by the EC.

2. *The EC is based upon inequality between nations and peoples.*

The EC's all-European models are unequal and discriminatory. The EC has presented a model of 'concentric circles', where non-members would be connected through different treaties and associations to the EC, which would constitute the unchallenged centre of Europe. The European countries would be divided into different classes, from the dominating EC 'superpowers' (Germany and France), to today's peripheral states (like Denmark), then to the EC-adapted EFTA states, all the way to the fourth- or fifth-class EC satellite states, such as Turkey, Cyprus, and the Eastern European countries.

3. *The EC is becoming a 'Fortress Europe'.*

In the EC, there are obvious tendencies towards Eurocentrism as opposed to internationalism. Most EC countries have a colonial past. In the security police collaboration effort now being shaped (Trevi, etc.), there is a tendency to view Europe's nearest neighbours on the other side of the Mediterranean in a negative light. When it comes to non-European industrialized countries, such as the United States, Japan and Southern Asia, the EC is thinking more in terms of competition than collaboration. In many parts of the world outside Europe, it is feared that the EC may become a 'walled Europe' with barbed wire around it.

4. *The EC suffers from a huge 'democratic deficit'.*

The EC members are democratic countries, but the EC itself is no democracy. This is openly admitted and debated within the EC, but true democratic reforms do not seem to be under way. Therefore, any dependency on the EC's present decision-making process constitutes a defeat for democracy.

5. *The EC concentrates power in Brussels to decide even the most minute details.*

The EC is being built up as a pyramid which reduces local and regional influence. EC institutions are taking over more and more of the decision-making power of the individual countries. When it comes to Denmark, close to 90 per cent of all the laws that Danish people are subject to were passed in Brussels, while a mere 10 per cent were passed in Copenhagen. The chairman of the EC Commission has stated that around 80 per cent of all the decisions within the EC countries will be made by EC institutions in future.

6. *The EC basically demands the same rules everywhere and excludes pioneer prototypes and models.*

EC harmonization means that all important safety regulations relating to merchandise, consumer protection, environment, etc. must conform to a standard level. This means a decreased standard for some countries. To a large extent, this is what the harmonization of laws and policies of EFTA countries with those of the EC is about. For this reason, there are many problematic areas for EFTA to consider regarding everything from storage of chemicals to consumer protection. This is why the EC has criticised EFTA for demanding too many exemptions. The fact is that for EFTA countries EC harmonization would mean a lot more adoptions in a downward direction than in an upward direction.

7. *The 'economic dynamics' of the EC internal market have been shown to have a negative impact on the environment.*

It has been proven that the EC model causes great strain on the environment. This is shown in the analysis of the environmental effects by the Task Force on the Environment and the internal market requested by the EC Commission in 1989. The same so-called dynamic effects that are thought to be beneficial to economic growth, such as increased trade, are in the environmental analysis report estimated to lead to increased lorry traffic, breakdown of rural communities due to lack of services, increased air and water pollution and destruction of sensitive ecosystems.

8. *The EC is creating new borders between European countries.*

EC integration is expected to create increased freedom of movement for citizens of EC countries, but at the same time new borders could be drawn up between the EC and the rest of Europe. The EC efforts to create a common 'outer border' may cause great hardship for Eastern and Central Europeans. New mobility problems may arise between neighbouring countries in several parts of Europe, for example between different Nordic states. Austria has, as a step towards harmonization with the EC, closed its borders to some of the Eastern European countries and even posted military personnel at the border with Hungary. Instead of various degrees of border control for each country (passport rights and regulations, visa demands, complete checks, random checks, etc.), the EC will enforce a complete removal of all internal borders while a unified, very restrictive, external border control will be enforced.

9. *The EC is becoming more of a centralized bureaucracy than either the USSR and the US.*

Within the EC many decisions concerning thousands of details within all areas of society are made at a supreme level. When the Economic and Monetary Union (EMU) is ready, all economic policies will be decided at a central level, and one single state bank will release a common currency. The political union is intended for a common security and foreign policy, according to the EC's own plans. The authority of the EC is likely to become greater, if possible, than that of the Supreme Soviet or the federal government of the United States when compared to the respective republic or state governments of those countries.

With the above in mind, it becomes evident that the economic-integrative model of the EC is hardly the most suitable organization for an all-European collaborative effort striving to save the environment and promote peace.

A Case Study:
Sweden between Independence and the EC

When members of the European Parliament met MPs of the EFTA countries in Vienna on 22 May 1990, to discuss a closer relationship between EFTA and the European Community through a treaty about a joint European Economic Space (= EC plus EFTA), several MEPs showed openly negative attitudes towards the EFTA ambitions.

Sweden, as the EFTA president until 30 June 1990, has played a major role in the EFTA attempt to enter the EC through the back door without telling the full truth to anybody, either the EC or the peoples of the EFTA countries.

The heart of the matter is that Sweden is trying to get all the commercial benefits from the internal market without paying a price. Sweden is also trying to gain covert access to the EC decision-making process in order to influence the EC in a different direction from the present one. As a matter of fact, almost every Swedish representative considered to be 'pro-EC' argues that only with a seat in the EC decision-making bodies could Sweden change the present development of the EC, in the direction of a European union, into a more functionalist EFTA-like approach.

A leading Swedish Liberal has stated that he wants Sweden to apply for membership in the European Community. But he does not want to abolish the checkpoints at national frontiers! Some Swedish teetotalers believe that Sweden might, as a full EC member, retain its restrictive alcoholic beverage policy, because after having had the chance to listen to Scandinavian lectures on the subject, Central and Southern Europeans will understand the dangers of alcoholism. Swedish trade unionists believe that they will create a Swedish labour market situation in the EC (Sweden has less than a quarter of the average unemployment of the EC).

These situations are typical of most of the pro-EC mood that is now sweeping over Sweden (and other EFTA countries). Those who want to join the EC do not want to join the EC that exists in reality, but an entity that only exists in their dreams or might come into existence after subversive EFTA activity inside the EC.

The government, which delivered its application for membership to the acting president of the EC Council on 1 July 1991, makes it quite clear that what Sweden wants to join has only superficial similarity with the European union that is on the agenda of the European Parliament.

Thus Sweden is completely morally corrupted by these contradictory influences — from the economic-integrative needs of big business and from the ecological-cooperative needs of the people, the environment and the traditional policy of independence and neutrality.

One pretty absurd aspect is the exploitation of language to conceal realities. The fact that the Swedish government in the Swedish parliament has set up many severe conditions for its harmonization with the EC rules, concerning everything from health and environmental commodity standards to a sovereign financial policy, has been kept unknown to the EC by a policy of non-translation. The Swedish government, as well as parliamentary committees, have refused demands by the Green party that the relevant parliamentary decisions from 1988 and 1989 be translated in their entirety into EC languages. Thus it is not known that, while Swedish delegates have promised the EC to apply the Cassis Dijon principle, parliament has decided the opposite, stating that no goods that do not comply with Swedish standards may be imported. (According to the Cassis Dijon principle, any commodity which complies with the legal standards of its EC country of origin should have free access to all other EC countries or EC-harmonized members of the internal market.)

At the same time, EC regulations are not well known in

Sweden. Most Swedes don't know that 14,000 pages of EC rules must be given legal status in Sweden in order for Sweden to achieve 'harmonization'. (In the case of full membership the number of pages rises to 80,000!) The majority in parliament has decided that EC laws could receive legal status in Sweden without existing in the Swedish language.

Further, it is known neither to the EC, nor to most Swedes, that several Swedish authorities have made investigations into possible effects of Swedish adoption of the 'community attainments' and concluded that very often Swedish harmonization with EC rules would mean a decrease of health and environmental safety standards. These reports have in part been classified. The following, however, are excerpts from some of the documents that are available (in Swedish only) to the public:

- In a pamphlet from the Ministry of Environment it is claimed that 'in most sections the environmental requirements are tighter in Sweden than in the EC, e.g. in the cases of chemical control, environmental border control, exhaust control and sulphurous emissions.'
- In a memorandum from the National Environment Protection Board it is stated that 'at the present time it is not possible to harmonize the Swedish rules about freons with the regulations of the EC.'
- The National Food Administration has stated that the EC allows higher levels of pesticides in fruit and vegetables than Sweden does.

In May 1990 the Swedish government in a confidential 'Problem Analysis EES' listed about 50 important points where harmonization with the EC would present serious problems; thus the Swedes would have to demand exemptions from the 'attainments'. It stirred considerable debate when I revealed, in an article in *Dagens Nyheter*, the existence of this paper and referred to some of its contents. Such reports are of course the factual background for the repeated warnings by EC president Jacques Delors and the European Parliament that the EFTA countries cannot get any real exemptions, only transitional arrangements.

In June 1990 all seven EFTA countries together presented a drastically shortened list of demands to the EC. This list has been kept secret even to parliamentarians in Sweden and, as far as I know, all EFTA countries. The abbreviated EFTA list, dated 12 June, is headlined: *Strictly confidential. Issues of fundamental interest to the EFTA countries.*

The list contains 12 main groups, and with subgroups 22 demands altogether, for exemptions from EC regulations. Sweden demands only eight exemptions. Thus, without public debate, without consulting even the EFTA delegation of the Swedish parliament, the government of Sweden has unilaterally deleted dozens of earlier very important demands. Among the deleted demands are those which concern Sweden's stricter rules on chemicals, nuclear safety, biotechnology, emissions from cars, lorry traffic, tax control, 'sick houses', etc.

In summary, the Swedish government has made contradictory promises to the EC and to the Swedish public. Therefore, if Sweden manages to bluff its way into the EC by giving up all demands for influence on decision-making and retention of Swedish rules, thereby belying its promises to parliament and people, the only choice for the Swedish government after an EES treaty (or EC membership) would be to *act as an anti-union mole inside the EC*. There would be an endless number of controversies between the EC central bodies and the Swedish authorities. Possibly the same applies to other EFTA countries.

Sweden, however, may be the sourest grape for the EC to swallow. Not only is Sweden neutral, it also has a history of almost sixty years of Social-Democratic political rule which has influenced all parties into acceptance of the basic elements of the 'Swedish model', including a huge public sector, high taxes, strong trade unions and intensive intervention by authorities into the activities of private enterprises in order to protect health, consumers, environment, etc. It is typical that the leader of the Liberal party told an audience of businessmen that Sweden would not have been much different than it is, had the Liberals instead of the Socialists ruled since 1932! Even some Swedish Conservatives would look like Socialists in many EC countries. How could such a country be integrated into the present EC whose internal market, EMS and European union are based on principles which are at odds with every important aspect of the 'Swedish model'?

If the Swedish government doesn't fight with the EC bodies every day for its policies it will lose all credibility at home. A possible EES treaty would not be honored. Swedish full membership would be even more complicated than the case of Denmark.

An Ecological-Cooperative Model for Europe

My opposition to EES and the EC does not mean that I don't want cooperation with the 'twelve'. On the contrary. But such a collaboration should rather be based upon the ecological- cooperative model.

The present global development is threatening the survival of humanity and many other species in many ways. The risk of nuclear war and the disappearance of the protective ozone layer are probably the most alarming issues in the short term, followed by the increasing greenhouse effect and the dangers of nuclear power and its wastes. Other global threats include:

- the rapidly decreasing capacity of our planet to supply a rapidly increasing population with drinking water, food and fuel;
- increasing shortages of non-renewable natural resources.

These threats call for global cooperation and solidarity.

All human activities must be undertaken in harmony with life and nature. Continued concentration in business as well as increased private economic power must be stopped. More economic small-scale activities, decentralization and increased regional self-reliance are structural reforms necessary to bring consumption and lifestyle in harmony with life and nature and coming generations.

The Green movement's vision for Europe — comprising East and West — is a continent of national democracies, regions with diversified economies, and a functional mix of self-reliance and international economic cooperation, based on sustainability and solidarity among all humanity, with future generations and with nature.

Part of a common statement of a conference of Green parties of the countries around the Baltic held in Kotka in the summer of 1989 describes a model of networking:

'By assisting in the establishment of a network of ecological groups and individuals we hope to see the birth of an alternative model of society based on an ecologically sound and socially just economy. This model can then serve as an alternative to the unsustainable economic policies which we have witnessed both in the socialist societies of Eastern Europe and in the capitalist societies of Western Europe. In other words we seek to establish a society distinct both from the COMECON model and from the model conceived in the EEC in Brussels. Instead of furthering the demands of central governments and private industries, this new society will have as one of its primary goals the healthy restoration and preservation of the Baltic region.'

Existing institutions such as CSCE and the Council of Europe should be developed into instruments for all-European cooperation. Within the European Council (which is open to all European democratic countries), culture, democracy and human rights have been in the forefront. The Commission and Tribunal for Human Rights are examples of models for an all-European controlling authority for environmental protection with the jurisdiction to supervise and intervene against violations of treaties.

Another possible platform for all-European cooperation is the regional UN body ECE — Economic Commission for Europe, with 31 European member states in East and West. The UN Environmental Programme (UNEP) with its global framework has an important role to play in defending environment and nature. Within ECE and UNEP numerous environmental conventions have been worked out, e.g. the so-called '30 per cent club' for the reduction of sulphur emissions, the Montreal Agreement for reduction of freon emissions, and the Basle Agreement to stop the hazardous waste export to Third World countries.

It has long been obvious that the ongoing EC harmonization will not lead to the longtime result that EFTA has envisaged, unless the EFTA countries are forced to make a commitment to submit fully to future EC decisions, without power to influence them, and to make the sort of concessions on environmental protection standards, welfare and social services that the governments of EFTA have promised never would be made. Not surprisingly, the negotiations between the EC and EFTA about EES broke down on 31 July 1991.

In this situation, EFTA must initiate efforts to create a different form of collaboration from the one the EC offers as the sole alternative.

I therefore suggest that EFTA immediately invite all the European governments together with representatives from ESC, ECE, UNEP, the European Council, the EC, the Nordic Council, and other European collaborative organizations, to a conference to discuss coordination, effectiveness and expansion of the all-European collaboration.

This conference would also discuss possibilities to partially anchor this all-European work at a *regional* level and give regions and minorities room for independent action. I therefore suggest that representatives of national minorities and indigenous peoples also be included, such as Sami and Basques, as well as delegates from special regions and states. The Baltic states are a natural choice of course, but also Soviet republics, German and Yugoslav states, Scotland, Wales, Northern Ireland, Greenland, Aaland, the Faroe Islands and similar regions and autonomous nations in other parts of Europe.

Maurice Strong, the first head of UNEP, is quoted in *The State of the World 1989* as having stated that people have learnt to enlarge their circles of loyalty from the family via the tribe, the village, the town and the city to the nation state and now are called upon 'to make the next and final step, at least on this planet, to the global level'. The director of the Worldwatch Institute, Lester R. Brown, and his collaborators agree, but add: 'This does not mean an end to the national governments. Just as people did not give up allegiance to family or town when nation states were created, so national governments can exist within a strengthened world community. *The solutions to many problems are close to home – often within a local government or grass-roots organization.'*

Thus the solution to the problems of global interdependence is not to create huge pyramidical hierarchies where the local community is crushed under the weight of world or EC bureaucracy, but to spin wide overlapping networks where local and regional entities may retain and even enlarge their sphere of autonomy, while at the same time becoming linked to the total ecological context with which they exchange influences.

According to the *Yearbook of International Organizations* there are at least 3,000 international organizations with members in Sweden, 250 of which are intergovernmental. Out of these, 500 non-governmental and 30 intergovernmental are European organizations. The number of regional and international environmental treaties must be counted in hundreds.

Those who want to coordinate all this into a single global structure, maybe a World State, are virtually looking to repeat the failure of Eastern European central planning. The vision of one European state, to deal with the environmental crisis, is just as fallacious as Lenin's dream to build justice and equality through Gosplan.

There should be a permanent body for discussion and cooperation, a United Regions of Europe, just as there is a UN of the world. There should also be an environmental equivalent of the European Court of Human Rights in Strasbourg and the International Court in The Hague. Treaties should be kept and transgressions should be met by sanctions. But just as real justice between individuals presupposes that every individual is free, so an international order must be based upon the autonomy of local communities and regions.

James Robertson

New Commonhealth: The Real Significance of 1992

No, it's not a misprint. I believe that commonhealth will be one
of the energizing ideas of the 21st century. In twenty or thirty
years' time, it will seem no stranger than commonwealth does
today. Indeed, the two ideas will reinforce one another, as new
insights spread about health and wealth and the links of both
with ecological sustainability.

That is what this chapter is about. It weaves together strands
that a mechanistic culture has dealt with separately. The first
section is about the movement for a new public health, which
emphasizes health, rather than sickness. The second is about the
movement for a new economics, which emphasizes wealth as
well-being. The third is about the need to integrate these new
approaches to health and wealth with one another, and with a
new approach to natural ecosystems — a vital aspect of the post-
Brundtland '1992 Process'. The concluding section discusses
the particular significance of all this for Europe.

Health, Not Sickness

One aspect of the modern secular culture which stemmed
originally from Europe but now dominates the whole world, is
that we pay more attention to sickness than to health. Health
workers and others in the health business have been able to
make a better living out of sick people than out of healthy

people, and politicians have found more votes in sickness than in health. So much so that the word 'health' is now used more often than not to mean sickness. Our health services, health professionals, health statistics, health policies and health insurance, for example, are primarily sickness services, etc. Our Health Department is a sickness department, and our Health Ministers are sickness ministers.

This modern tendency to treat health from a remedial point of view, after the event, has been paralleled by our approach to the environment. As the Brundtland World Commission on Environment and Development reported:

> environmental management practices have focused largely upon after-the-fact repair of damage: reforestation, reclaiming desert lands, rebuilding urban environments, restoring natural habitats, and rehabilitating wild lands.[1]

In just the same way, health policies and health services have concentrated on remedying sickness once it has occurred rather than on positively promoting healthy conditions of life and enabling people to be healthier. Economic policies have reinforced this remedial approach. Far from aiming to improve health and the environment, they have treated health and environmental risks and damage as unfortunate but inevitable side-effects of economic progress, to be minimized and then remedied — if possible — after the event.

That is one way in which the idea of commonhealth cuts across today's conventional approach to health. Another is that it recognizes health as something more than an individual condition. Conventional health services have concentrated on the provision of care to individuals. Conventional health education and health promotion have been mainly designed to encourage individuals to look after their own health — an approach that all too easily degenerates into 'blaming the victim', when ill-health is due to social and environmental circumstances outside people's control. Community medicine and public health have come low in the pecking order of the medical and health professions.

Commonhealth, by contrast, emphasizes our common interest in creating and maintaining conditions that will enable us to live healthy lives. Such conditions include physical, social, political and economic environments that make 'the healthier choice the easier choice' — for politicians, public officials and businesspeople, as well as for people in their personal and family lives.

Another point of difference between the idea of common-health and the conventional approach to health is the emphasis conventionally placed on new drugs, new equipments and other new medical technologies. The conventional assumption is that advances in health — and in all other fields — are to be achieved primarily through scientific research and the development of improved technology. The commonhealth approach does not dispute the importance of technology, any more than the concept of commonwealth disputes it. But it emphasizes that the key to health creation, like the key to genuine wealth creation, lies in the social and environmental factors which determine how technology is actually developed and used.

It would be wrong to think that commonhealth is just a pie-in-the-sky idea. Since the early 1980s the European Regional Office of the World Health Organisation (WHO-Europe) has been alerting us to the need for a new understanding of health and a new approach to health policy. The 1982 publication *Health Crisis 2000*, based on the WHO European Regional Strategy for Attaining Health for All by the Year 2000, warned that:

> there could be a health crisis by the year 2000 unless radical steps are taken by the public, the professions, industry, and the governments of the region. This is no idle warning. A careful analysis of trends in health and disease, made over the past three years by repre-sentatives of the medical profession and the health ministries of the region's 33 member states, has produced ominous signs that our health policies since the Second World War have set us on a dangerous course. The glittering attraction of high technology and the public's demand for 'miracle cures' have meant that we have almost abandoned the principle

of self-care in a 'caring community'... Instead of promoting health and preventing disease, we have invested the bulk of our health budgets in 'disease palaces' which have really only cured our acute illnesses.[2]

Through the 1980s WHO-Europe has taken the lead in WHO's work on lifestyles and health, health promotion, health education, healthy cities and healthy public policies. Key milestones have included: the Ottawa Charter for Health Promotion, issued at the first International Conference on Health Promotion in 1986; the launch of the Healthy Cities project in 1986; the second International Conference on Health Promotion in Adelaide in 1988, which concentrated on healthy public policies; and the European Charter on Environment and Health, issued in 1989. A third International Conference held in Sundsvall, Sweden, in June 1991, focused on creating supportive environments for health.[3]

The impact of these efforts on actual developments may have been disappointing so far. But the ideas behind them have laid the foundations for rapid progress when the breakthrough comes. They can be briefly summarized as follows.

The Ottawa Charter affirmed the importance of fundamental living conditions and resources, including a stable ecosystem, as prerequisites for health. It defined health promotion as the process of enabling people to take control over and improve their health, and stressed the importance of community empowerment. It outlined a comprehensive strategy for health promotion based on healthy public policies, supportive environments, community action, the development of personal skills, and a reorientation of health services. It pointed towards a new approach to public health, in keeping with late 20th century needs.

The Healthy Cities project in Europe covers 30 cities in 19 countries, committed to achieving greater support for healthy local policies from political decision-makers and local communities. The project office in Copenhagen reviews progress, and disseminates innovative approaches.[4] The spread of the healthy cities idea has, in fact, gone much wider than the cities directly participating in the project. A total of some 300 are now involved.

The Adelaide recommendations stressed that healthy public policy must involve all sectors of government decision-making, including especially those not specifically responsible for 'health'. Public policy in such fields as agriculture, education, social welfare, housing, transport and economics, should ensure that everyone has equitable access to the prerequisites for health. New systems of political accountability should make policy-makers answer for the health impacts of their policies.

The European Charter on Environment and Health was issued in December 1989 by the Ministers of Environment and of Health from the European Region of WHO, meeting together for the first time. The Charter lays down entitlements and responsibilities for a healthy environment, principles for public policy, and priorities. It has been endorsed by the European Commission as a guideline for future action by the Community. Its Principle 6, that 'the health of individuals and communities should take clear precedence over considerations of economy and trade,' has been ignored so far in the process of creating a European single market – as indeed have environmental considerations. The Charter must be brought to bear on further economic integration in Europe up to and beyond 1992.

Wealth As Wellbeing

A worldwide movement for a new economic way of life and thought has been gathering strength through the 1980s. Elsewhere I have described the principles of the new economics, outlined how they can be applied across the whole range of economic life worldwide, and proposed an agenda for the 1990s.[5] Here a brief summary must suffice, together with a few words on the connections between new economics and commonhealth.

The conventional way of economic life and thought now prevalent worldwide has been based on European cultural assumptions and principles. These stemmed originally from

17th-century thinkers like Descartes, Hobbes, Francis Bacon and Newton. They were crystallized into a general system of economic understanding by Adam Smith in the late 18th century. They include the following:

1. Human life is a competitive struggle for power. Among the main aims of economic life are: to increase the number of people dependent on you, for example as customers or employees; to become more powerful than your rivals, such as competing firms; and, generally, to be better off and 'climb higher up the ladder' than other people. Since losers, as well as winners, are a natural and inevitable product of such a system, today's economic order naturally and inevitably makes large numbers of people relatively powerless, poor, and unhealthy.

2. It has been given to humans to harness the resources of the natural world to meet our needs and wants, and to treat the natural world as a limitless pool of resources and a limitless sink for wastes. As the human population of the world has grown, this approach has inevitably and systematically damaged natural ecosystems to the point where catastrophe now threatens.

3. Economic life centres on nation states. For Adam Smith economics was about The Wealth Of Nations, and ever since his time economists have taken the nation to be the key unit in economic life. In the decentralized one-world human community of today and tomorrow this is doubly out of date.

4. People's economic behaviour is determined by self-interest. The whole web of their economic activities and relations is best understood as if it were a value-free system, governed by impersonal natural laws. So moral considerations are out of place in economic life. The name of the game for homo economicus is simply to maximize his own self-interest. The invisible hand of supply and demand will ensure that all comes out for the best in the best of all possible worlds. Unfortunately, the real world doesn't work like that. Whether the outcome is good or bad depends on who you are — rich or poor, powerful

or powerless, winner or loser.

The new economics reverses all these assumptions and principles. It looks to a new economic order for the 21st century that
will be enabling for people and conserving of natural ecosystems, that will be organized as a multi-level one-world system,
and that will recognise the right and obligation — the freedom —
of all people to give expression to moral choices in their
economic lives.

So far as health is concerned, conventional economic policies
have had many damaging effects. For example, conventional
economic growth involves treating as additions to well-being
such things as the expansion of the tobacco industry and the
arms trade, investments in unhealthy products and lifestyles.
The European Community announces stronger health warnings
for cigarette packets and will give 11 million ECU to cancer
research in 1991, but it will also spend 1.34 billion ECU to
promote tobacco growing in the Community.

In industrialized countries of both east and west Europe,
conventional economic development fails to solve the problems
of poverty and deprivation that lead to ill-health, and all too
often makes matters worse. Pollution of air, water and land
present problems everywhere. (See Teo Wams and Maria
Guminska.) In Third World countries, economic development
creates even more health problems — for example by depriving
peasant peoples of their traditional livelihoods.

Underlying the health-damaging effects of conventional
economic practice is the assumption that the creation of wealth
and the creation of health have nothing to do with each other.
Effort expended on safeguarding or improving health is actually
regarded as a cost — as a drag and a constraint on economic and
business growth. A new understanding of wealth creation is
needed. Health creation must be seen as an aspect of it, and
investment in health must be recognized as an economically
valuable form of investment.

This means questioning the misleading ideas of conventional
economics about what are wealth-creating and what are wealth-
consuming activities. It is absurd, for instance, to accept that

tobacco manufacture creates the wealth required to support the medical services needed to deal with lung cancer. And this is just one example of where we are led by those who tell us that conventional economic growth is a necessary prerequisite to social progress and so must be given priority over it.

We urgently need new indicators of economic, social and environmental well-being, as a basis for setting economic policy targets and for measuring economic achievements. The inadequacy of Gross National Product (GNP) for these purposes is much more widely appreciated now than it was even five years ago. It needs to be replaced, or at least supplemented, by more concrete indicators of the state of economic and social well-being and of the natural and man-made environment. The infant mortality rate and the under-five mortality rate are good measures of the general health and well-being of a population.[6]

Health, Wealth and Ecosystems: Towards Brazil 1992

Over the past two decades — from the Club of Rome's first report and the United Nations Stockholm Conference of 1972[7]— awareness has been growing that the world faces serious environmental problems. During the 1970s and early 1980s the issue was commonly seen as being about trade-offs between environment and development — about reaching compromises between acceptable levels of economic activity and acceptable levels of environmental damage. By the later 1980s it had become more widely understood that, if economic activity is to become ecologically sustainable, a new marriage between ecology and development is needed. The Brundtland Report reflected this shift:

> Economics and ecology must be completely integrated in decision-making and law-making processes — not just to protect the environment, but also to protect and promote development. Economy is not just about the production of wealth, and ecology is not just about the protection of nature; they are both

equally relevant for improving the lot of humankind.[8]

It was unfortunate that this call by the Brundtland Commission for a new direction — or new paradigm — of development was muffled and largely obscured by its simultaneous, more conventional call for a new era of economic growth. But at least the '1992 Process', leading up to the UN Conference on Environment and Development in June 1992 in Brazil, is now focused on the need to deal with the worldwide environmental threats and the widespread failures of economic development as aspects of a single world crisis. That is useful progress in itself. A crucial part of the 1992 process from now on must be to get it understood that conventionally measured economic growth is neither good nor bad in itself but is a meaningless target or measure of progress.

So where does health come in? Brundtland made the right noises, at least so far as the Third World is concerned:

> Good health is the foundation of human welfare and productivity. Hence a broad-based health policy is essential for sustainable development. In the developing world, the critical problems of ill-health are closely related to environmental conditions and development problems...
>
> These health, nutrition, environment and development links imply that health policy cannot be conceived of purely in terms of curative or preventive medicine, or even in terms of greater attention to public health. Integrated approaches are needed that reflect key health objectives in areas such as food production; water supply and sanitation; industrial policy, particularly with regard to safety and pollution; and the planning of human settlements...
>
> Hence, the WHO Health For All strategy should be broadened far beyond the provision of medical workers and clinics, to cover health-related interventions in all development activities.[9]

Good, as far as it goes. But two further points are outstanding. First, the need to integrate health, environmental and economic decision-making applies to the industrialized countries of the so-called First and Second Worlds as well as Third World countries. Second, activists for 'the new public health' — including those involved in the WHO initiatives on health promotion and healthy public policies outlined earlier in this chapter — must find ways to engage effectively in the negotiations leading up to Brazil 1992.

Europe and the Challenge of 1992

Unfortunately, parochial west Europeans — from the business, financial, political, bureaucratic and professional classes — think of 1992 as the year in which the European single market is to be achieved. They are mostly unaware of its larger historical significance.

They do not feel concerned about the 'other 1992' in Brazil where for the first time in human history representatives of *all* the peoples of the world will come together in an 'Earth Summit' to discuss our common future. They will probably not notice either that 1992 will also be the 500th anniversary of what, with ingrained cultural arrogance, European peoples have been taught to think of as Columbus' 'discovery' of America. That event marked the beginning of the aggressive expansion of European Christianity and subsequently European secular culture all over the globe. This has led to the dominance of today's mechanistic, amoral, economistic world view over those of other cultures. And it is that which now threatens the health and very survival of the human race and even of life on Earth.

Thinking of 1992 as an occasion for a worldwide reorientation of the most radical kind, rather than merely another business opportunity, presents the peoples of east and west Europe with a threefold challenge.

First, we must put our own house in order. This means switching to a new development path all over Europe, in which the creation and maintenance of healthy living conditions for people and the restoration and maintenance of natural ecosystems are among the primary objectives of personal lifestyles, business goals and economic policies. The principles evolved by WHO-Europe over the 1980s must be brought into economic decision-making.

Most importantly, this new European path of development must be inclusive, not exclusive. It must bring in all the peoples of Europe, including those living in the EFTA countries and the countries of central and eastern Europe. It must enable all Europeans to share in creating their new commonhealth. As I have argued elsewhere,[10] it must reject the idea of developing the present European Community into a self-contained superstate with economically dependent, neocolonial satellites in the other parts of Europe.

Second, by making this switch ourselves, Europeans must offer to the rest of the world a new model of economic progress — much less rapacious and much more benign towards people and the Earth than the model we have propagated over the past half-millennium.

Finally, commonhealth has a global dimension. As Europeans, in transforming our own economic order, we can take a lead in transforming the present worldwide pattern of economic dominance and dependency between rich and poor countries — together with the UN, Bretton Woods and other international institutions which reinforce it. By helping to create a new, more equal system of economic relations we will be helping today's poorer peoples to create healthy and sustainable economies, and healthy and sustainable natural environments, for themselves.

Notes

1. *Our Common Future* (Oxford, 1987), p.39.
2. O'Neill, Peter, *Health Crisis 2000* (Heinemann, 1982).
3. Information about all these initiatives, and more generally about health education and health promotion at the European and inter-

national levels, can be obtained directly from Dr Ilona Kickbusch and her colleagues at WHO-Europe, 8 Scherfigsvej, 2100 Copenhagen, Denmark.

4. Healthy Cities Project Office, Krystalgade 7, 1172 Copenhagen K, Denmark.

5. *Future Wealth: A New Economics for the 21st Century* (Cassell, 1990). See also the chapter 'Health is Wealth' in Ekins, Paul (ed.), *The Living Economy* (Routledge, 1986). Also my booklet *Health, Wealth, and the New Economics*, published by The Other Econoimc Summit, 1985, available from New Economics Foundation, Universal House, 88-94 Wentworth St, London E1 7SA.

6. Anderson, Victor, *Alternative Economic Indicators* (Routledge, 1991). Also South Commission, *Towards a New Way to Measure Development* (Caracas, 1989).

7. *The Limits to Growth* (Pan, 1972). Ward, Barbara and Dubos, Rene, *Only One Earth* (Penguin, 1972).

8. *Our Common Future*, pp.37-8.

9. ibid., pp. 109-110.

10. 'Towards a Multi-Level One-World Economy: The Wider Significance of 1992': *New European* quarterly review, spring 1990, vol. 3, no. 1, 14 Carroun Rd, London SW8 1JT.

Sandy Irvine

An Overcrowded Continent

The population time bomb is no longer ticking away. It has already started to explode. Yet across Europe there is a deafening silence about this tremendous crisis. Many Europeans protested about the possibility of nuclear war yet very few are prepared to face the realities of overpopulation. From the radical pressure groups to the more progressive groupings inside all the major parties, there is a consensus that the problem of human numbers simply does not exist or that it will go away of its own accord. Many environmentalists too seem to think that we can save the planet simply by changing the washing powders we use and buying lead-free petrol or cutting down on more extravagant luxuries. Even amongst those who recognize that there is a problem, many view it as an issue for the so-called Third World; they are unable or unwilling to address the problem when it comes to the rich countries.

Full Up

According to the Brundtland Report, 'The population in North America, Europe, the USSR and Oceania is expected to increase by 230 million by the year 2025, which is as many people as live in the USA today.' Europe is already the world's most crowded continent. Using more optimistic estimates from the UN, it seems that the population of Europe (excluding the USSR) will rise from 484 million in 1980 to 512 million in 2000 and 522 million by 2250.

Britain's population, for example, rose last year to 57.1 million, with the crude birth rate increasing by 1.8%, a continuation of a trend over the last five years. According to Eric McGraw's figures, if everyone wanted to go to the coast at the same time on the same hot summer's day, there would only be about 10 cm of seaside per person. (Of course, as he also notes, the resulting congestion on the transport system would be such that they would never get there but the point illustrates how the quantity of numbers restrict choices open to society.)

Figures such as a percentage growth rate of 1% might seem very small but it would double a population's size in a lifetime. The figure of a 0.3% growth rate of Europe's population logged by the American Population Reference Bureau in 1989 would double Europe's population in 233 years. The USSR's seemingly small rate of increase of 0.9%, for example, would mean doubling its population in about 80 years. In neighbouring Poland, the population seems set to rise by some 4 million more people by the year 2020, making its housing and many other problems harder to solve.

In some European countries, the growth in human numbers has levelled off. It is, however, dangerously complacent to assume that in Europe a once-and-for-all demographic transition to stability has taken place. The trend has only existed for a very short period of time and might easily change. In Sweden, for example, the total fertility rate seems to be rising again. Worse, the comparative stabilization in Europe's population has occurred at an unsustainably high level. Despite the social and environmental problems this creates, examples of which are discussed later, some governments such as that of Germany are trying to encourage population growth while many churches and other groups still oppose birth control and other reproductive rights.

In any case, falls in the birth-rate can be misleading unless set against the equally important death-rate. Here medical science is working hard to enable people to live longer. It should also be remembered that the Green movement, more than any other grouping, stands for policies to reduce the death-rate by its policies in areas such as transport, food quality, workplace health and safety, measures that seek to reduce dramatically the toll of premature and avoidable deaths that plague industrial society.

Though the discussion in this chapter focuses of course on the European dimension, the size of Europe's population cannot be separated from that of the rest of the world. Since no issue is so personal, it is more honest to express the matter in personal terms. If the typical couple of child-bearing age deliberately parent three children, it is the same in terms of effects as saying that the world can not only cope fine with over 5 billion people but that this figure is not high enough. To express the issue in terms of social policy, the simple truth of the matter is that to refuse to act and develop an effective population policy in today's circumstances is not a life-affirming act. It is the very opposite.

Enough Food

Perhaps the most popular argument which diverts attention from the crisis of human numbers is that there is more than enough food to go around if only it were distributed evenly.

In fact this is simply a paper calculation with not much relevance to the real world. The argument depends upon a series of false premises and illogical deductions. For a start, it is wrong to assume that current levels of food production by intensive high input/high output farming can be sustained. Barriers of rising resource costs, pollution and soil erosion, for example, are likely to mean that we cannot maintain what is temporarily a very productive system but one that is undermining its own foundations. Large-scale farming in Europe is in fact more like a non-renewable extractive industry than anything remotely sustainable.

It is also misleading to aggregate local food production figures (of uncertain accuracy) to give a global total which then is divided by the number of mouths in the world. To those mouths, however, must be added many billion farm animals who depend upon humans for their food supply. Then there are very real problems of transportation, storage, local dietary patterns, local farmers' markets and so forth which many people ignore in order to make the global population/food supply equation balance.

Already stocks of food are not keeping pace with the rising number of mouths to be fed. Through the last decade, the amount of cropland available for growing food declined by 7%. Underground water aquifers, that vital ingredient for sustainable food supply, are being depleted faster than they refill. The productivity of the world's rangelands and fisheries is equally under threat. According to figures quoted in the *British Medical Journal*, a magazine which, unlike more 'radical' ones, recognizes the seriousness of the population crisis, current food production just feeds the world's current population with around 20% of it hungry. A basic vegetarian diet might provide for six billion.

A host of fixes are proposed to meet the pressure for more food. These include: cultivating more land, increasing crop and animal yields, more irrigation, farming the oceans, synthetic foodstuffs and even colonizing the moon and outer space. All create more problems than they solve — soil erosion, deforestation, water pollution, rapid depletion of oil and other scarce resources. Furthermore, global pollution, increasingly unpredictable weather patterns and rising sea levels will probably reduce food production quite dramatically in the next century. No wonder that Paul Ehrlich has argued that 'the claim that the world can feed eight billion people is the most frequently repeated imbecility of all time'.

In fact, of course, people don't live by bread alone and most definitions of the good life include a whole variety of other things — clean water, shelter, furniture and furnishings, open space, privacy, various consumer goods, travel etc. — the provision of which can only be undermined in our finite and interconnected world by the extensification and intensification of food production. More land under crops and herds of domesticated animals must mean less land for other uses — forestry, energy production, recreation, space for wildlife and so on.

Dense

Another popular argument goes like this: 'Look how crowded Holland is yet the Dutch don't starve.' Not surprisingly this is sometimes called 'The Netherlands Fallacy' but it should be renamed for it is becoming more common to point to Third World 'miracles' such as Hong Kong and Singapore as 'proof' that there is no need to worry about population growth.

However it is inadequate to think just in terms of population density (which brings serious enough problems of its own in today's giant cities). The real issue is the resource base drawn upon (present and future). Taken as a whole, Europe's population exists in its present numbers today because it can command the resources of other peoples ('ghost' acres mainly in the Third World), of future generations and of other species. The Netherlands Fallacy fails to recognize that crowded but affluent countries survive because other countries are not — yet — like them. Instead of talking about Europe having made a demographic transition, it would be more accurate to speak of a demographic takeover.

The EEC, for example, is been heavily dependent on imports from the poor countries, the source of over 50% of its raw materials. In some cases, the dependence is quite dramatic: around 92% of cobalt, 85% of tin, 68% of phosphate consumed in the European Community comes from the Third World. The more affluent countries of Western Europe regularly import three or four times as much food from developing nations as they return to them. European livestock also consume Third World resources since this is the source of much of the protein concentrate fed to them. The situation is worse when it comes to items such as tropical hardwoods, coffee, tea, cocoa. Many 'wholefood' shops too depend upon resources that the Third World badly needs for its own people. As a result of such patterns of resource use, each additional European does far more damage to environmental life-support systems than, say, one more Ethiopian.

The raising of Third World living standards will of course

mean that they will consume resources that now fill European tables, decorate their houses, feed their animals and supply their factories. We cannot avoid this problem by 'baking a bigger cake'. Using the detailed figures provided by Trainer's exhaustive study *Developed to Death*, it can be seen that to give even the current world population European standards of living would exhaust several key minerals within a lifetime while oil, gas and uranium would not even last that long. More disastrously, the pursuit of more production must mean more pollution and environmental degradation, since the laws of thermodynamics dictate that this is the entropic price of all resource usage.

Affluence… The Best Contraceptive?

Many people blame poverty as the cause of population growth. There is much truth in this argument but it is only part of the picture. Large families are of course not unknown amongst the well-to-do. In countries like Britain a major factor in renewed population growth has been the middle-class couple who do not stop at two children but proceed to parent three or four. A whole host of cultural factors are involved, not least the male machismo that measures potency in terms of number of offspring. There are many men who won't do anything about curbing their own fertility because they fear for their 'masculinity' or because they see it as a 'woman's problem'. UN and many other surveys have shown that women do want to control their own fertility for the sake of their own health, that of their children, and their general well-being, but lack the freedom, information and materials to do so.

Population increase is also the product of what has been called 'the tyranny of small decisions'. The link between ecological ruin and the size of individual families can seem somewhat far-fetched to a couple who decide to parent more than two children. Yet the big problem is nothing more than all those little decisions added together.

More Humans... Fewer Non-Humans

It is the expansion of human numbers that is the major cause of the contraction of non-human life forms with whom we share the planet. The American magazine *Discovery* recently put the rate of destruction at a staggering 17 species of plants and animals each hour.

Its primary cause is not overexploitation (destructive though these causes are in the specific cases such as marine mammals massacred by Norwegian whalers or birds shot down by Italian 'sports' enthusiasts). Neither is it pollution, though again some species such as birds of prey have been devastated by agrochemicals. Rather it is habitat destruction which in turn is directly related to the amount of land we humans exploit to provide the basics of water, food, clothing and shelter. The rapid increase in this holocaust of non-human life forms is of course due to the clearance of tropical rain forests.

The endangering and extinction of Europe's flora and fauna is less in absolute terms simply because the biological richness of temperate forests is less than that found in the tropical forests. In relative terms, however, the impact of population growth has been as catastrophic for the non-human life forms that once inhabited the continent. From the bare moors of Scotland to the equally denuded hillsides around the Mediterranean, there is evidence of a deforestation that has left only clumps of old growth woodland, mainly in Eastern Poland. Much of the surviving tree cover is in biologically impoverished plantations. Other key wildlife habitats such as wetlands have similarly been destroyed. In Denmark, for example, 15% of the total area of wetland was destroyed in 15 years between 1960 and 1975.

Down the centuries, beavers, bears, bison, boars and many more species had to make way for more people. The diminished biodiversity of today is still dwindling. Once common species from song birds to the frogs and toads, all of which were until recently part of our local environment, have been more and more scarce. 195 of Europe's birds, 33% of the total are, for example, threatened and 29 in danger of extinction. 108 species of flowering plants are threatened with immediate extinction and 1,400 have become very rare. On the 'red list' of seriously threatened species are 36 species of mammals, 72 birds, 47 reptiles, 13 amphibians, 104 fish and 96 butterflies. Of 13 terrestial carnivores indigenous to central Europe, only five now occur in numbers that put them (at the moment) safe from risk.

Movement

The problems of population size are compounded by its distribution. Movements of people have always happened, particularly when the local 'nest' has become so fouled in one way or another that life elsewhere seems a better proposition. However this solution is often at the expense of the social and ecological communities on the receiving end of the migration. Nothing illustrates this better than the destructive eruption of Europeans into all four corners of the globe. It might have eased many tensions back home but the price was paid by the environments and peoples of the new worlds they conquered. In many ways, the whole episode set in motion further large-scale movements of people both within the ex-colonial countries and between them and the imperialist heartlands.

Migration can also damage the community left behind since it is often the more prosperous, qualified or youthful who are best placed to exercise the option of moving elsewhere. The result is a drain of social resources out of the country they leave behind. People, for example, who have educated at the expense of one country go and sell their talents in another. The free movement of labour has also served as a tool to undermine gains won by local working people. Take, for example, the bitter struggle against brutal exploitation waged by American farm labourers in the sunshine states of the South-West USA. Their courageous leader Cesar Chavez has long campaigned for an end to illegal immigration from Mexico because of its adverse affect on hard-won pay and conditions. Guest workers are similarly used in many European factories.

It is the sheer scale of modern populations that makes the problem so volatile today. In the USA, for example, immigration itself is a major factor in continued population growth. But the problems are equally great in terms of movements within countries. Again this has been dramatically illustrated in the USA by the environmental and social disasters that have happened in Southern California and Florida as a result of the internal exodus to warmer climes. Los Angeles, for example, has a population some ten times greater than local water supply can satisfy and therefore is forced to plunder areas way beyond its borders in very destructive water schemes.

Europe faces the same problems. Sometimes it is the product of seasonal movements which, for example, have set more and more of the Mediterranean coastline in concrete to provide hotels for summer visitors. At other times, people are moving more permanently. In West Germany, the influx of East Germans is worsening the housing shortage. In England, more than a million new houses will be needed by the year 2001, most of them in the already crowded South-East. The deteriorating global environment will worsen such pressures creating many million 'environmental refugees' fleeing pollution and climatic change. Acording to many forecasts, for example, the impact of the greenhouse effect on North Africa will trigger vast movements of people northwards.

Controlling Population Movement

Local communities must have the right to regulate the influx of outsiders to avoid all these unsustainable and exploitative pressures. There can be no principled objection to such a policy. After all, fire regulations control the number of people in a public building while many nature reserves are closed to the public some or all of the year. Similarly, anyone wishing to see traditional tribal peoples survive in places such as Amazonia and Borneo must support the strictest of immigration controls over would-be settlers and other exploiters of their lands. As Garrett Hardin put it, under conditions of overpopulation 'to claim the right of immigration would be to assert the right of invasion'.

Restrictive though such measures might seem upon individual freedom to settle wherever one fancies, they are essential tools to provide a viable and attractive future for local populations as a whole. Unfortunately, knee-jerk radicalism seems incapable of separating the use of immigration control measures to keep populations in balance with local ecological carrying capacity and the racism that lets in people of one colour but not another. The Green alternative is to make places better for people to stay, to meet their needs locally rather than at the expense of somewhere else.

Population Policy and Human Rights

The tradition of both European liberalism and social democracy has been to discuss abstract human rights without any reference to the real impacts on the environments and local communities. There has been a general failure to pose, let alone answer the question 'what then?': what are the real- world consequences of values and policies?

Documents such as the UN Declarations of Human Rights treat the individual as having an unqualified and socially underwritten right to parent as many offspring as desired. This philosophy is reflected in the pro-natalist welfare systems created in countries such as Britain and in the assumption that large families are deemed to be entitled to the same variety of grants, allowances and general support as small ones. Similarly enshrined is the right to move and settle freely. Such sentiments are perhaps the classic example of bad ideas born good. At the time they did challenge the repressive and discriminatory practices of contemporary society, but now they justify social policies which have opened a dangerous chasm between power (to reproduce/ to move and settle freely) and responsibility (to control family size/to avoid overcrowded areas).

Contrary to the glib rhetoric about reproductive rights, there are no liberties that will increase if there are more people and many that will decrease (not least those of other species) unless today's generation are prepared to exercise intelligent restraint. Garrett Hardin spotlights the essence of the issue:

There is a cliché that says that 'freedom is indivisible'.
Properly interpreted, this saying has some wisdom in
it, but there is also a sense in which it is false. Freedom
is divisible — and we must find how to divide it if we
are to survive in dignity. There are many identifiable
freedoms, among which which are freedom of speech,
freedom of assembly, freedom of association, freedom in the choice of residence, freedom of work, and
freedom to travel. You can make the list as long as you
like. After you have finished, ask yourself this question: Is there one freedom on the list that would
increase if our population became twice as great as it
is now? Freedom is divisible. If we want to keep the
rest of our freedoms, we must restrict the freedom to
breed. How we can accomplish this is not at this
moment clear; but it is surely subject to rational study.
We had better begin our investigations now. We have
not long to find acceptable answers.

The harmful impact of greater human numbers on the liberty of
each individual is particularly clear in cities. One reason why
there are so many restrictive planning controls there is the need
to contain the consequences of population density. Many measures put forward as an alternative to direct population policies
— population redistribution (e.g. to relieve city-based problems), reductions in personal consumption, switches to a vegan
or vegetarian diet — may themselves create even greater restrictions upon personal liberty than anything currently being proposed by those denounced as 'ecofascists'.

Population Policy

Quite clearly, it is no longer any use simply describing the
population problem in the manner of the Brundtland Report
and most other discussions of the problem. It is time to do
something about it.

The prevention of excess deaths (both of people and other

species) depends upon the prevention of excess births. Most people rightly dislike instances where very restrictive policies (e.g. China's one-child families) have been introduced. Yet that situation has only come about because more socially acceptable measures were not implemented in the past (Mao, like Fidel Castro and many others, used to denounce family planning as an imperialist plot).

The only solution is a whole package of social and economic reforms. At one level they are the mirror image of those being offered by the West German government to encourage population growth. If it's right to bribe couples to have more children, it cannot be restrictive to do the same for the opposite goal and reward those willing to exercise responsibility in their lives.

Greens stand for education, free family planning and other incentives — not restrictions — to achieve the goal of population stabilization and then reduction. There is of course the argument that this would create a population with too many old people. This point of view is in fact another form of prejudice. Improvements in lifestyles as a result of Green health, basic income and other policies would help far more of our senior citizens to play an active part in society than is the case today in countries such as Britain.

Paul Ehrlich once commented that 'Whatever your cause, it's a lost cause without population control.' There are many, of course, who hide behind accusations of ecofascism to avoid facing reality. They should listen to something else Ehrlich and his wife Anne wrote: 'It is essential (to) hasten as much as possible the arrival of zero population growth, followed by a prudent reduction in numbers... If the human population cannot be soon curbed by humane means, Nature will do the job for us — and she is not noted for her kindness and compassion.'

Ranchor Prime

The Pursuit of Progress and the Search for Inner Meaning

A child of twentieth-century Europe, conditioned to think that indoor toilets and refrigerators are indispensable for civilized life, looks back at the way people lived in western Europe as recently as a hundred years ago, without electricity or running water, and wonders how life was possible in such primitive surroundings. Even though they did get by somehow, the child thinks, they couldn't have had much fun without television, cars and the whole range of gadgets which signify 'progress'.

If developments in computer design and the creation of artificial intelligence continue at their present pace (a big 'if'), children of the twenty-first century will view life in our own century with similar disbelief. Northern civilization has long assumed that its progress is something inevitable: we accept it as an article of faith that, as each generation succeeds the last, we have become more sophisticated and the quality of our life has been enhanced as we advance ever closer to the perfect human society — a utopia of plenty. In contrast to this our past is an obscure and uncomfortable place.

How would a future historian, perhaps from another planet, see this obsession with progress after observing the course we have followed over the last hundred years? Has the twentieth-century development of human society, with its increasing dependence on advanced technologies, been a healthy thing?

Until now, the very word 'modern' has been a euphemism for 'desirable'; but modern technology, modern medicine, modern cars and modern kitchens have now been joined by modern environmental problems, modern diseases, modern traffic and the stress of modern life.

Today's technologies require a vast range of raw materials to fuel them: materials which are becoming more and more difficult and costly to obtain. The warnings of Green economists that our present rate of economic growth cannot be sustained can no longer be dismissed as exaggerated or alarmist. It is clear that we are going to have to learn a simpler way of life, not only for our own survival, but also for a fairer world whose limited resources are more evenly distributed. Yet due to psychological dependence on the comforts afforded by today's technologies and our addiction to 'progress', this prospect is hard to come to terms with.

'What! Live without my washing machine and have to go down to the stream to do my washing? How horrible!' The prospect of being without the benefits of modern technology is deeply disturbing — it strikes at the heart of the doctrine of progress, the pursuit of which treats all forms of physical work as drudgery to be eliminated by ever improved comforts and conveniences.

Belief in the inevitability of progress has meant that traditional knowledge and understanding have been made redundant simply because they are old. It has created a society in constant need of change and 'improvement', never satisfied to remain as it is. The ideal which is held before us in education is to discover, to push forward the frontiers of knowledge, to create new possibilities and new solutions. There is a great arrogance in this: it assumes the inadequacy of the past and the superiority of the present generation. It has created a strange and disturbing psychological condition, fed by constant propaganda, which prevents us from ever being satisfied with the present — instead of appreciating what we have received from previous generations and learning to live within our means, we are taught never to be satisfied, always to yearn for more.

Voices of wisdom have warned against the misconception that satisfying material desires can bring happiness:

> One who is undisturbed by the ceaseless flow of
> desires — which pour like rivers into the limitless
> ocean which is always being filled yet remains steady
> — achieves peace; not one who strives to fulfil those
> desires.[1]

Alienated from our past and dissatisfied with our present, we
train our children as scientists and technicians in order to keep
up the pace of growth and progress, seemingly forever, but we
do not teach them the inner wisdom to live with what they have
created.

There are alternatives.

Many of the world's cultures have preserved the wisdom of
their past with reverence. They have not rejected the simple
lifestyles they have inherited, but have seen them as an essential
part of their identity and as the cradle for their spiritual growth.

The old Sanskrit histories of India record the wisdom of the
past for future generations. The original spiritual teachings were
orally transmitted from generation to generation by the system
of guru and disciple. The guru's task was to pass on the sacred
tradition without changing it, but the time came when it was
necessary to write down the teachings because the people of the
coming age, it was believed, would be misguided and disturbed
and unable to memorize the words of the Vedic hymns. Writing
therefore, far from being a sign of advancement, was understood to be an unavoidable necessity to counteract the general
decline in wisdom and the power of memory.

These people had a very different view of progress from our
own. They saw they were in danger of losing something of great
value with the passage of time and their task became to sustain
and preserve their way of life, not to change it. They were happy
with their tradition because it had spiritual depth and an
understanding of truth, therefore they chose to live in such a way
as to be able to pass on to the next generation a culture and
quality of life which had not been debased by new ideas.

Discovery and progress had different connotations in the
world of spiritual India: they referred to the inward journey

through the secret landscape of the spirit; to the search for inner meaning and spiritual wisdom which alone was capable of fulfilling their true desires:

> When you have that wisdom which destroys all ignorance, your knowledge will reveal everything, as the sun illuminates the day.[2]

It is the sense of inner meaning which is missing from Northern culture. The belief that there is significance and value to each and every part of life in the universe in and of itself, quite apart from its practical value to humans, is an essential part of the Indian spiritual world-view. When life is lived in this consciousness it becomes possible to find peace and fulfilment even in very simple surroundings. In fact, far from bringing fulfilment, pandering to the unlimited sensual and mental appetites of the human species and creating ever more complex arrangements to satisfy them obstructs the search for inner meaning:

> The wise do not take delight in sensual pleasures, which are short-lived and are themselves the source of suffering.[3]

There is a story of a man who bought an ornate antique birdcage to decorate his home. He carefully restored it, cleaning and polishing it all day. Inside the cage was a bird, but he took no notice of that, not even bothering to feed it. When he proudly displayed his birdcage to his friends, they were shocked to see that despite the beauty of the cage the poor bird was dying of hunger. Northern culture has effectively built a very elaborate cage in which the human spirit is now languishing, imprisoned by its own material excesses. Despite the sophistication of the cage, this civilization has failed to see the inner meaning of life, and the bird inside is dying.

The view that in previous times great wisdom existed in society is still commonly held by spiritually-minded people in India. They see the modern age and the all-pervading influence of 'modern civilization' in their lives as part of a general decline over the thousands of years of Kali Yuga, the age of quarrel and hypocrisy, leaving them with only the remnants of a greater wisdom.

This world-view and the one predominant in the North appear to be quite different, and both have their limitations. One encourages tradition at the risk of creating a fatalist and inward-looking society, while the other encourages innovation at the cost of losing what is good from the past and produces a society of disoriented, rootless individuals obsessed with finding satisfaction through careers and possessions. In reality it is the search for a balance between the two extremes which is required. Combining the mystic wisdom of the old world with the pragmatism of the new, the handicaps of both can be neutralized, like the lame person riding on the blind person's shoulders.

The Indian spiritual tradition teaches that wisdom is something inherent in life itself, pervading the universe. It is something which one can receive and discover for oneself from the world about one and at the same time it exists within each one of us. Truth is not the prerogative of any one tradition, but is present in all. Indian spirituality does not lend itself to institutionalized religion, which divides the world up into religious boxes: this belongs to that religion, this belongs to the other one, and anything outside my box cannot be true. It teaches that each of us possesses an inner wisdom which we have somehow lost sight of; that we are looking outside ourselves for what is already within. Because our attention is directed externally, we need to be re-directed within. This re-direction is the essential role of the teacher and the religious tradition.

In the great cycle of the *Mahabharata*, the epic history of old India, spiritual teachings are set in the classic tradition of the teacher showing wisdom to the disciple. At the heart of the epic is the Bhagavad Gita, or 'Song of God', where Krishna teaches his warrior friend Arjuna, who is presented with an awful dilemma: whether to fight in battle against his own relatives and dear friends, or to allow the forces of evil to overrun his kingdom. Taking this as a metaphor, Arjuna finds himself in a position of great danger where confusion obscures his path and his duty is not clear. He says to Krishna, 'I'm confused; I'm frightened; I don't know what to do. Please advise me.'

This has obvious parallels with today's overwhelming environmental and social problems. Humanity is caught by dilemmas of increasing perplexity where the right path is never clear. We have created a civilization of great complexity in which the economic and social needs of people are intricately woven into a global web of cause and effect over which we have less and less control. The whole edifice, being based upon the principle of trying to replace the natural order with an artificial one aimed at satisfying material desires, is highly insecure and dangerous. We are trying to solve our problems through a pragmatic approach. Making constant adjustments to the balance of life, without any clear knowledge of what their consequences may be, we stumble on without knowing where we are going.

The further we progress along this path, the deeper our illusion becomes. We think that we are making progress, but our progress is like that of the deer in the desert who chases after a mirage. The poor animal runs deeper and deeper into the desert until eventually it can go no further. Led on by its burning thirst, trapped by its blindness and misjudgement, it eventually lies down to die in the wilderness.

What we have lost is faith in our own wisdom. The voices of wisdom are many the world over, but we no longer hear them. They have become a quaint historical footnote for us, which we no longer feel the need for. We believe we have now come of age, and we have no more need for superstitious or romantic ideas of worshipping some superior being.

At this crossroads of the closing years of the twentieth century we need to pause and take stock. We need to ask ourselves whether we can afford to cast off the ropes and drift off into the midst of the storms and vastness of history and the universe with nothing to hold on to. We need to question our arrogance in being unwilling to sit at the feet of the wise to learn.

In re-examining the world's stock of wisdom we can now take advantage of the fact that we are a global community. We are no longer limited to looking at only one tradition. There are many sources of understanding still left to us all over the world. In particular our Northern civilization needs to find a new balance and harmony which it has all too clearly lost. It will benefit by examining the wisdom traditions of India. Having exposed most of the rest of the world to our own traditions, and having largely abandoned them ourselves, we now need to learn from others; to put down our swords and guns, our computers and micro-scopes, our cars and televisions, and have the courage and the vision to journey in new territory where these things will be of little value for us.

Spirituality has first to be practised before it can be taught, and those who teach it often fail, so we must have patience. One of the greatest injuries our modern way of life has inflicted on us has been to take away our patience, to make us believe in the instant solution. Those who accept reincarnation (a quarter of the British public and about half the world) can readily under-stand that it takes time to learn about truth.

Reincarnation is a good example of a teaching which has been largely ignored by Northern civilization, despite the fact that it has always existed in one form or another in the unofficial religions of our countries, and dates back beyond our current doctrines. It is important because it stresses the equality of all life forms and their transience too. It does not support the anthro-pocentric humanism of Northern culture which permits human society to terrorize the animal kingdom and dominate the cycles of nature for its own conveniences. Nor does it support the empire-building mania of European societies, who wanted to possess as much of the world as they could, believing that they only had one life in which to do it all. It is these attitudes that have encouraged us in our present path of industrial and technologi-cal war upon nature and the world.

There are many important principles in the Bhagavad Gita, such as the soul, karma, rebirth and liberation, which have not as yet found resonance in the Northern tradition. Coming as they do from a very different culture, these principles are immensely relevant to the debate about the search for a new set of values or for rediscovering the old ones. In times of fear and confusion these principles provide a valuable alternative per-spective and are worth exploring. They could well point to the next phase of spiritual understanding which Northern civilization, with all its problems, might be capable of achieving.

Crisis is a creative experience. Crisis in our own lives brings anxiety and stress, but it also brings understanding and renewal. Very often it is through struggling with our destinies that we come to understand who we are. Seeing our strengths and weaknesses enables us to progress to the next level of self-awareness, to grow as persons. Sometimes, through crisis, we rediscover a truth that we had forgotten, which we had thought was no longer important, or whose relevance we had not understood and when we come back to it we see it in a new light, understanding its relevance in a way we were not able to before.

The crisis of survival and direction now faced by the world does not have to be a destructive experience. It can be a time of redefinition and rediscovery; a time of finding truths where we previously thought none existed; a time of hope and fulfilment. No one can pretend that the coming years are going to be easy; there will undoubtedly be great hardships and suffering; but if we are to survive the challenges which now face us we must be prepared to learn, to grow and to change, both as individuals and as societies.

Notes

1. *Bhagavad Gita*, chapter 2, verse 70.
2. ibid., chapter 5, verse 16.
3. ibid., chapter 5, verse 22.

Ilona Cheyne

Environmental Issues in Europe and the Role of the International Law

It is a truism that environmental issues affect all of us and take little notice of political boundaries. Legal systems, on the other hand, are designed to serve particular political and social organizations. The content of law — and the way in which that content is created or changed — is an indication of the distribution of power within those organizations. This is as true on the international plane as it is in domestic state affairs. This essay will look at some of the implications of the relationships between law and political system for the regulation of environmental issues in relation to public international law.

Public international law is a product and a reflection of the political organization of the international community. It is based at present on the existence of numerous and independent states which are approximately equal in the sense that no single state is able to impose its will upon all the others. The international system, therefore, is essentially atomistic and consensual; it promotes the right of states to maintain their political independence from each other and to protect their sovereign powers over internal affairs and foreign policy.

In international law this means that all states are recognized as sovereign with equal legal capacities, rights and duties. These duties may be varied by undertaking new legal obligations. But each new legal obligation must be consented to by each sovereign state, and each is free to grant or withhold that consent. There is no general law-making institution which can impose acceptance of an obligation upon an unwilling minority. In practice, of course, many factors will affect the decision whether or not to give consent and in some cases the freedom of choice may be more apparent than real. But once consent is given, for whatever reason, that state is bound by the obligation until or unless it is changed by legitimate means.

There are several reasons why a state might choose to accept the restraint of binding legal obligations without being compelled to do so. In very general terms, there are clear advantages to living in an ordered society where promises may safely be given and accepted, and where the behaviour of the other members of the community is for the most part predictable. Resources can then be committed to productive and beneficial activities, the benefits of cooperation enjoyed and common interests pursued. Global, institutional cooperation has been a steady, though slow, development over this century.

The concern here, however, is not so much with the general question of support for a legal system, but with the need to encourage acceptance of specific obligations directly relating to the protection of the environment. There are two main reasons for a state to accept a restraint voluntarily. First, the principle of reciprocity in international law means that states are only bound by a legal obligation in relation to other states that have accepted the same obligation. A state will accept restrictions on its own freedom of action when it sees sufficient benefit in other states being likewise restricted. Secondly, but not so often, states may see a value in binding themselves to a certain standard of behaviour regardless of whether there is a directly reciprocal effect. So, for instance, the Geneva Convention of 1949 relating to the treatment of civilians in wartime applies to the parties regardless of whether the other belligerents are bound. In this case, the rationale may be purely humanitarian. In other cases, such as preferential trading arrangements for less developed countries, humanitarianism may be accompanied by less altruistic motives.

The highly individualistic nature of international society is both the cause and effect of the comparative absence of institutional structures, both for law-making and for general law enforcement. The result is an unusual form of legal system which must, for the most part, look for its strength elsewhere than in the imposition of rules and supervision supported by coercive enforcement. Instead, the stability of the legal system depends in large measure upon its reliance on individual consent and the benefits, both long-term and short-term, of reciprocity. In other words, the high degree of compliance with international law that is evident in everyday international relations is a direct result of the voluntary creation of its obligations.

The fact that compliance arises from a system of reciprocal benefits gives rise to important implications for the protection of the environment. When states fail to comply with their international legal obligations, enforcement is commonly effected by negotiation, backed if necessary by withdrawal of reciprocal benefits. This form of sanction works well in areas where international cooperation has a high perceived value, such as in the international postal system or air services. In the area of environmental protection, however, the perceived value is often the avoidance of a potentially dangerous situation which may occur some time in the future and to which individual states contribute only incrementally. In particular, the practical effect of the restrictions varies from state to state. The ability of other states to ensure compliance by withdrawal of cooperation is therefore likely to be reduced.

At the other extreme of sanctions is the use of force, but this is clearly inappropriate for at least two reasons. First, the use of armed forces is difficult to agree upon multilaterally and is always likely to be out of proportion to any environmental offence. Secondly, the possibility of abuse and the potential for human and environmental disaster render such a means of enforcement impracticable. There is, in other words, no easy analogy to be made between the coercive measures available to the individual state in dealing with recalcitrant individuals and those available to the international community in dealing with offending states.

In addition, another important effect arises from the absence of an institutional legislature with responsibility for acting for the good of the whole community, coupled with reliance upon individual consent. We see in the international system an unusually close identification of legal regulation with the self-interest of the law-makers. The agenda for international law-making is inevitably tied to the preoccupations of the individual countries, ranging as they do through developing, newly industrializing and developed states. Economic development has been, and continues to be, their predominant concern and this can be seen from the most cursory glance at law-making negotiations, declarations and agreements of recent years. These include complaints against protectionism, promotion of free trade measures, assertion of national control over natural resources and regulation of exploitation of shared resources in the deep seabed. Although the Stockholm Declaration on the Human Environment was made as long ago as 1972, and despite the projects conducted under the auspices of the UN Environmental Programme, international efforts to discuss and protect the world environment pale in comparison with the time and energy devoted to economic matters. The pressures of international economic relations, and those from domestic, industrial and other interest groups, have dictated that governments have had very little choice but to favour economic development over environmental interests. It is particularly unfortunate, therefore, that economic development so often has harmful environmental effects.

International rules for environmental protection may be particularly subject to domestic pressures for another reason. Where states see the benefit of reciprocal obligations in their international actions, and are prepared to adopt common regulation in international affairs, they are acting as individual subjects with broadly similar interests in their external affairs. Within the international system, therefore, they may be treated for most purposes as unitary actors. Where, however, international law becomes increasingly concerned with matters that impinge upon domestic regulation, such as human rights or protection of the environment, it is no longer justifiable to treat states as unitary actors. The acceptance of, and ultimately compliance with, international obligations necessarily becomes more susceptible to the complex domestic interests and pressures of each state. As a result, the perception of shared benefit on the international plane is weakened and the natural tendency to comply with the law is compromised. The task of persuading governments that global and cooperative protection of the environment is to their benefit is therefore highly complex and one in which international lawyers can play only a partial role.

Assuming, however, that states agree to accept environmental protection measures, there are two methods by which legal obligations can be created — by international customary law and by treaty.

International customary law comprises a body of general rules and principles that are binding on states. It is created through the operation of state practice accompanied by the belief that the practice is legally binding. This belief, termed *opinio iuris*, is not only an acknowledgement that the state is bound by law to act in a particular way, but also an expression of expectation and reliance that other states will behave likewise. The state practice does not have to be universal, but it must be demonstrated by a majority of states including those most closely concerned by the practice. In many cases, this will be evidenced by mere acquiescence rather than a positive act. A newly-created state is deemed to have accepted any rule of international customary law in force at the time of its entry into the international legal community. This is probably best explained as a 'membership fee' for joining the club of sovereign states.

Such a system for creating and changing rules gives considerable stability because of the wide measure of agreement that lies at its foundation. At the same time, however, the process has certain inherent disadvantages. It is cumbersome, and often requires the passage of considerable time before a sufficiently consistent practice may be developed. Finding satisfactory evidence of state practice — and interpreting that evidence — is often a difficult and time-consuming task. More importantly, the growth of law through state practice is better suited to a claim of exclusive rights against other states than to the development of the detailed, cooperative legal regimes required for proper environmental protection. For this reason in particular, international customary law is unlikely to be the most appropriate vehicle for the protection of the environment.

Treaties are contractual agreements between states which, at first glance, avoid the disadvantages of international customary law as a method for creating legal obligations. Treaties are made in writing and are binding only on the parties. There is little problem in discovering the content of the rules and the identity of the states bound by them. It is this very certainty, however, that leads to difficulties. States that might have acquiesced in a general practice will not necessarily be prepared to commit themselves to a precise obligation through a deliberate act of ratification or accession. As the international community has become larger and more diffuse, so it has become more difficult to attain common agreement on innovative draft treaties. This problem became so acute during the last United Nations law of the sea conference that the need for positive acceptance of each draft article was abandoned. Instead, a 'consensus' procedure was adopted which allowed draft articles to be passed unless objections were raised. This passive form of acceptance certainly allowed a draft treaty of some 320 articles to be finalized, but it also led to a drafting style designed to avoid any wording that might stimulate resistance.

This had two important results. First, many of the most controversial provisions of the draft treaty were worded so vaguely that they may be interpreted in several different ways. Secondly, the essentially passive nature of the consensus procedure merely disguised (and therefore postponed) disagreement over the nature of the obligations. Despite the successful negotiation of the draft text, several states, including the UK and the USA, have refused to sign or ratify the treaty. Although written agreements are preferable to international customary law when protecting the environment, it is important to avoid an over-ambitious global treaty which will fail to attract crucial support.

The requirement of consent for the creation of, and compliance with, international law means that it is futile to consider imposing restrictions on unwilling states. Both traditional methods of developing rules, custom and treaty, are unsatisfactory for environmental protection. In addition, agreements reached on the international plane also require compliance, supervision and enforcement at transnational and national levels. The willingness to implement environmental policies, including control over both foreign and national companies, is an essential part of making these international obligations work. The United Nations Environmental Programme (UNEP) therefore plays a valuable role in facilitating coordination among UN specialised agencies, governments, non-government organizations and other interested persons.

UNEP, however, has had comparatively limited success in getting technical agreements on environmental protection widely ratified. In addition, it has become identified with an approach to environmental protection which is closely tied to the development concerns of Third World countries and is not viewed with complete sympathy by developed countries. As a result perhaps, the latter have tended to operate through other organizations that more obviously reflect their concerns, such as the OECD and the European Community.

A notable feature in recent years has been the highly publicized, high-level conferences on specific issues concerning, for example, protection of the ozone layer. These conferences have demonstrated the willingness, even the eagerness, of developed countries to take environmentally protective measures and to be seen to do so. Although the publicity attracted to these law-making conferences undoubtedly benefits environmental causes, they do raise two concerns.

First, the very high-level participation of governments in environmental treaty conferences imports a political agenda that is not entirely helpful. The public support given by heads of government to environmental protection and their willingness to accept restraints on industrial practices for the common good should be gladly accepted. But it was in the interests neither of the governments involved nor of the treaty supporters to focus attention on the allegations made by many of the scientific community that the measures agreed upon to protect the ozone layer were at best partial solutions and constituted an unnecessary surrender to the interests of the industrial lobby. Secondly, the concern must be that such high-level participation and support is vulnerable to political fashion and the changing priorities of international relations. The interest and goodwill currently displayed by governments is likely to be exhausted by continuing a series of piecemeal, issue-related treaty conferences.

What is needed, therefore, is an arrangement that can harness the present tide of environmental concern and provide for a continued, scientifically-informed debate. A model that might be followed is that of an agreed charter of legal principles, subject to detailed implementation and supervision by an international organization. The Stockholm Declaration of 1972 and the establishment of UNEP represented the beginning of an international political regime for environmental policy with only a small legal component. The wide-ranging provisions of the World Charter for Nature presented to the UN General Assembly in 1982 attempted to create mandatory principles but failed to construct a procedural and supervisory framework in which they could be made to work. The time has now arrived to crystallize the principles and rules that have developed in a rather haphazard fashion since 1972 into a legal regime. This would promote a set of binding legal standards rather than voluntary cooperation, and would consolidate the progress promoted by the UNEP process. It would not replace it, but rather would be complementary to, and supportive of, that process. Existing organizations exist from which instructive lessons may be learnt, in particular GATT, the International Labour Organization and the proposed authority to be established to supervise exploitation of the international seabed area. They not only offer positive examples to follow but also, and more importantly, they suggest certain pitfalls to avoid and negotiating difficulties that are likely to arise.

Negotiating issues are likely to involve a number of sensitive issues. These would include:

- whether the body would make binding decisions or only recommendations and voluntary negotiated agreeements;

- whether voting would be by majority or by unanimity; if by majority, whether member states would be given weighted votes, and if weighted, whether any state or group of states would have a veto;

- the provision of independent technical and scientific support to the executive body;

- the possibility of financial support and rewards for countries introducing environmental protection measures at the expense of their economic development;

- the acceptance of a dispute settlement procedure, possibly with a quasi-judicial function.

All of these need more detailed examination than is possible here. The UN Conference on Environment and Development to be held in 1992 is an ideal opportunity to consider these issues and to entrench the considerable progress made over the previous 20 years.

The difficulty of achieving this kind of agreement should not be underestimated. It may not be possible at present to find sufficient common recognition of problems, causes and solutions in an international community of over 160 states with widely differing political and economic agendas. But the debate is particularly important for Europe both as a significant creator and as a victim of environmental degradation. European states both create and suffer transboundary pollution. Many of the west European states depend heavily on a highly industrialized economy, and there is increasing pressure, especially in the east European states, for both agricultural and industrial development. The urgency with which these issues must be tackled means that the European Community and the non-EC governments in Europe should take the opportunity in the 1992 Conference to push for an integrated legal regime. If, however, a global legal regime cannot be created for the time being, this should not be allowed to delay the establishment of a specific regional institution which is more specialized in environmental affairs and with a wider membership than the existing European structures.

A European regional organisation of the kind discussed above is feasible because of the common interests and objectives of the region, and if such common purposes can be harnessed then such an international law regime would be not only desirable but also workable. The future of the European region holds many risks as well as many hopes; willing cooperation and trust based on experience will be needed to create an economically and environmentally sound regime which can act as a model for future global management. This is most likely to be nurtured within a clear structure of legal principle, enforceable undertakings and progressive development of sound environmental policies.

Freda Meissner-Blau and Paul Blau

The EC as a Parasite on the Third World

The title of this contribution rests on two assumptions: a protracted timeframe and the present character and goals of the European Community. If a shorter timeframe is taken (less than twenty years or so) or if the EC undergoes fundamental change in this time, then the fiasco of severe economic collapse and ecological breakdown is perhaps avoidable. In what follows we present this notion in six theses.[1]

1. Permanent Material Growth is Impossible in a Limited World.

In the three decades from 1950 to 1979 the global consumption of fossil fuels multiplied fourfold, as did economic production. In the EC gross production has increased by a further 24% from 1979 to 1989, and by 27% in the whole OECD area.

Car production increased from 8 million per year in 1950 to 21 million in 1979, and by 1988 15.2 million new cars were produced in the USA alone. Out of the 'world population' of cars in 1985, the USA contributed 139 million, Japan 30.7 million, Germany 26 million and China 1.2 million.

In 1988 5.7 billion tons of carbon were released into the atmosphere, chiefly by power generation, motor traffic and steel production; a further 1 to 2 billion tons came from burning of forests.

The effects are well-known: increased CO_2 content in the atmosphere and the greenhouse effect, leading to a change in regional, then global climate, rise in sea level and so on. Against the preindustrial CO_2 level of 280 parts per million, the 1987 figure was 348, an increase of 24%. The tendency is accelerating.

China alone plans to double its use of coal by the year 2000. It is not hard to imagine what this means in environmental burden with a population of over a billion (1.28 billion by 2000). China already contributes some 594 million tons of the 5.7 billion ton carbon emission. In ten years this would increase to the present US level.

Already in Europe (excluding European Russia) a fifth of all forests (31 million hectares) are damaged. The ozone hole over the Antarctic has grown to twice the area of the United States (18.8 million square kilometres).

Two major factors are particularly decisive for environmental stress: energy consumption and population growth.

World energy consumption has increased fourfold in recent decades and is still rising at around 1.5% per year — if significantly slower than in the 1950s and 1960s. Yet per capita consumption varies enormously.

One of the most striking differences in the present global distribution of energy use is the enormous disparity between developing and industrialized countries. The 70% of humanity that lives in developing countries accounts for only 30% of global energy consumption. In fact, if only oil, natural gas, coal, and electricity — the so-called 'commercial' energy sources — are considered, the developing countries' share of global energy shrinks to less than 20%. The disparity is even more striking on a per capita basis. On average, each person in the developing countries consumes less than one-sixth of the energy consumed by people in the industrial countries, and less than one-tenth as much as the average US citizen.

In absolute terms, the average per capita consumption in the developing countries is 506 kg oil-equivalent per year (1986), the average in the OECD countries 4,954 kg.

Yet there are wide variations even within these groups. The developing countries range from 21 kg per capita in Ethiopia, through 208 kg in India, to 1,427 kg in Argentina. The EC countries range from 1,284 kg in Portugal to 5,201 kg in Holland. The EC average is 3,465 kg. Canada is the world leader with 8,945 kg, followed by Norway with 8,803 kg, and the United States with 7,193 kg. The former Soviet bloc countries show astonishingly high figures: the Soviet Union 4,949 kg and the GDR 5,915 kg.

This means that a more just distribution of resources in the context of ecological responsibility can permit a further rise in per capita energy consumption only in the Third World countries.

The same goes for nutrition. Figures for calory consumption are not an adequate reflection of the differences, for the rich countries consume far more animal products, and the poor countries chiefly vegetable foods. To extract the same amount of calories from animal food, however, requires five to twelve times as much plant production. The developing countries showed in 1985 an average daily per capita consumption of 2,460 calories, with Mozambique as low as 1,617 calories. Given that even in the poor countries, the upper classes live in luxury, it is easy to understand the high level of undernourishment even where average calory intake is relatively high. Brazil, for example, shows a figure of 2,657 calories per day, scarcely lower than Japan with 2,695. Yet according to official statistics, 70% of the Brazilian population are undernourished. The famines in Ethiopia and the southern Saharan countries are already daily news. In the Sudan they threaten to reach an even worse level.

Average 1985 consumption in the OECD countries stood at 3,357 calories, with the EC showing 3,386. Here too the Soviet bloc came surprisingly high, with the USSR at 3,332, Czechoslovakia 3,473 and the GDR 3,769 (against 'only' 3,519 in West Germany). As is so often the case, statistics give a very incomplete reflection, even if they are reliable as far as they go.

World hunger today is an enormous problem, which is intensifying with the growth of population and environmental destruction. The present annual population growth of 88 million needs an extra 28 million tons of grain per year to keep step. Yet every year now 14 million tons are lost through environmental destruction. Air pollution and acid rain, and the loss of soil through erosion (24 billion tons per year — in the 1980s alone equal to half the topsoil in the USA) are the main causes. As much as a third of the world's cultivated area is threatened by soil erosion. Deforestation in the Himalayas leads to floods in the plains. While in 1960 19 million hectares in India were affected by flood, in 1984 the figure was 59 million. In 1988 two-thirds of the cultivated land in Bangladesh was flooded for a day or more. While in 1980 there was a global average of 0.16 hectares per capita for grain production, this figure had fallen by 1990 to 0.13; forty years ago it was 0.23 hectares.

2. Redirection of the Flow of Resources from Rich to Poor Countries is a Moral and Political Duty.

Between 1987 and 2000 the population of the present EC countries is projected to increase from 323 million to 330 million. In the same period, the developing countries are expected to show an increase from 3,761 million (1986) to 4,926 million, who will obviously demand their share of the Earth's riches.

These figures alone indicate the political dimension of the growth question. Can we expect the great majority of the world's population in the next century to accept in good spirit that the lion's share of energy resources and other non-renewable raw materials should benefit a small minority in the rich industrialized countries, who are also imposing the heaviest burden on the environment?

The USA alone consumes a quarter of the world's fossil fuel and emits (1987) 1.22 billion tons of carbon (more than 5 tons per capita, i.e. five times the world average). We should not forget that the military weight of the Third World is also growing. China and India already have nuclear weapons, and other developing countries (for example Pakistan) are certainly close to this. The most current example is provided by the Gulf crisis. Iraq, like other developing countries, 'owes' its chemical

weapons and other modern means of destruction to the industrialized countries, who in this fashion are building their actual
enemies of today and their potential enemies of tomorrow into
military equality.

The demand for a new world economic order, as raised
already in the Coyoacan declaration some fifteen years ago,
should be conceded out of prudence alone, if not from moral
considerations. A social volcano is forming on a global scale,
whose explosion will make previous revolutions seem like storms
in a teacup.

*3. Western Europe, with its small size, is especially vulnerable (density
of population, industry, communications and weapons), and particularly dependent on raw materials.*

One consideration here is generally neglected by economists
and politicians. All production of goods and services makes
demands on the environment (energy, raw materials, waste,
etc.). This means that given the same output and comparable
technology, the stress on the environment is greater or less
depending on the economic space (if we ignore the export of
environmental damage and waste — which then affects other
people — and the net effect of clean-up measures). The following
picture results from a comparison of the economic powers of the
Western world and Japan:

Table I

	EC	USA	Japan
Population in millions (1986)	325	246	121
Area in million square kilometres	2.3	9.4	0.4
GNP in billion US $ (1988)	3151	4818	1528
GNP per capita US $	9718	19558	12458
GNP per sq. km. US $ million	1.37	0.51	3.82

Thus while in the USA value creation per capita (in money terms) is about double that in the EC, the environmental burden per square kilometre is 2.7 times higher in the EC. Japan shows an even greater difference: GNP per capita is under two-thirds of the US value, yet the stress on the land is over seven times greater.

To conclude: even taking into account all topographic and other differences, the EC space experiences a far heavier environmental burden than the USA and is thus ecologically that much more vulnerable. Japan is a more extreme case of this. Japan's rightly praised environmental legislation derives far more from necessity than from a greater insight on the part of its politicians and businesses. If this were really the case, Japan would not pursue a ruthless policy of robbery outside its own frontiers (e.g. in fisheries and the clearing of tropical forests, in Malaysia above all).

Yet our comparison shows even for the EC countries that an environmental stress which is still containable in the USA (or the Soviet Union), could lead here to collapse. On this point, a prudent environmental policy must be given especially high priority. But in contrast to this, in November 1990 the EC made cuts in its already modest environment programme.

4. The EC is programmed for further material growth, which a) undermines its own ecological foundations, and b) through exploitation and plundering of the Third World becomes a provocative parasitism and a joint cause of global environmental catastrophe.

This thesis can be firmed up by two examples. First of all the actual and projected growth rates:

Table II

Actual and projected percentage change over previous year

	1988	1989	1990	1991
GNP	+3.8	+3.5	+3.0	+2.9
GNP per capita	+3.4	+3.0	+2.4	+2.5
Personal consumption	+3.0	+2.5	—	—
Gross investment	+8.5	+6.3	+4.0	+4.0
Industrial production	+4.1	+3.8	+3.3	—
Income from employment (gross)	+4.0	+3.5	—	—
(net)	+4.0	+3.0	—	—
Income from enterprise and wealth (gross)	+10.0	+5.5	—	—
(net)	+10.5	+4.5	—	—
Unemployment per cent	10.4	9.6	9.3	9.1
in millions (excl. Portugal and former GDR)	14.55	16.06	—	—

What also becomes clear from the last column is the almost programmed widening of the income gap between owners and employees. Long-term unemployment on a mass scale is also forecast.

The EC is thus set firmly on the path of growth that the World Bank has predicted for all rich industrial countries until 1995. Since the developing countries, starting from an infinitely worse basis, are assumed to have a growth rate only marginally higher, it is clear that a widening and deepening of the gulf betewen rich and poor is considered the natural course of history, as shown in the following figures:

Table III

Real Percentage Increase in GNP

	1977-1986[I]	1987	1988	1989	1990	1991	1992-1995[II]
Industrialized countries	2.8	3.5	4.4	3.5	2.7	2.9	3.1
	1972-1981						
Developing countries (annual average)	5.0	3.8	4.1	3.0	3.2	4.5	
(per capita)	2.3	1.6	2.0	0.9	0.1	2.4	

[I] annual average
[II] projected

The plundering of the Third world results also from the development of exchange between these and the rich industrialized countries:

Table IV

Growth of Exports by Volume and Value
(annual percentage average)

	1972-1981	1982-1989/90
Industrialized countries		
volume	+6.1	+45.5
unit value	—	+18.0
Developing countries		
volume	+2.1	+38.0
unit value	—	+ 0.72
fuel exports		
volume	-1.6	+10.0
unit value	—	+ 0.49
other exports		
volume	+6.3	+63.3
unit value	—	+ 0.92

Terms of trade (change in per cent per year)

	1972-1981	1982-1989/90
Industrialized countries	- 2.0	+16.4
Developing countries	+ 7.0	+ 0.83
fuel exports	+17.8	+ 0.46
other exports	- 0.9	+ 0.99

World Trade Prices (per cent change in annual averages)

	1972-1981	1982-1989/90
Finished products	+10.1	+26.0
Raw materials (excluding oil)	+10.5	+ 0.97
Oil	—	+ 0.61

Export Prices for Developing Countries
(per cent change in annual averages)

	1972-1981	1982-1989/90
Fuel	+11.2	+ 3.66
Non-fuel	+ 9.6	+ 1.60
Manufactured Goods	+ 9.8	+ 0.92

The rise in exports from the developing countries, which among other things is also enforced by relative prices (and by interest on debt), accelerates in turn a large-scale environmental destruction. The destruction of the tropical rain forests, as in Brazil, provides an impressive illustration.

The second example concerns the catastrophic development of nuclear industry and air traffic. Despite energy surpluses, the governments of France and Britain, above all, but also the German (most recently against the growing resistance of the population), are forcing the further expansion of nuclear power stations. In France, the Superphénix fast-breeder reactor at

Creys-Malville was even started up again 'provisionally' in January 1989, after having to be closed due to a leak in the sodium tank, despite serious warnings from French and Swiss experts.

The EC plans to double air traffic from 1985 to the end of the century. Quite apart from military traffic, the complete overburdening of airways and airports with hours of waiting and delays is only too well-known, as is the increasing danger of collisions. An ever denser network of nuclear installations and an overfilled air space increase the likelihood of an airplane crashing onto a nuclear power station with potentially the most serious continental contamination. The assertion that nuclear plants are safe against such collisions is crass misinformation. In the case of a low-flying military plane, kinetic energies of a quarter of a million tons could be involved. The crash of a French Mirage in 1988 occurred a few flight seconds from the OHU nuclear plant in Bavaria. The crash of a jumbo jet over Scotland in December the same year was also in the vicinity of a nuclear power station.

The following German figures show that accidents of this kind are no rare event. From 1973 to the end of 1988 372 military aircraft crashed in Germany. In 81 cases buildings were damaged. 19 of the jet crashes, according to official figures, were 10 to 20 kilometres from 'nuclear installations' (30 to 60 flight seconds), three were 5 to 10 kilometres (18 to 33 flight seconds) and one was 3 kilometres (11 flight seconds). (Government reply to a question from the Greens in the Bundestag, 22 December 1988.)

5. The present balance of power in the EC rules out any radical change of course in the near future, in the realms of nuclear policy, transport, agriculture, etc. The change that is needed will thus probably come only in the wake of serious breakdowns.

This is based on numerous statements and declarations of intent from leading EC politicians, and on the large-scale projects already under way. Besides the doubling of air traffic (with the necessary expansion and construction of new airports), we can mention the expansion of high-speed rail lines and associated works, the building of new mountain crossings and the like. As far as large-scale chemicals goes, a sharp upswing is expected despite the poisoning of the biosphere that is already out of control and the unresolved problem of waste. Of the 80,000 or more industrial chemicals in production, less than 5% have been toxicologically tested. At present some 1,000 new substances are discovered per day. The present total of some 8 million chemicals is increased each year by around 300,000 combinations which have never before existed in our living space.

Genetic technology with its new and hardly suspected risks is being powerfully pursued. Under the increasing pressure of the USA at the Uruguay GATT round, the EC's agricultural policy, which has already led to the collapse of peasant farming in Western Europe, is being driven ever further through the rapids of concentration into steadily greater agro-industrial factories. The removal of remaining barriers to trade which is now demanded will accelerate still more the export drive to the Third World and with it the destruction of nature and traditional cultivation there. But in Europe too, the further chemicalization and mechanization will bring with it devastation of landscape and biotopes on a large scale.

Indeed, the EC space is already affected by partial ecological catastrophes, whose health-damaging and economic consequences cannot yet be grasped in their full scope. The threatening upset of the North, Baltic and Mediterranean seas affects first of all the coastal fishery and tourist trade, but later the fishing industry as a whole, as it is inshore spawning grounds that are worst polluted. The death of the forests leads to emergency clearances and an oversupply of wood, before making wood exporters into importers.

Water shortage and soil erosion, which in the past were above all Third World problems, now threaten as further consequences of agricultural, industrial and settlement policy. The concept of 'environment refugees', known first of all from Asia, Latin America and the USA, came home to Europe for the first time with the poison spill at Seveso in Italy in 1976. A decade later, the Sandoz fire at Basle narrowly missed leading to a similar result.

The poisoning of air, water and soil harms children most of

all, both directly and indirectly through the food chain. As chronically sick adults they later become a growing burden on the already financially stretched public health system and state budget. The longer life expectancy resulting from medical progress is no longer by itself an adequate measure of the general quality of life. 'The state of human health cannot be separated from that of the Earth,' as the Worldwatch Institute wrote in their State of the World Report for 1988- 89. In large parts of the world the average life expectancy has indeed been significantly increased, but with it the life expectancy of homo sapiens as a species has been dramatically reduced, unless a radical change of course takes place in the industrial countries.

The relatively modest economic growth rate of 3% predicted for these countries should not conceal its exponential character. This still means a doubling in 23 years, and the EC's ambition goes far beyond this. If the growth in production of goods and services is maintained, all environmental legislation and measures can in the best of cases lead only to a slower growth or shift in the total burden (for example the fitting of catalytic convertors on a doubled volume of motor traffic).

For two reasons, it is impossible to map out a specific 'stress scenario' which could predict when ecological collapse and the inevitably following economic collapse would result. First, the 'time bombs' and past burdens that are lurking on all sides are in many cases unknown (new ones are discovered almost daily), as are also the long-term effects of countless commercial chemicals. Secondly, there is complete uncertainty as to the synergetic effect of many of the stresses involved. We do not even know whether in some cases irreversible damage has not already been done, and whether for example endangered animal and plant species can still be saved; still less what effects their disappearance from the life cycle will have also on human beings.

To sum up, almost everything that is dear to the EC governments (and those of other industrial countries) must gradually be abandoned, to make way for new goals. But then this would no longer be the EC as we know it — and as it knows itself.

6. The political transformation in the former Soviet bloc countries will increase still further the danger of ecological collapse and the plundering of the Third World.

The transition now under way to a 'free-market economy', which the governments and peoples of these countries, in their ideological vacuum, anticipated helplessly yet for the most part still full of illusions, is proceeding according to the dogmas of the growth religion and the desires of western corporations. Its spearheads are the motor manufacturers and nuclear industry.

The scarcity of automobiles (according to one US study the Soviet Union alone needs at least 86.7 million new vehicles) is to be remedied by 'joint ventures', and the shortage of energy by the building of 'safe nuclear power stations'. In the transition period, a reduction in social security and massive unemployment are declared unavoidable, in countries where nothing is more urgently needed than the new labour-power of willing hands, and where the signals must point to an environmentally bearable transport system (rail instead of road) and a similarly appropriate energy supply (through a combination of increased efficiency, reduction of waste and expansion of renewable energy sources).

In this respect rail is incomparably superior to road. To transport the same volume by road takes five times as much energy as by rail, producing up to 40 times more pollution and vastly more noise, using two and a half times as much land, and causing 29 times more deaths and 75 more injuries.

Still more ominous is the pressure of the nuclear lobby. Against all logic, Framatom (France), Siemens (Germany) and their like are abusing the backward state of information in the eastern countries, and their present technological and economic emergency, to drive them into the nuclear cul de sac:

> The problems that have led to the commercial demise of nuclear power in almost every part of the world remain unsolved: without massive subsidies nuclear fission remains economically uncompetitive with alternatives; the international ramifications of nuclear

accidents are inhibiting; the safe operation of nuclear reactors continues to be hostage to human frailty, and the problems of permanent nuclear waste disposal are unsolved... while new designs for so-called 'inherently safe' reactors are being explored, such reactors are not available and cannot be considered a near or intermediate term solution.[2]

Since western diktat allows no restrictions on speculation and enrichment, even from dubious sources, we have to reckon with great social tensions and political dangers that go beyond the kindling of nationalism and racial hatred. An environmental destruction that is already far worse than in the west arose chiefly from a situation where these countries had to exploit their own resources. The West on the other hand is able to import raw materials and energy sources from wherever it likes, at convenient prices. West Germany and Austria, moreover, had been sending toxic waste to eastern Germany against hard currency.

Banks, casinos and luxury hotels, those temples of the consumer society, are now shooting up in the big cities of eastern Europe, to satisfy the lucky few while the mass of the population suffer more than ever. Yet should in due course broad layers here too make it to waste of the western kind, it will also place the burden on their own future and the poorest of other regions of the globe. Overcoming the West-East divide will intensify yet further the North-South divide.

Rethinking Values

All governments in the EC member countries are committed to further economic growth. Even the much trumpeted Brundtland report on the gap betwen rich and poor countries presents further increases in production, consumption, raw material and energy use, even in the countries of the waste economy, as a way of solving the problem. The meaning of work is turned upside down; in the industrial countries, with an almost stable population and saturated market, production is allegedly needed to maintain jobs, instead of to meet needs. In the best case it is argued that profits from an increased growth rate should be used to 'repair the environment'.

The international press celebrated the new increase in growth rates in the rich countries. Terror would have been a better reaction. An exponential growth of 4% per annum means a doubling in 17 years ('just right' according to the economists).[3] At this rate, children born in 1990 would need sixteen times the volume of goods and services by the time they reach seventy, simply to avoid market crises.

Three illusions characterize the loss of reality on the part of the technocratic political leading stratum in our countries:

First, the illusion of a 'technical fix', the belief in the unlimited problem-solving capacity of science and technology.

We can recall the once-prized 'high chimney policy'. Waste products were disposed of in the upper atmosphere where they were diluted to an unmeasurable degree. Today we know what these wastes from England, Germany, Poland and the Soviet Union mean for instance in Scandinavia. Today we know that Dilution Is No Solution.

The same goes for the sea, with the North and Baltic, Mediterranean and Black seas stricken by algae and dying seals, tourists with skin rash and ruined fisheries.

Incineration and export of toxic waste are still presented as the recipe for waste disposal. Though this only means shifting the problem in space and time within the biosphere, no consistent strategies for avoidance of waste have been produced.

The same goes for the battle against cancer. Resources are used on a grand scale for research, equipment and surgery; while a considerable portion of the GNP helps to cause cancer, preventive measures lag sadly behind.

The second illusion is that of perfect people. The nuclear accidents at Brown's Ferry and Harrisburg in the USA, as well as the Chernobyl catastrophe, are put down to poor training, carelessness and irresponsibility on the part of the reactor staff. The response in the countries not affected is that 'It can't happen here.' When in the 1970s the International Atomic Energy Organisation held a conference in Salzburg on the nuclear fuel cycle, the speculation in the corridors was that the first large-scale nuclear accident would happen in the Third World, as people there were not properly trained in the handling of complex technical installations. By an irony of history, the accident happened on the territory of a superpower.

However, at the conference on reactor safety held by the IAEO in September 1986, three childish conclusions were drawn. First, nothing like Chernobyl would happen again. Second, in case the impossible did happen, information should be exchanged at the earliest possible date. And third, atomic power could in no way be abandoned. Since then, there have been the Transnuklear and Nukem scandals in Germany. And French experts maintain that the cooling circuit risk in the Superphénix fast breeder reactor at Creys-Malville is less than in a conventional heavy water reactor, even though Superphénix is cooled by liquid sodium, which explodes on contact with water or air.

The third illusion is belief in the unrestricted market. Everyone wants to produce more and to export more once their home market is saturated. Industrial imperialism has displaced the old-style military imperialism and is growing ever more aggressive.

But the countries of the world are communicating vessels, and the planet itself a living organism. What affects one part also affects the other. The old success recipe of exploitation has reached its limits. Damage and waste, the inherent compulsions of industrial society, must cease. We have to live off income, not capital. This means that each step to replace non-renewables by renewables is a step in the right direction. This principle must be the compass that guides us in future.

Notes

1. The figures in this essay are taken from the World Bank's World Development Report for 1988, the Worldwatch Institute's State of the World reports of 1988 through 1991, the United Nations Annual Bulletin of General Energy Statistics for Europe 1990 (for 1988), the

International Monetary Fund's World Economic Outlook for May 1990, and similar sources.

2. Prof. Josef Goldemberg, 'Lifestyles, Energy Choices and Development', Proceedings of the 39th Pugwash Conference on Science and World Affairs, July 1989, Cambridge, USA.

3. Report on Working Group 7, 'Development, Environment and Security', Proceedings of the 39th Pugwash Conference, ibid.

4. Against this, a 2% rate of population growth is seen as an 'explosion'. A further example of a schizophrenia divorced from reality.

Edward Goldsmith

The Big Financial Institutions

It is generally true that customs are gentler
wherever people trade.

Montesquieu, 1749

In February 1854 Commodore Matthew Perry of the United
States Navy arrived in Japan with a powerful squadron of
warships. Being thereby in a strong negotiating position, he was
able to force the Japanese (who until then had followed a policy
of strict seclusion from the western world) to open two ports
(Shimoda and Hakodate) to trade with the USA and to provide
for an American consular representation in Japan. In this way,
Japan was slowly brought within the orbit of world trade. Fifteen
years before, British troops had invaded China whose government had refused to allow the import of opium grown by British
planters in India.

Such events were a far cry from the gentle customs that a
century before Montesquieu supposed would stem from trade.
Yet these incidents, and one could cite hundreds more, serve to
show to what lengths western government have been willing to
go to 'open up' and thereby obtain access to new markets for
their planters, manufacturers and traders and for the modern
corporations that have now taken over much of the planting,
manufacturing and trading on an international scale.

To 'open up' international markets and at the same time
obtain access to new investment opportunities as well as cheap

and plentiful supplies of labour, food and raw materials has always been and remains today the overriding goal of the foreign policy of those countries which dominate international trade. What is more, *in spite of all the rhetoric to the contrary*, all considerations, whether human, social, ecological or climatic, remain as ruthlessly subordinated as ever to the achievement of these goals.

For example, at present it is US policy to assure that grain is made available to US grain merchants at a price that is below the cost of production, the farmer receiving subsidies known as 'deficiency payments' as partial compensation. This has enabled UN grain merchants to establish a very low price for grain, thereby eliminating local competition and gaining a correspondingly increased share of the global market for US grain exports.

As the then Senator Boschwitz, an ally of the mammoth Cargill Corporation, argued in a letter to *Time* magazine during the US Congress debate on the 1985 Farm Bill: '... if we don't lower our farm prices to discourage other countries now, our worldwide competitive position will continue to slide and will be much more difficult to regain. This should be one of the foremost goals of our agricultural policy.' Which of course it is, with horrendous consequences, not least to the growing number of small so-called 'Third' World farmers it drives out of business, out of the countryside and into the urban slums.

They are replaced of course, but by large plantations not only geared to exporting at the expense of producing local food for local people, but also largely dependent on *imported* agrochemicals and destructive agricultural techniques.

This forms part of the pattern of US policy which is to force poor countries in particular to maintain conditions which favour US commercial interests, under threat of retaliation against their exports. The US Trade Representative (USTR) is actually empowered by Congress to do just this. At Carla Hill's confirmation hearing as the current USTR she undertook to use these powers 'as a crowbar to pry open foreign markets', which is just what she is attempting to do in the latest round of negotiations in the General Agreement on Tariffs and Trade.

Similar self-interested goals are shared by bilateral aid agencies such as Britain's Overseas Development Agency and the USA's Agency for International Development. Something like 75 per cent of money they give to poor countries is in the form of 'tied aid', which means it must be spent on the donor country's produce or manufactured goods — whether or not these are desired by the recipient country.

There is no better illustration of this point than the insistence by the British government a few years ago that India purchase (against its will) 22 Westland helicopters under threat of having its aid from the UK cut off. Under such conditions, Third World aid is little more than an export subsidy. Worse still, it also serves to create a need among recipient countries for the donor country's produce. In this way, African countries such as Nigeria and Tanzania have been 'hooked' onto American and Canadian hard wheat.

Such policies were effectively institutionalized in 1944, when the main western nations met at Bretton Woods to plan world economic policies for the post-Second World War period. The primary concern was to plan the world economy so as to diminish the possibility of another 1929-style slump. It was decided that the *means* of achieving 'economic stability' would be a tighter interweaving of the interests of the western manufacturing nations with those of the primary producing nations. Achieving this required two main strategies. First, a development of the capacity of the primary producers to produce raw materials for the manufacturing nations and, second, an expansion of their power to purchase manufactured products.

Three principal institutions were set up at that and subsequent meetings to implement these policies: the International Bank for Reconstruction and Development (IBRD or World Bank), the International Monetary Fund (IMF) and the General Agreement on Tariffs and Trade (GATT).

The World Bank's task was primarily to finance the physical infrastructure required for development; the ports, highways, bridges, dams for hydro-electricity and thermal power stations. It also became involved in 'rural development', backing vast irrigation projects and livestock rearing schemes. Because of its great power and influence, the World Bank set the direction followed by other multinational development banks and by private banks as well. The social and environmental destructiveness of many World Bank schemes in Third World countries has been amply documented in the last few years and strongly criticised by environmentalists. Several US Congressional hearings have been held to enquire into the Bank's activities, while the US representative on the Bank's board has even withheld funds from some of its most potentially disastrous projects. A US senator went so far as to state that if the public knew just what its money was being spent on 'they would be out in the streets.'

The Bank has even promised to reform, but it is difficult to see how it can do this and still fulfil its function of lending about $20 billion a year to Third World countries. However tightly embroiled it may be in the spiralling debt crisis, the Bank's overriding priority remains to lend as much money as it can.

The IMF's role since the war has been to help countries tide over what was once expected to be temporary balance of payment difficulties so that they could remain effective trading partners. Those which had 'overborrowed' were forced to accept IMF 'conditionalities' for putting their house in order. This basically involves increasing export earnings, reducing imports and cutting back on government expenditures on social services, including health, education, environmental standards and even food subsidies for the very poor.

GATT is actually only a 'provisional' treaty, merely a contract agreed by governments rather than a definitive treaty. Nevertheless, GATT is subscribed to by 100 countries (contracting parties) which between them control 90 per cent of the world's $3,000 billion trade. The objective of seven 'rounds' of trade negotiation which have taken place over the last 40 years has been 'the substantial reduction of tariffs and other barriers to trade'. As I write, the eighth round of negotiations is expected to fail. Attempts to extend the round to include services, agricultural products, foreign investment and intellectual property — in short, transnationalize the world economy to an unprecedented extent — have frightened too many 'contracting parties'.

318 Green Light on Europe

And no wonder. For example, in the rapidly expanding trade in services such as transport, travel, banking and insurance (of which the USA is the world's largest exporter), it is proposed that any firm from any country may set up, as of right, in any other country. Any discrimination in favour of local companies can be penalized by retaliation or even *cross-retaliation* in other areas of trade or business. It requires little imagination to see that the big transnational companies already dominant in various service industries are bound to have the same effect on small Third world service companies as the US grain merchants had on small Third World farmers — put them out of business. Similarly the inclusion of 'trade-related intellectual property rights' would effectively require that royalties be paid for patents on, say, genetically 'improved' seeds. This could cost Third World countries who are 'obliged' to buy them anything up to $60 billion a year and further speed the loss of the older but non-patentable varieties.

It could even become 'GATT-illegal' to restrict the export of hazardous wastes to Third World countries. 'It would not be desirable,' a GATT document states, 'for any country to adopt measures designed to stem such flows of investment and trade as might result from international differences in pollution control norms.'

The hugely public battle between the USA and the European Economic Community (EEC) over agricultural subsidies exposes the ruthless reality of international trade deals. The most powerful actors indulge in a bare-fist fight to protect their own interests while the longer-term interests of the Third World, where agriculture is central to economic performance if not survival, are ignored. Ben Jackson of the World Development Movement reckons the knock-on effects of the GATT proposals to the Third World environment would be severe. It cannot be an accident that the Environment Committee set up by GATT officials in 1971 has never sat.

Neither can it be a coincidence that 'experts' advising GATT negotiators come mainly from the transnational corporations which have the most to gain from turning the world into a vast 'free trade zone'. Virtually all technology is monopolized by a few TNCs and they are responsible for much of the world's capital investments. They already have tight control on trade, controlling, for instance, 80 per cent of all the world's land devoted to export crops. Between 80 and 90 per cent of the trade in tea, coffee, cocoa, cotton, forest products, tobacco, jute, copper, iron ore and bauxite is controlled by the three to six largest corporations in each of these particular fields.

There is no doubt that some have benefitted greatly from the 'opening' of world markets and the 'rigour' of the economic discipline dished out by the Bretton Woods institutions. Since 1965 alone world trade has increased six-fold, and the total economic activity of the world is now thought to be well over $10,000 billion.

However, of the 100 biggest economic entities on Earth, only about half are countries, the other half are 'megacompanies' and none of them are to be found in the Third World. Indonesia's environment minister, Emil Salim, sums up the effect of two decades of the development of the world economy to his country like this: 'Today we have to export three times as much timber to buy one tractor as we did in the 1970s.' The bottom line of the search for economic efficiency and free trade on a global scale is that the growth of the richest economies is being subsidized by the environment and the well-being of the poorest countries.

Astonishingly, despite all the evidence that something is going badly wrong with the world economy and that its negative effects on people and the environment are multiplying alarmingly, the opening up of the so-called Second World — eastern Europe — was heralded by the west, not as a triumph for democracy and human courage, but as 'proof' that the west had won the battle of political and economic ideology.

Economic, trade and commercial agreements set up between the EEC and individual east European countries, for example, all contain conditions concerning the continued commitment of the governments to market economics as well as pluralist democracy. In summer 1989, the Organization for Economic Cooperation and Development (OECD or G24) countries delegated all responsibility for handling aid to and trade with eastern Europe *on their behalf* to the European Commission (the 'civil service' of the EEC). The Commission's PHARE programme originally set up to support Poland and Hungary but now extended to Bulgaria, Czechoslovakia, Romania and Yugoslavia, requires a commitment to economic liberalization with a view to introducing market economies from its recipients.

Although it is a motive kept well in the shadows, economic self-interest as a condition for a trade or other international relations is, as I have already argued, old as the hills. However, to enshrine as a principle a commitment to political and economic transformation in the articles of a multilateral bank is quite unprecedented. Yet this is what the new European Bank for Reconstruction and Development (EBRD) has done.

The idea for the bank was proposed at and endorsed by an EEC summit by President Mitterrand of France in December 1989. The first meeting to set up the EBRD took place in January 1990 and with amazing speed the Articles of Agreement were ready for initialling five months later in May. The bank expects to open for business sometime in 1991 once the articles have been ratified by two-thirds of the total shareholding.

The purpose of the Bank could not be more explicit. Its first article reads as follows:

> In contributing to economic progress and reconstruction, the purpose of the Bank shall be to foster the transition towards open market-oriented economies and to promote private and entrepreneurial initiative in the Central and Eastern European countries committed to and applying the principles of multiparty democracy, pluralism and market economics.

The second unique feature of the EBRD is its focus on loans and investment for the private sector. Sixty per cent of the Bank's exposure in any country over the first five years must be to the private sector and the remaining 40 per cent is restricted to public sector project finance rather than government programmes.

In becoming the first multilateral development bank to make provision in its articles for promoting 'in the full range of its activities environmentally sound and sustainable development' the EBRD seems to have heeded at least some of the lessons of its model, the World Bank. However, the heavy emphasis being given to developing eastern Europe along west European lines with environmental concern 'tacked on' will not be enough for the EBRD to avoid the same pitfalls.

Indeed, there could well be serious conflict between the overt political objectives of the EBRD's president, Jacques Attali (a close friend of President Mitterrand, and a politician not a financier) and both the constraints imposed by the environment and the deteriorating world economy. Attali sees the EBRD as 'an embryo of a larger Europe and a larger European entity... the tool for helping eastern European countries reach the same level of development (as the EEC).'

Therefore, replacing the Trabants of east Europe with Fiats or Volkswagens, for example, may reduce local pollution somewhat but the overall increase in number of cars will not only cancel that out but also greatly increase emissions of carbon dioxide, the main greenhouse gas. Furthermore, the recent publication by the OECD State of the Environment Report noted that despite its level of development the sewage of 40 per cent of its population remains untreated.

Article 2.2 of the EBRD's charter states that it will work in close cooperation with, inter alia, the IMF and the World Bank. If they, in concert with the new EBRD, 'open up' the markets and prescribe a financial regime in eastern Europe in the same way as they have done in the rest of the world, then it could not be too long before the Second World joins the Third World in subsidizing the First World.

There is evidence that some, if not all, of the fledgling east European governments are aware of this dilemma, even if most of them have little power to do anything about it at the moment. The pressures to go ahead with reforms in order to meet the immediate needs of their peoples are overwhelming. It could be that another revolution will be needed before gentle customs result from the new relationships between east and west.

Karen Christensen

With the Earth in Mind: the Personal to the Political

Living in a way that reflects our values, though hardly a new idea (indeed, the goal of religious life for centuries), has become not only a personal statement but a political one. Ecological living — from buying green to being green at heart — reflects individual commitment and sensibility as well as a change in the way we perceive our responsibility to the Earth.

Ecological living means different things to different people, depending on their society and position. In the west, it some- times seems to mean little more than choosing a cruelty-free lipstick or unleaded petrol. Beyond these superficial (but not negligible) changes, a new way of life depends on developing a responsiveness to the natural world, to the richness of human experience and to our potential for effectiveness and creativity. This means the evolution of a consciousness based not on individualism, isolation and passive consumption, but on com- munalism and a sense of our real interconnectedness with the forces and systems of the Earth, and with our fellow humans and other living creatures.

A new consciousness will lead to changes in the way we go about our daily lives: carrying a canvas shopping bag, eating organic foods and less meat, choosing sustainably harvested timber and nontoxic varnishes, or refinishing a set of second- hand cupboards instead of buying something new.

It must be clear that changing the way we live also means different things in different countries. The present situation in

Europe — the east struggling to find a new path and new leaders, the west preening itself as a social model — presents a dilemma. Green consumerism, vaunted as a potent force for change in the west, must look ridiculous and self-indulgent to people in developing countries, just as the US appetite for diet foods appears to most Europeans (who wonder why Americans don't have the sense to stop eating so much).

In western Europe, women's sanitary products are advertized as 'chlorine-free' or 'biodegradable', while in the east one often cannot buy such disposable products at all. Britons buy tiny plastic trays of organically grown parsley, while Czechs queue to get basic foodstuffs, never mind the pesticide levels.

Both regions need to keep in mind two essential truths. First, the social and economic pressures that keep west Europeans consuming — and that are now leading the people of eastern Europe and the developing world to want to consume at the same level — are based not on need but on dissatisfaction and unhappiness, on powerlessness and vulnerability, and on the illusion that by buying more, possessing more, these emotional and psychological ills will disappear.

Second, the real measure of a satisfactory society is not a 'standard of living' measured in terms of consumption but rather what might be called sustainable satisfactions — stable relationships with the natural world and our neighbours, good work, skilled crafts, spiritual commitments, learning and the arts, creativity and love. For both east and west, the real challenge is to find a way of dismantling the consumer society and replacing it with a society wealthy not in terms of GNP but in those sustainable satisfactions which are available to all people.

The question for westerners is no longer how to achieve an ecological lifestyle — several dozen books and publications provide that information regularly — but whether such individual changes really affect the destructive forces of modern industry and commerce. It has been said that the emphasis on individual lifestyle change shifts the blame for environmental problems, and hence the quest for solutions, away from the corporate and government agencies that are fundamentally to blame. To that I can only reply: personal change leads to public change, and it is public attitudes that will force the necessary changes in industry and technology. Personal change leads people to reassess their lives, to resist the insistent pressures of advertising and see more clearly the harsh and desensitizing culture we live in. To stand against the prevailing tide is an experience of liberation. Personal change helps people to become powerful, active in the world around them.

And individual actions add up. As John Seymour, co-author of *Blueprint For a Green Planet*, wrote in a letter to *The Ecologist*:

> It is our contention that such people can do things,
> and abstain from doing others, to help to save our
> planet... You and I cannot influence governments,
> nor big business, but we can conduct our own lives in
> a way calculated to save what we can of the biosphere.
> This may not seem much but it is as much as we can
> do.[1]

And even then Seymour is much too pessimistic, because green consumerism and various environment campaigns have proved that we can influence government and business. One example of pressure being brought to bear on a major industry was seen in 1989 when British disposable nappy manufacturers made a rapid switch to non-chlorine-bleached paper pulp following a widely publicized campaign launched by the Women's Environmental Network.

The question of how to influence people outside the committed green centre is, rightly, of growing concern to environmentalists. The answers are not all in, but many different tacks are being tried. Magazines aimed at the general public, local pressure groups to tackle community issues, and education projects in schools, are a few examples. Some people thought the answer would be handbooks on simple-things-you-can-do, which made saving the Earth sound like an easy project. The Earth Island Institute in San Francisco countered with a list of 'difficult things you can do to save the Earth'. The first was: 'Bury your car.' They later decided that this would waste resources and changed it to: 'Send your car to a recycling plant.'

Self-righteousness is tempting, when you try harder than your friends. But widespread social change won't come about if we underestimate the complexity of adopting a new way of life in a society which is geared to consume rather than conserve. Long-term, substantive change will require drastic shifts in attitudes, and, of course, in the way we organize our communities. The truth is that I've found myself lying about just how much I do, how little effort it takes. And I suspect that smugness about the proportion of household rubbish you recycle is not, really, any better for the soul than the consumer smugness of a company executive who always has the latest model car.

Well-meaning people often feel beleaguered because there is so much information available about energy-efficient light bulbs and recyclable packaging that no one can possibly do it all. They end up feeling depressed and guilty, thinking that a green way of life is so much effort that it's a clear choice between saving the planet and helping their football team win the league championship. Increasing the involvement of people who care but who know they can't do everything right, is an essential part of the green movement, and the responsibility of green activists. No one should underestimate the power of personal example — using cotton diapers, saving the leaves for the compost heap, or riding a bike to the company picnic will inevitably influence other people. This isn't a matter of making them feel guilty, but of showing what is possible by putting ecological principles into action.

I see the current surge of interest in the practical side of environmentalism as divided into three main areas: green consumerism, home ecology, and voluntary simplicity. Each has a useful contribution to make.

'Green consumerism' — a deliberate irony according to its author, John Elkington — hit Britain in the autumn of 1988. It seemed to catch environmental groups by surprise. Many of them, though not the UK Green Party, were involved in the 'Green Consumer Week' organized to promote the *Green Consumer Guide*. There is little doubt that green consumerism has the potential for reducing the environmental damage done by industry. The availability of products which have been made from recycled paper or which have not been tested on animals is a good thing, and having 'green' products on supermarket shelves is a potent method of spreading information.

Green consumerism does not, however, address the question of the quantity we consume, or of consumerism as a basis for a culture or civilization. It presents itself as a method of personal empowerment. 'People's ordinary spending is the most powerful agent of change they possess' may sound good. I see myself at the till, voting with my choice of environmentally sound products. But the implication that people are capable of no more than putting a different brand of washing-up liquid in their shopping trolley is damaging and demeaning.

Small businesses are profiting from a growing interest in nontoxic, cruelty-free products, but multinational companies also use greenspeak to sell highly questionable products and practices. In addition, 'economies of scale' remains a tenet of the green consumerists, who say that we should encourage the multinationals by buying their 'green' products, because in this way the companies will be encouraged to make greater changes in the resources they use, in their production methods, and in dealing with the waste they create. The underlying assumption is that the multinationals will continue to prosper — and that lower prices for less damaging products is the most we can hope for.

A serious impediment to the success of green consumerism is that it is difficult to market green and ungreen products together. In Britain, Safeway has been the leading mainstream marketer of organically grown produce. Their labelling stresses 'organically grown for better flavour', not mentioning the health or environmental benefits of buying food produced without pesticides. Since organic produce does not always taste dramatically better than chemically grown produce, maintaining high volume sales is likely to be difficult.

A second kind of change, which I think of as 'home ecology', concentrates on how we do things rather than on what we buy. A number of practical handbooks have been published in the past couple of years, replete with tips and checklists on everything from ecological eating and composting to choosing a holiday destination and deciding what to feed your dog.

Astonishingly, the American version of the *Green Consumer Guide* tries to separate shopping from other forms of behaviour change:

> By choosing carefully, you can have a *positive* [my italics] impact on the environment without significantly compromising your way of life. That's what being a Green Consumer is all about... It wasn't very long ago that being a Green Consumer was a contradiction in terms. To truly care for the environment, it was said, you had to drastically reduce your purchases of everything — food, clothing, appliances, and other 'lifestyle' items [since when, I wonder, is food a lifestyle item?] — to a bare minimum. That approach simply doesn't work in our increasingly convenience- and consumption-oriented society. No one wants to go back to a less comfortable, less convenient way of life.

Books on 'home ecology' contradict this at every turn, pointing out the ways in which our notion of convenience is skewed. They concentrate on principles like appropriateness, durability and repairability, on making the home energy-efficient, on using natural materials and on home design which emphasizes our connections with the environment outside.

Of course one can carry this too far, and some of the writing about lifestyle change has become downright silly. One list of tips suggested: 'Write small so you use less paper.'

A worrying tendency is that some people become obsessed with the hazards of modern life and concentrate on creating an insulated and filtered indoor environment, while cheerfully allowing the world outside to become a wasteland. This is reminiscent of the survivalist mentality at the height of the Cold War: 'I can't do anything about the Bomb, but I can build a shelter in my basement.' The triumph of consumerism is, I suspect, closely connected with the nuclear threat, with uncertainty and pessimism about the future — 'Eat and drink for tomorrow we die.'

The third strand in ecological living has to do with choosing 'enough' rather than 'more', and 'better' rather than 'bigger'. This choice is driven not only by the 'push' of the Earth's limitations, and the realization that a high-consumption life is wasteful and polluting, but by the 'pull' of genuine personal satisfactions and a desire for social stability. People are beginning to realize that a low-consumption way of life can give us more time (that commodity so scarce in western society) for the things and people we care about, as well as less stress and disease (the plagues of technological civilization).

I'm a little concerned, however, about the legalistic tone which some writers fall into when discussing a voluntary simplification of the way we live. Duane Elgin, for example, writes:

> Let go of idle gossip and wasteful speech. Wasteful speech can assume many forms: distracted chattering about people and places that have little relevance to what is happening in the moment; name dropping and building social status by association...

This is puritanical, as well as anti-intellectual. Elgin, author of *Voluntary Simplicity*, has defined it as 'a way of life that is outwardly simple, inwardly rich'. The latter is obvious enough, but I think we ought not to understand the first as being monkish or austere in a material sense. For not only is there pleasure in material objects of quality — a well-crafted chess board, for example, or a beautifully glazed plate — and in the design and creation of such objects, but they remind us of the natural world from which they come. We can learn a new kind of materialism, not the modern consumerist view which devalues the things of the Earth — their manufacture 'untouched by human hand' — but a reverence for the beauty and bounty of nature and for fine human handicraft. Alan Durning of the Worldwatch Institute writes about 'a true materialism that does not just care *about* things but cares *for* them'. A creative, ecological way of life will be outwardly as well as inwardly rich — rich in the beauties of texture, colour, and sound, full of the vibrant energy of the natural world.

Thankfully, some east Europeans are concerned about wholesale adoption of the consumer lifestyles of the west, and the discarding of the cultural identity of the east. The Czechoslovak president Vaclav Havel has talked of avoiding 'the omnipresent dictatorship of consumption, production, advertising, commerce, and consumer culture'. People in the east are understandably keen to enjoy some of the benefits of a free market — Levis, personal computers, and pizza — but this economic transition should not be bought at too high a price.

It could mean continued environmental degradation, with long-term costs impossible to calculate, as well as an accelerated cultural degradation. This is not only because western materialist society has little to offer in terms of real human satisfactions but because culture and local traditions are fragile, an endangered living heritage which can be destroyed all too easily by the juggernaut of western commerce. Religious rituals can become tourist spectacles, and traditional handicrafts mere souvenirs. Once these are lost as fundamental parts of a society's shared language, restoration will be difficult, if not impossible. They are the roots which hold a society, the soil in which humans grow, together. The loss of regional identity and local traditions in the west may explain why we feel our culture is crumbling and washing away.

In order to strike a balance between the economic and social changes which are undoubtedly needed in east European countries, and the precious regional differences which should be preserved, it would seem desirable for at least three ideas to be kept in mind:

First, there is a great deal in the time-honoured, traditional ways of life in places often scorned as backward or primitive that is far more ecologically sound than the 'advanced' ways of the industrialized west. The baby of tradition, and the rich, textured cultures and long-established communities of the east, should not be thrown out with the bathwater of communism — nor be laundered in the detergents of capitalism. I remember buying cold drinks in Krakow from a tiny cart where the glasses were rinsed out and reused. I bought kefir in returnable bottles from the corner shop, and tiny bouquets of violets, tied with a bit of straw, and bunches of dandelion greens from a farmer's market. Would life be better in the east if there were paper cups and plastic bottles, if flowers came wrapped in plastic and vegetables were shipped from the other side of the continent?

Second, to shore up the traditional ways that make ecological sense, and avoid the destructive practices of the high-tech world, we should encourage alternative technologies based on efficient and renewable energy sources. At this moment many in eastern Europe would like a taste of 'development', but there is no reason that it should be achieved with the notoriously costly, large-scale, unhealthy methods of capitalist production instead of with the notoriously costly, large- scale, unhealthy and inefficient methods of socialist production. There is a third way, of low-impact, localized technology, perfectly matched to the essentially decentralized and communitarian societies of the east. The moment for its introduction should not be lost.

Finally, it is possible to plan an ecological society — trying to avoid the pitfalls that the unplanned, rapacious systems of the west have blindly stumbled into — and the bureaucracies of the east certainly have enough experience in planning to make a brave attempt at this. Instead of the wholesale introduction of the automobile, for example, there is still time to rationalize systems of production and consumption, workplaces and residences, so that extensive transportation is neither necessary nor desirable. Instead of taking on the capital-intensive ways of western agribusiness, there is still time to examine the record of western societies and see that the most efficient producers are small family farms and the most ecological methods of cultivation involve the efficiency and economy of horses.

The lesson for both east and west is surely that it is necessary, possible, and actually desirable, to reduce wasteful consumption. We can reduce the extraction of nonrenewable raw materials and the degradation of fragile ecosystems, improve our towns and cities, and increase human health and happiness by concentrating on all the desirable things in life which cost nothing. Psychologist Paul Wachtel points out that 'The growth that will improve our lives at this point is a growth in generosity and equity, two non-polluting commodies of which we truly can never have enough.'[2]

Our failures may prove the most valuable lessons the east can learn from the west, and westerners who understand these failures may be the best advisors we can send to the east. Another responsibility for the west to shoulder is the fact that our personal choices influence ordinary people in other parts of the world, not only economically but because we set an example. The marketing of artificial baby milk in the developing world depends in part on the fact that a smaller proportion of western women breastfeed; bottles are therefore 'advanced'. And unless we actively adopt alternative technologies, the people in other parts of the world who are offered them may feel that they are getting secondhand clothes while we wear designer jeans.

One of the things we need to develop in our lives and communities is an appreciation of individual creative expression. This is a fundamental part of human life which has been swallowed up by consumer culture. Crafts have become hobbies. People spend their time 'collecting'. Music and dance have become consumer items — things to pay for — instead of a form of self-expression and shared experience. Baking bread, painting pictures, and dancing on the village green are ways of establishing different values in our lives, and in the long term may be as important in creating a sustainable society as eating low on the food chain or fitting solar panels.

Another thing we need in order to blunt the power of consumerism is community, and the cultural heritage of family and place. Social change hinges on changes in personal relationships. A society centred around the nuclear family maximizes consumption and de-emphasizes community values, leaving us at the mercy of the commercial values of the market and making it difficult to put lifestyle ideas into practice.

What a human being will settle for is little indication of what he or she will thrive on. People are deeply dissatisfied with their role in modern society, and even small changes in the way we live are bound to lead to personal action. With this will come an increased sense of aliveness, of engagement with the place we live and with other people. Learning to compromise appropriately, finding ways to talk about human values that everyone recognizes, and convincing people that change is not only essential but possible — this social activism will be the result of a consciousness of our connections with, and responsibility to, the ecosystems we live in.

Bill McKibben has written that the threats and uncertainties of life in a greenhouse world will make people cling to their present ways of doing things:

> Now, as the familiar world around us starts to change, is the moment when every threatened instinct will push us to scramble to preserve at least our familiar style of life... A voluntary simplicifcation of lifestyles is not beyond our abilities, but it is probably outside our desires.[3]

I disagree. I feel sure that people are waiting to be moved to action, to passion. Passion means love and anger, and we need both — anger at the folly and injustice of industrial society, love for each other and for the natural world. With this passion will come the courage to make bold personal choices, and major changes in the way we live. Here lies our real hope for saving the Earth.

Notes:

1. John Seymour, letter published in *The Ecologist*, vol. 19, no. 3, 1989.
2. Paul Wachtel, *The Poverty of Affluence* (New Society, Philadelphia, 1989).
3. Bill McKibben, *The End of Nature* (Viking, 1989).

Thanks to Alan Durning and Kirkpatrick Sale.

Petra K. Kelly

We Must Feminize Power!

Where would we get to
if everyone said
where would we get to
and no one went
to have a look
where we'd get to
if we went.
                    Kurt Marti

When Die Grünen, the West German Green Party was founded,
I coined the term 'anti-party party'. I wanted to define the new
type of power (non-violent counter-power) we were talking
about and trying to enact: the power of non-violent change and
non-violent transformation of institutions; power that is something common to everyone, to be used by all for all. 'Power over'
was to be replaced by 'shared power', by 'the power to do things',
by the discovery of our own strength as opposed to a passive
receiving of power exercised by others, often in our name. Not
power to dominate, not power to terrorize or to oppress, but the
power of non-violent change.

The Hungarian philosopher and writer György Konrad expressed it well with his notion of 'anti-politics' as a moral force:

> Anti-politics strives to put politics in its place and
> make sure it stays there, never overstepping its proper
> office of defending and refining the morals of the

game in a civil society, and civil society is the antithesis
of military society.

Feminism and the power of non-violence are to me very
essential concepts of Green politics. Male-led revolutions have
been, so often and so tragically, merely power exchanges in a
basically unaltered structure, leaving behind dramatic accounts
of their crisis and heroism. Think of the siege of the Winter
Palace or the taking of the Bastille, for example. Furthermore,
those revolutions were often based on the concept of *dying* for
a cause, while a feminist conceived transformation (non-violent
revolution) is all about daring to *live* for a cause.

When I think about feminist-conceived transformation, I
think about the nuns in the Philippines, for example, who
brought about the non-violent fall of Marcos; or the women of
the Chipko (Save The Trees) movement in India; or the Argentin-
ian Mothers of the Plaza de Mayo with their white scarves; or the
women in the Swords Into Ploughshares movement in the USA.
I think about women like Katya Komisaruk, the imprisoned San
Francisco peace activist; or Maneka Gandhi, who tried as a
minister to block dam projects and set up environmental courts
in India. I think about the brave and courageous women who
have taken part in the non-violent revolutions in east Germany,
Czechoslovakia, Poland, Hungary, the Soviet Union, and initiated the concept of Round Tables there.

Yet although we women represent *half* the world's population
and over one-third of the labour force, we receive only one-tenth
of the world's income and own *less than one per cent* of the world's
land. We are also responsible for two-thirds of all hours worked.
Not only do females make up the majority of the poor, starving
and illiterate, but women and children also form more than 90
per cent of all refugee populations. Women outlive men in most
cultures and therefore are the elderly of the world as well as
being the primary carers for the elderly.

In industrialized countries we women still are paid only half
to three-quarters of what men earn at the same jobs, we are still
stuck in the ghetto of low-paid, female-intensive jobs and we are
still the last hired and first fired. Women in poorer countries are

responsible for more than 50 per cent of all food production, 50 per cent of all animal husbandry and 100 per cent of all food processing and child care.

Toxic pesticides, herbicides, chemical pollution, leakage from nuclear wastes and acid rain usually take their first toll through a rise in cancers of the female reproductive system, and in miscarriages, stillbirths and congenital deformities. It is mostly women's work which has to compensate for the destruction of the ecological balance. For example, deforestation results in a lowering of the water table which in turn causes parched grasslands and erosion of topsoil; women, as the world's principal water-haulers and fuel-gatherers, must walk further to find water, fodder for animals and cooking fuel.

The overlooked factor in the power of women as a world political force is the *magnitude of suffering combined with the magnitude of women*; women constitute not an oppressed minority but a majority of almost all national populations and of the entire human species.

As the human species approaches the capacity to eradicate all life on this planet, women can and *must feminize power to reverse all these trends*. The goal is not only to change drastically the powerless status of women, but to redefine and transform nonviolently all existing patriarchal social structures and modes of existence. The revolutions in eastern Europe have shown the west that it is possible to non-violently transform repressive and barbaric Communist systems and secret services and use the power of the people against the ultimately useless power of guns, tanks, and oppression. Although there have been dramatic political changes and some hopeful signs of transformed polities, power has not yet been feminized and the women who were at the forefront of the revolutions are or have been edged out of leadership positions. Only in Czechoslovakia, the foreign service seems transformed by strong women ambassadors.

Robin Morgan has stated: Sisterhood is global — the most pernicious of all patriarchal tactics has been to keep women a divided world caste. I believe that indigenous feminism has been present in every culture in the world and probably in every period of history since the suppression of women began. For example, it is not generally known that Mahatma Gandhi's non-violent resistance strategies were acknowledged by Gandhi himself to be copied from a nineteenth-century Indian women's movement. Nor is it widely known that it was a courageous women's action in Poland which inspired the Solidarnosc movement.

Feminism, non-violence and ecology have always been profoundly revolutionary ideas working against the artificial divisions in the world. The Israeli and Palestinian women who dared to open and continue a dialogue for genuine peace knew their lives as women mattered more than the politics in the region would admit.

Women, bearing scars from the way men have used power, often want no part of established power themselves. Yet the male concept and use of power has left a world of acid rain, global warming, torrents of toxic and chemical waste, heaps of useless weapons and disappearing species, topsoil, forests and fresh water sources. In this world, women must intervene and come to understand the systems of patriarchy which underpin both capitalism and state socialism. It matters less which came first, more that we understand how our societies are affected now. Male domination under any ideology is oppressive for women and restrictive for men.

I believe norms of human behaviour can and do change over the centuries and that attitudes based on sexism or racism can be changed. But first we must be able to envisage a world, a society in which balance comes from the existence of a dynamic inter-relationship between men and women, body and mind, spirit and matter; a reconnection between the Earth and all living things. For me, ecological feminism is one hopeful perspective, political and spiritual, that integrates these concerns.

What is needed in political theory and practice is a change of both form and content, a vision that is holistic and coherent rather than separated and compartmentalized. The current fragmented way of solving problems, as demonstrated so floridly by Chancellor Kohl in Germany and President Bush in the Middle East, must be replaced by new, non-violent problem-solving strategies which consider the complex dynamics of interconnected living systems.

But we must also change our daily consciousness about our own lifestyles and our own attitudes. We must be acutely aware of our own habits and behaviour and the ways in which our personal actions can contribute to the perpetuation of the present system of wasteful consumption in the industrialized countries. We will have no way of bringing any Green or feminist vision into reality, if we do not begin with transforming our personal lives and attitudes.

Above all, we women must explain to men in power that we are not weak, nor are we meek, but we are in fact very angry people — angry on our own behalf because of the continual wars, large and small, waged against us every day and angry on behalf of the entire planet Earth. Our anger makes us strong.

In striving for an ecological society, women do not want it to be one where the men build windmills and women silently listen, bake bread and weave rugs. There must be a sharing, a coming together of men and women — the rigid divisions of roles and the competitive struggle imposed by a social structure which pits human against human crushes us all and has led to the present frustration felt by both men and women.

The sort of society women seek is reflected in the principles of the Green movement in both west and east Europe. Peace has a wider meaning than simply the absence of certain weapons or armies, but is the positive internal and external conditions in which people are free to grow and develop their own potential. Most of our world today is suffering from all types of violence — including structural violence. And there is usually indifference and silence, even if mass murder continually takes places, as in Tibet for example. Tibet has been occupied by the Chinese for over forty years and one could say a holocaust has been happening on the roof of the world. Daily, Tibetans are tortured and killed, Tibetan women are sterilized, forced to have abortions. All this suffering is going on while western governments, even after the massacre of Tiananmen square, do business as usual with China. Even former German Chancellor Helmut Schmidt visited Peking and praised Deng Tsiao-ping as one of the most important and exemplary statesmen of this century. There

338 Green Light on Europe

seems to be no moral basis in politics. Human rights are indivisible and must be at the core of all politics — at home and abroad.

The question of non-violence has posed a big challenge to established Green parties in east and west Europe. How, on the road to power, by (say) taking part in a coalition government, does one deal with the violence inherent in the state? How can the structural violence often inherent in current government policies be dealt with? What can a Green minister of the interior, for example, do to transform his or her area of responsibility? Is it not violent when, as part of the richest industrialized countries, we waste at least 50 per cent of the energy we generate, overproduce and overconsume and then dump our often highly poisonous waste in poor countries? The cash payments made to tempt poor countries to accept our waste are often large enough to tempt them to mortgage the health and safety of their people as well as their environmental integrity. This is surely nothing but garbage imperialism. We in the Green parties have not yet found a satisfactory answer as to how to transform or reduce the structural violence inherent in the state once the Greens participate in power-sharing at the top.

The grossly unequal distribution of wealth and power in the world is intrinsically violent and one of the most serious threats to our future security. Deepening poverty for two- thirds of humanity and environmental degradation are not separate problems.

The 1980s have ended in political upheaval. As the Swedish disarmament minister May Britt Theorin said: 'Reality has outdone fiction.' As Bob Dylan prophesied, in one of the anthems of the 1960s, 'the times they are a-changing.' If, at the beginning of the 1980s, anyone had predicted changes like those we are now witnessing, she or he would have been scorned as a dreamer or someone out of touch with reality.

However, not all the changes are going in the right direction. The Soviet Union has begun a course of conversion for its armament industry and plans to shift 60 per cent of its military factories into civilian, socially useful production. But will this trend survive the recent violent clampdowns in the republics?

And the trend toward more and more nationalism and internal disintegration? Despite the Soviet military and political disengagement from east Europe and the collapse of the Warsaw Pact, NATO states did not responded in anything like the same way, and due to the war in the Gulf seem less likely to now than ever. Do governments and parliaments have enough influence in either the Soviet Union or the USA to withstand the pressures of their military-industrial complex, part of a $1,000 billion global industry representing one-tenth of all world economic activity? I am not so sure.

I was born in a small Bavarian town called Günzburg and raised in a German Catholic convent school. I have also lived in the United States, Holland and Belgium for many years so have also viewed Germany from the outside. Like my friends in the German Green party, I was not in favour of the way and speed with which east and west Germany were unified. Our model was one of a confederation, two German states growing together, cooperating with each other as closely as possible but also competing for more ecological ways of doing things, more democracy, more women's rights, more social justice.

The east German revolution was the first revolution ever to take place on German soil. It was led by very strong women, including Bärbel Bohley, one of my best friends, Ulrike Poppe, Katja Havemann, as well as by many brave and courageous men. It was these friends from the independent, ecological, women's and peace movements in east Germany who suffered oppression for many years and who were also imprisoned. During those difficult years, they received very little by way of solidarity from the left in west Europe. Travelling back and forth for many years, together with Gert Bastian, I visited my friends in their subversive kitchens, in their small living rooms and even saw them being taken away to be questioned by the state security police. I will never forget those long discussions in those kitchens when the non-violent revolutions were being planned nor will I forget when, finally, in the autumn and winter of 1989, those revolutions finally took place in East Berlin, in Leipzig, in Dresden, in Prague and in many other towns and cities.

But the inspiration and the spirit of the east German revolution were so quickly snuffed out and reversed by Chancellor Kohl's reunification plan, by the west German banks, by the west German businesses, by the west German and west European companies who were falling over themselves to make east Germany and eastern Europe a new Sicily for the west. The east German revolution was cancelled out by established west German politicians peddling their blueprints for our so-called perfect western capitalist society. The draft constitution, a radical new document prepared by the east German Round Table, was hardly discussed, and the west continually told the east how to live their newly liberated lives. All the ecological ideas for the soft rebuilding of east German society were ignored, and the old, misguided forms of politics and economics were perpetuated.

Suddenly nothing was of any value in eastern Europe — suddenly nothing was of value in east Germany, not even the widespread provision of creches for children, or the more liberal abortion law, or the new law for conscientious objectors. Suddenly the west, western economics and western politicians triumphed and acted as if they themselves had liberated eastern Europe and *personally* removed the Wall and the Iron Curtain! As Pastor Heinrich Albertz pointed out: '... a west German military invasion of [east Germany] would be more honest than what is going on now.'

In east Germany, the revolution which had been led by so many courageous women was quickly over, or at the very least, seriously interrupted, by an election which was won by all the arguments that told the east Germans they were bankrupt, literally and metaphorically. The election in east Germany was decided by the Deutschmark not by conscience.

Now the (male) media has forgotten those brave revolutionaries who stood firm in those days of October 1989 when there was nearly a second 'Chinese solution' carried out by Mr Honecker and his SED gang. So too have the western governments and western parliaments forgotten those women and men of the first hour in the rush to get on with business as usual. Very little has been learned about non-violent transformation, or change coming through grassroots direct action.

But the citizens' action movement in eastern Europe has not forgotten the ideals and the dreams which gave them so much strength in such difficult times. In the words of Martin Luther King Jr:

> Non-violent resistance... is based on the conviction that the universe is on the side of justice. Consequently, the believer in non-violence has a deep faith in the future. This faith is another reason why the non-violent resister can accept suffering without retaliation. For he knows that in his struggle for justice he has cosmic companionship.

Non-violent resistance has a long history, and, if women and Greens have anything to do with it, a great future. We must learn to give non-violent action and thinking a chance — and we must train it and pass it on, if we are to succeed. In one of the bitter ironies of history, Albert Einstein wrote a letter on behalf of atomic scientists struggling to prevent the arms race which resulted from their scientific endeavours. He warned that the splitting of the atom had changed everything save our way of thinking. In one of his last statements as president, Eisenhower said: 'There will come a time when the people will demand peace so loudly, that politicians had better get out of the way and let them have it.'

I hope that, despite recent setbacks, this time has truly come. The concept of women in power but using it differently from the way men have up to now is not new. There are quite a few historical examples; we need to highlight these and begin to believe that we women in the Green movement can make a very big difference — in both style and content of our Green politics. What is hopeful about today is the way women, not only in the ecological/feminist movement, but also ordinary women going about their everyday lives, are questioning the way things are. Whether they live in Europe, Africa, Asia or America, women know, all too often from first-hand experience, that environmental degradation and social deprivation go hand in hand and that they and their children are the first to suffer. Women in eastern Europe are now facing a devastating social crisis and are the first victims of the new poverty and unemployment.

In a joint letter written by east and west European feminists in the 1980s, we declared:

> ... [women] want fredom from exploitation and vio-
> lence: in our thoughts and actions, at our places of
> work, in our relationship with nature and the relation-
> ship between men and women, between generations,
> between states, between East and West and between
> North and South in global terms.
>
> Together we want to break this circle of violence
> and the anxieties created in us by this violence;
> anxiety about nuclear weapons, fearing the death of
> humanity and the end of the Earth, fearing the rape
> of our bodies and souls.
>
> (excerpt from *Open Letter From European Women*)

The Green non-violent revolution must go on! Women are at its heart and must take on leadership positions, even though men in Green movements and parties still cannot accustom themselves to that idea, as it means that they must give up their privileges. Women inside Green movements and parties might even succeed in altering the often loveless and alienating style of party politics, and in holding on to the spiritual and moral values of non-violence and feminism as the core of ecological politics. Maybe we have a real chance after all?

Jakob von Uexkull

Reflections on Parliament and Government

I would not presume to attempt to review here the rich and varied experiences and challenges of Green parliamentarians. My own experiences as a Green MEP for a few years are of somewhat limited applicability. The European Parliament is not a typical parliament, nor was I a 'typical' Green Parliamentarian — if there is such a thing. But, writing shortly after the election in which the West German Greens lost all their seats, I feel a look at Green attitudes to power may be useful.

The debacle of Die Grünen is a catastrophe which should not be underestimated. The symbolism of their failure has an impact far beyond the immediate practical effects, for the major achievements of Green parties have not been parliamentary victories (hardly possible for a radical opposition with less than 10 per cent of the vote), but the credibility which they have given to Green issues. What I have called parliamentary fetishism works: suddenly all sorts of 'alternatives' (some of them only Green in the broadest sense), become newsworthy and respectable because there is a Green party in parliament. I have experienced this in my own work with the Right Livelihood Award. In the UK, despite major efforts over the years, the media show little interest. In Germany, where we have no office, the award is front-page news. Incidentally, the interest in 1990 was greater than ever, so those Germans who blame public disinterest in

Green issues for their debacle are not being honest.

Now this ripple effect is working in reverse. 'Greenish' politicians in other parties complain about the difficulties of gaining support for ecological reforms because, to their uncommitted colleagues, the German result shows that 'there are no votes in it'. The ripples go further, for while there is much green talk and few green measures, there is even less green implementation. In the USA, for example, though Reagan found it very difficult to dismantle and repeal the Carter era environmental legislation, it was much easier to signal to the bureaucracy and judiciary that prosecutions should be as few and fines as low as possible.

It is time to admit the enormity of the Green failure. Over the past decade the global environment has continued to deteriorate. Most indicators of well-being for our soil, water, air and forests are still pointing sharply downwards. Numerous catastrophes have revealed the hollowness of the safety claims of experts and governments. The effects touch us all. 'The future generation now present in the sperm and ovum of living people is being damaged as the interior of the human body gradually assumes the polluted state of the outer environment' (Rosalie Bertell). Traditional knowledge in many areas is fast disappearing. The glorification of 'free trade' is making it impossible for communities — and even nations — to regulate the use of their natural resources or control harmful imports and investments.

Not radical activists but highly placed international civil servants like the director-general of UNEP now warn that the life-support systems of the planet are actually collapsing. The Worldwatch Institute concludes that we have not decades, but only years left to turn around! In one poll after another, in one country after another the environment comes at the top of the list of popular concerns.

Yet at the end of this momentous decade, the various Green parties hover somewhere between 2 and 10 per cent in the polls. The leaders of Die Grünen — in one of the most environmentally aware countries — express the pious hope that in 1994 they will climb back over the 5 per cent threshold and re-enter parliament! This complacency is not new. After five years in the European Parliament, the German Green vote in the 1989 Euro-elections remained static. Yet instead of analysing the reasons for this failure, the result was hailed as a success. The measuring-stick of Green success has become not the majority required to begin implementing our policies or the 15 to 20 per cent needed to become a major political player, but the threshold of parliamentary representation. In a collapsing environment, 8 per cent for the party which claims to be its representative is treated as a reason to celebrate! This failure of Green politics is even more remarkable, considering that the ground was already prepared.

The established parties have been paying lip service to green issues since long before the Green parties existed. The EC has had Environmental Action Programmes and even NATO has had an Environment Department for 20 years. Since Stockholm 1972 the environment has been on the public agenda. Pressure groups like Greenpeace have made sure its profile stayed high, yet the gap between words and deeds has remained enormous. It has been calculated that at the present rate, it would take 117 years to achieve agreed EC limits for the 129 dangerous substances on the 1976 (!) EC blacklist. Such examples could be continued almost indefinitely, and not just in Western Europe. So why have the Green parties been unable to fill the void?

The decision to create political parties, instead of remaining as broad-based citizen pressure groups, was very controversial among ecological activists. Many of us believed that it was crucial to enter the political arena, that only if you actually threaten their votes will you force other parties to act. If they did not, then the Greens would eventually gain power. So we thought. But the voters have not lived up to our expectations. The gap between their level of environmental concern and their readiness for personal sacrifices no doubt remains considerable. However, our failure to live up to their expectations is much greater. Instead of being at the forefront of the struggle to create and empower environmental awareness, Green parties have become the beneficiaries of this awareness — and sometimes its parasites, using Green votes to pursue their own agenda.

In Germany a regional election was held in the state of Lower Saxony a few weeks after Chernobyl. This was preceded by a national congress of Die Grünen in Hanover. Did the party focus its congress and campaign on ridding Germany of nuclear power, now that all the assurances of the pro-nuclear forces had lost their credibility and public worry was at its peak? Wrong! The main theme of the congress and campaign was the demand that West Germany leave NATO! Party strategists assumed that the Chernobyl-shocked voters would automatically vote Green and wanted to claim the expected increased vote as a sign of support for their anti-NATO campaign. The plan misfired: a conservative campaign to portray the Greens as a far-left fringe group succeeded in keeping their vote almost unchanged. The ripples were noticeable even in Washington where I was at the time: if they can't even win after Chernobyl, then how many votes are there really in Green issues, my American friends asked.

It has been said that a Green mistake was not to take parliament seriously, to remain in effect an extra-parliamentary pressure group inside parliaments. In my experience, the opposite is closer to the truth. From the day they entered, most Green MPs have done their best to prove themselves good and diligent parliamentarians. In the German Parliament, their per capita productivity (measured in questions asked, etc.) was so huge as to generate complaints from the overworked bureaucracy. In the European Parliament, even the postage bill of the Green-Alternative group (GRAEL) surpassed that of the much larger socialist group. As the GRAEL contained MEPs from five or (periodically) six countries, several of whom had national parliamentary experience, some of our experiences may have a wider relevance.

At no time did the GRAEL (or the national parties represented in it) debate or decide how far to integrate itself into the parliamentary structures. The majority of MEPs were of the opinion that no parliamentary post should be declined, no delegation trip refused, no issue ignored. The assumption seemed to be that this was what the voters expected. Thus the energy of the group dissipated and the workload soon became unmanageable. This was especially true for the German Green MEPs who were given neither an assistant nor a secretarial allowance. The funds provided by the European Parliament reverted to the party and were donated to the so-called Ökofonds, often to fund leftist fringe and solidarity groups. In my home town of Hamburg the local Green party newsletter reported that in 1987 only 0.3 per cent of this money went to ecological projects. This is perhaps an extreme case but it illustrates one problem: large sections of the most powerful Green party do not accept the overriding principle of the ecological survival issue. My local German Green magazine speaks of 'breaking the capitalist chains', of the 'courage to rebel permanently' and the 'need for oppositional, anti-state, progressive politics' — the agenda of the utopian left.

Warnings that we are not in parliament because of an increased social-revolutionary potential in the population, and that relegating Green issues to the back burner means that there will soon be no society left to debate in, fall on deaf ears. While other parties aim to appeal to the largest possible spectrum of voters, Green parties often seem to aim to alienate an ever larger spectrum!

For example, polls before the first election in which Greens were standing showed that even many conservatives hoped that the Greens would enter parliament. This soon changed. But today, almost ten years later, with the party in crisis, the local activists have learned nothing. Calls for rejuvenating the party list the many groups the party should work with. Ecologists seem to end up — almost as an afterthought — at the bottom of the list, far behind the squatters, the communes and the immigrants (who cannot vote).

The early impact of Die Grünen has caused many other Green parties to fall into the same trap. This is not a question of left or right: it is a tremendous achievement that Green parties have been able to combine a caring for nature with a strong stand on citizens' rights, justice and self-determination. Most pro-environment groups in history have been illiberal and frequently reactionary. Their writings abound with comparisons between the strong and healthy native tree, plant, bird, etc., and the foreign interloper reproducing all over the place and interfering with the natural order. Yet our success in combating such dogmas seems to have been bought at the price of our parties becoming captive to every 'radical' pressure group around.

The problem is not 'leftism'. Preserving and adapting the ideals of socialism (and liberalism and conservatism) within the new Green paradigm is vital. The problem is 'anti- statism'. To most Greens the state and the government itself—not its present occupants — are the enemy.

Green parties are thus caught in a vicious circle, subjecting themselves to all the vagaries of parliamentary politics while refusing to play the game for real. If Green parliamentary politics is to have an impact commensurate with the enormous effort and sacrifice which has gone into it (depriving many pressure groups of their most effective activists) then a choice needs to be made. The Greens can become a 'proper' political party with effective structures and a clear identity. In this case the 'fringes' may leave and set up their own parties. But a left-liberal Green civil-rights party may well emerge as a potential coalition partner in several countries, giving it an influence in excess of its size. As the environment continues to dominate public aware-nesss, major parties on the left and right will compete for the attentions of such a party and be ready to concede various eco-taxes, 'green bans', etc. in return for its support. As Greens believe both in empowering the individual, freeing the local and informal economy from the constraints of the centre and in social justice, both in letting market forces work better (e.g. to kill off nuclear power) and in longer-term planning, both right and left will be able to find arguments to compete for Green support without unduly alienating their own voters. Once intro-duced, many reforms such as eco-taxes, environmental impact studies, 'green' GNP accounting, etc. will be almost impossible to reverse and will lead inexorably onwards as their limits become clearer.

Those Greens who arrogantly look down on the 'pale greens' in other parties ('If they were serious, they would join us!') should ask themselves whether their own party really provides a platform for serious political work.

Green parliamentarians and political activists have had some remarkable successes — often seeing their best ideas snapped up by other parties. But as long as Greens enter parliament as a loose alliance of individual activists with different agendas, their achievements will fall woefully short of their potential and of the needs of the planet.

To overcome this weakness, we need to follow the example of the anti-colonial liberation movements. The participants knew that their individual ideas on the future of their country varied widely. But they all agreed that without independence none of their ideas could bear fruit. Today we face another even more overriding challenge. If the life-support system of the planet does break down, then none of our visions can be implemented. The only division of importance in Green politics is between those who are prepared to adjust their actions and thinking to this state of emergency and those who are not. The latter are not Green (if the word is to have any meaning) and to pretend that they are can only cause confusion. Once this line is drawn, the Greens can and need to remain broad-based. It will be instantly understandable if Green parties declare themselves, like the anti-colonial liberation movements, to be a one-issue coalition to counter the unique threat to the planet. On other matters Green MPs will vote according to their conscience — or abstain. On all issues regarding the environment, they will endorse the most effective solutions put forward, always favouring those which incorporate measures to make sure that the burden does not fall on those already disadvantaged, while recognising that most of the working class in the rich countries also belongs to the privileged global elite whose lifestyles are not sustainable. This will give the party an instantly recognisable identity as the one whose constituency is not a special interest group but the future of all of us.

Our demands, being the planet's demands, are not for compromise, but we will support any realistic step along the way, recognising that there needs to be room for alternative paths, trial and error, once the direction is right. A Green party in the USA will no doubt put greater emphasis on using market mechanisms than will the French or Swedish Greens. A consensus may yet emerge. In California last November over a third of the voters endorsed the 'Big Green' initiative, which demanded a remarkable degree of regulation. On the other hand, Die

Grünen have been forced by the influx of former East Germans to reconsider much of their socialist rhetoric.

A political party is a limited vehicle playing a limited role, which will break down if overloaded. The 'liberation movement' role can be played successfully on the parliamentary arena — it has been done. But a party with any chance of success cannot also be a giant encounter group, experimenting with new types of structure and leadership and acting as if the Green paradise is already here. If you wish to remain a perpetually protesting outsider, then a political party is a waste of your time.

Greens need to overcome their mistrust of success and learn to celebrate good leadership in their midst, rather than fearing and denying it! One activist describes how he was 'on the verge of getting the ear of the mainstream when the attacks from within began'. Sounds familiar? Perhaps — to quote one American Green — 'the types of interpersonal changes we want take at least three generations to become established.' But I for one do not believe that the internal anger and abuse which has done so much damage to Green politics can be explained because 'most of the participants grew up in authoritarian and anger-producing environments' (Jerry Mintz in *New Options*, 31 December 1990). This is a nice new-age non-judgemental explanation. Everybody is assumed to be honestly working for what they believe is best.

Such naivety may yet be our downfall. Are we really not aware how much fear the prospect of Green power must cause the beneficiaries of the status quo? Have we forgotten what they are capable of? In West Germany, the small groups on the far left were infiltrated by the various secret services to such an extent that in one case, two agents from different services, knowing nothing of each other, reached the top in their respective groups and signed a cooperation agreement with each other. From the beginning, the Greens have been flooded with members of these groups. Yet no one has even suggested that, like in East Germany, the files of the western secret services should also be checked by an independent commission.

It would be very surprising if other Green parties have not been subjected to similar attentions. Such infiltrations will not be limited to one wing of the party. In the case of Die Grünen one of the most suspicious episodes was the bogus 'financial scandal' used by the 'Realos' to overthrow the fundamentalist party leadership in 1988. Who gave the false information to the media? Obviously a party unwilling to fire or expel anyone (except self-proclaimed fascists) provides optimum working conditions for every agent-provocateur around.

The greatest danger to Green politics is the complacent belief that it does not really matter if we make mistakes because the deteriorating environment will do the job for us, ensuring that people turn to the Greens one day. There is indeed the possibility that the old parties will fail to muster the political nerve to do what needs to be done and consequently will lose all credibility. As the philosopher Ernst Bloch wrote, the great moment may encounter too small a people. However, if that moment comes, I fear the democratic Green movement will also have lost its chance. When the ecological breakdown 'hits home', parliamentary democracy will be the first victim, as the eco-fascist ('forget the poor') or eco- stalinist strongmen take over. When the next day breaks the polluters may well be in jail. But, judging by historical precedents, we are more likely to join them there than to be asked to enter the government.

Vello Pohla

The East European Greens and the European Model

One and a half years ago, the Estonian Green Movement became a member of the European Greens — the first national Green party from the Soviet Union to do so. We soon learnt that it would be very difficult for the Estonian Republic and also for other liberated east European countries and republics in what we call the Free East to be admitted to the European Community.

Even among Greens there were different visions about the new European model; visions and models depended on the situation in which people are living. But it seemed that the difference between our time-space and the rest of Europe was up to a hundred years. There had been the colonial empire, totalitarianism, concentration camps for nations. The Soviet people were a product of socio-political-genetic engineering, a dead economy and a destroyed environment. And then began the breakdown of the empire, our material misery and political and psychological troubles.

To come into the European Common Home we have to ask for hard currency and technology, we must accept European established ideology, its value system and all the associated information. We must sell our natural resources and labour. But we have to be successful. In short, for us it may mean slavery again. We may find ourselves in a new empire, in an integrated, unified, centralized Europe; a glorified model of a Europe that is quite familiar. We have experienced it for 50 years, although in a different context.

Maybe we are too sensitive, emotional; maybe we are more awake, maybe we were forced to eat too much fruit from the tree of good and evil. We are not yet so tied down in our everyday life to the European way of life, to the American way of life, to the world's definition of prosperity, that we cannot ask whether it is worth paying the high price for it that humanity is paying now.

We have to get closer to the Earth

In our loneliness and doubts we got support and understanding from one mysterious nation in Europe and in the world — the Green nation — which in some sense is living hidden like the natives of the Earth described in the book *Urantia*. During the last year and a half, we learned to look behind the political environmentalism of the Greens in west Europe and their endeavour to describe an alternative world order, and they learned to look behind our national radical aspirations to all human liberty. Greens from northern countries especially acted as a connecting bridge to spread understanding of our *ethno-ecological* political position. In Budapest and Venice, Greens made radical statements about national self-determination and the diplomatic recognition of the Baltic states.

After all, we were not living in a different time-space — the world is indeed one and life is one, everything repeats itself on a new level. Freedom is one, violence is one — be the chains made of iron or of gold.

What kind of model for Europe would the Free East Greens like to have, what kind of Common Home? First of all — what kind of model will it be? We think that the structure of a European model consists of at least three dimensions:

   1. **Functional:** to pursue economic growth and military strength, to follow the technological necessities of the international financial order, or to produce for people's real needs.
   2. **Understanding, or type of thinking:** is it based on

rationalism and formal logic — based only on the right hemisphere of our brain, or is it holistic, systemic, synthesized — based on both hemispheres, uniting thinking processes with existential life?

3. **Values:** are these values real or alienated? Are the questions about the meaning of life, about life as a biocentric value in itself?

The last two dimensions touch on the mind and the spiritual side of life. Looking from the side of the 'emotional' Free East, it appears that the so-called new happy Europe — the Europe of the EC, Gorbachev's Common Home, Mitterrand's Federation of Europe, or the United States of Europe — all are founded mostly on the first dimension only, on functional effectiveness, on the rational and technological. Deep values and spiritual meaning are left aside, 'progress' is unbalanced; it may lead to a new totalitarianism. Man will be used as a means again. What it already means for nature and the environment we know quite well. We in Free Europe don't like these models of Europe. A *Third Way* is our dream.

The dimensions which favour spiritual and real values are the alternatives for the new model for society, for Europe. They will carry the new ideology and politics for all of us. We — the Green nation — are not merely environmentalists, not merely seekers for sustainable 'development'; we know we have to be awakened to survive. This is the hope and mission for global Greens.

What model of Europe would we like to see then? In human society there are three types of production:

1. Production of energy and material things and information. Kilowatts, tons and bytes. On the whole, we can make these everywhere.

2. 'Reproduction' of spiritual activity, soul, culture and customs.

3. 'Reproduction' of nature and environment.

These last two are not possible just anywhere; they link us to the Earth, to life and soil in concrete places. For us it is not a question of theory. In its deepest meaning, culture and environment are inseparable from ethnic nation and settlement (habitat). That's why Europocentric modern culture, technology and 'one-dimensional man' without ethnic structures are more and more alienated from life. This sort of person cannot protect nature.

> *We have to get closer to the Earth*
> *to touch the soil*

Therefore as we seek to abolish the Soviet empire and transform it into a civil society, we use the holistic word (or rather the notion) *ethno-ecology* to give the word nation its true cultural and environmental, and therefore properly ecological, meaning.

The nearest model of Europe based on ethno-ecology is the concept of a Europe of regions which we use to counter the one-sided, one-pole, concentric integration of Europe. We would go further, make our model even more holistic and talk of a Europe of bioregions. One example is the concept of a Baltic bioregion prepared by the Green parties of Sweden, Finland and Estonia and presented to the Helsinki parliamentary conference on cooperation in the Baltic Sea area in January 1991. According to this concept, regional interests and environmental demands, national cultures and historical traditions will serve as a synthesis for common policy. It foresees the founding of a Baltic Sea Council, consisting of parliamentarians of the region. Bioregional cooperation, like that around the Baltic Sea, presents a political challenge to the building of a highly centralized European Community.

Why do we have so many national conflicts today? We think that one of the reasons is that people are living their national lives in a way which clashes with the nature of their surroundings. Economic and technical unification, monetary systems, and the interests of those in power lead to the violence of alienated values. Think about the Gulf War! And this nightmare started as a liberation of Kuwait! When people are permanently in a state of war with nature, they cannot have a natural, human life.

Let's take the problem of economic refugees, an urgent one for west European countries. Political hypocrisy deals with it as a question of human rights. Is it a human right that I should be allowed to leave Estonia to go to a richer country which accepts me as a refugee? Or does human rights mean I can live happily in my homeland, *in my own home*, where my roots are in the nature and the culture which give me my human identity? The refugee and the immigrant is a very unhappy person.

As a matter of fact, to be *forced* to wander, to emigrate is caused by an unbalanced economic and social life, by the religious dictatorship of goods, by militarism and unbalanced use of energy and resources. The Free East wants the model of Europe to be one where we don't need to leave our home for the European Common Home. We've already tried one Common European Home here, in the Soviet empire! We want our rights in our own home. Small is indeed beautiful and it is there we can find our identity. Only then can we understand other people, other cultures, minorities and refugees. People should not be living in order to produce and consume, either information or TV sets. These are only tools for living. We live in order to listen to the gentle gust of wind rustling the leaves in our own backyard.

Does this make us nationalists, extremists, separatists? Estonian Greens are working on their own project for an Estonian Green Freedom State, as a third way for human society. Are we against the future of Europe, or against just one kind of Europe? We believe in the Free East, where people can reach existential reality by means of grassroots settlement, national culture and an ethical link with nature, where there is value in diversity as well as historical and genetic identification. And of course, by self-determination and national independence. If the model of Europe does not contain all this, Europe will be one-dimensional, with no hope for survival.

The model we like will be holistic, deep ecological, non-violent, spiritual, with inner growth instead of economic growth as a goal.

We have to get closer to the Earth, to touch the soil,
to be one with life.

We think it will be a Green model for a new Europe.

BIOGRAPHIES

Sergio Andreis was born in 1952, completed high school in California, graduated from Milan University and took postgraduate courses in the history of philosophy at the Freie Universität in Berlin. He worked with international NGOs for several years, focusing on multilateral intercultural cooperation, spent 15 months in military jails after refusing to perform military or civilian service, and was active with the Italian peace movement. He was elected with the Greens in 1985 to the regional parliament of Lombardy and then in 1987 to the national parliament. He is a member of the Foreign Affairs Committee.

Zsuzsa Beres was born in Budapest in 1952. She went to school in Washington, DC, Hungary and England, then read English and history at Budapest University from 1970-75. She has worked as a translator and editor, and has also worked for radio and with western correspondents based in Budapest during the recent two years of political change. Not previously active in politics, she joined the Danube Circle at the time of the International River Dams Conference in September 1988, was a founding member of the Green Party of Hungary in November 1989, joined the Feminist Network in June 1990 and set up the group Green Women. Currently out of mainstream politics, she is now a journalist with Reuters' Budapest office.

Paul Blau was born in 1915 in Vienna, studied agriculture and philology, and was active in the resistance movement against Hitler, and on the executive committees of the Austrian Socialist Party and Trade Union Federation. He was a representative of the International Federation of Free Trade Unions at the International Atomic Energy Agency, editor-in-chief of the *Arbeiter-Zeitung* (the central paper of the Socialist Party of Austria), director of the Institute for Societal Affairs, member of the Austrian Pugwash group, founding member of Ecoropa, president of the Viennese Foundation for the Conservation of Nature. His publications include a book on the risks of ionizing radiations (1961) and numerous articles and lectures on the labour movement, work science, world politics, peace and disarmament, economics and energy, and ecology.

Ilona C. Cheyne, LL.B. (Edinburgh), LL.M. (London), barrister, lecturer in law at the University of Newcastle-upon-Tyne. She has been visiting fellow at the International Law Institute, University of Cambridge, and at the University of Michigan Law School. She also writes on international trade.

Karen Christensen, author of *Home Ecology* (London: Arlington, 1989), is an American writer who has lived in Britain since 1981. Her *A Smaller Circle: Community, Nature and the Arts* will be published by Rider Century in spring 1992, and she is working on *Words to Change the World*, a writing and media guide for social activists.

Guy Dauncey is an author and consultant in the fields of personal, social, economic and ecological change. He is a director of the Institute for Social Inventions (London), secretary of Voters for a Responsible Community (Victoria, B.C.), and a director of the Sustainable Futures Group (Vancouver, B.C.). He is author of *The New Unemployment Handbook* (NEC, Cambridge, 1987), *After the Crash: The Emergence of the Rainbow Economy* (Greenprint, London, 1988), and other titles. He lives at 2069 Kings Road, Victoria V8R 2P6, B.C., Canada.

Ecoglasnost was founded in April 1989 and became internationally famous in October of the same year when it staged demonstrations in Sofia during the Conference for Security and Cooperation in Europe governmental meeting on the environment. By skilfully combining the issues of environmental pollution and human rights, Ecoglasnost gained much popularity as an agent in the downfall of Bulgarian president Todor Zhivkov. In subsequent elections, Ecoglasnost won seats in the national parliament, but ambivalence over remaining an extra-parliamentary pressure group or taking part in the democratic process had already prompted leading members of Ecoglasnost to form a Green Party which is now represented in the Bulgarian parliament.

Per Gahrton was a founder of the Swedish Green Party in 1981, and is currently one of the 20 Green MPs. Active in international Green politics, he served as a co-secretary of the European Greens for several years. A prolific author, specializing in defence and Arab affairs, some of his works are: *The Struggle for Palestine* (1970), *The Swedish Parliament from Within* (1983), *Gold or Green Forests* (1983), *Our Doubtful Defence* (1985).

Johan Galtung, born 1930, a leading Norwegian social scientist and peace activist, founded the International Peace Research Institute in Oslo in 1959. Since 1951 he has written extensively on a variety of issues and themes, and from the 1980s has focused particularly on alternative defence (non-offensive defence), social cosmologies, cultural violence, environmental issues and economic theory.

Edward René David Goldsmith is the founder and co-editor since 1969 of *The Ecologist*. He is vice-president of Ecoropa. He stood for parliament in 1974 as a candidate for the People's Party, and for the European Parliament in 1979 for the Ecology Party. He is the author of *The Stable Society* (1977) and *The Great U-Turn* (1988); co-author of *A Blueprint for Survival* (1972), *Social and Environmental Effects of Large Dams* (1985) and *5000 Days to Save the Planet* (1990); editor of *Can Britain Survive?* (1971); and co-editor of *La Médecine à la Question* (1981), *Social and Environmental Effects of Large Dams Vol. 2* (1986), *Great Britain or Industrial Wasteland* (1986), and *The Earth Reports I* (1988) and *II* (1990).

Jacques Grinevald is a philosopher, historian of scientific and technological development, and member of the Faculty of Social and Economic Sciences of the University of Geneva. He is also a member of the Institut Universitaire d'Etudes du Développement and a collaborator in the Swiss Federal Institute of Technology's Man, Technology and Environment Programme. He is currently preparing a book about the concept of the planet Earth as a Biosphere and the rise of global ecology.

Maria Guminska was born in 1928 at Zakopane, Poland, near the Tatra mountains. After graduating in medicine in 1952, she specialized in biochemistry, clinical chemistry and biochemical toxicology. She obtained her Ph.D. in 1962 after presenting her doctoral thesis on tumour metabolism. Since 1980 she has been professor of biochemistry at the Copernicus School of Medicine in Cracow. Concerned with the impact of environmental pollution on human health since the first ecological disaster in the Cracow region, her research has included the adverse effects of fluorides, the interrelation of fluoride toxicosis and magnesium depletion, and the effects of lead and organic solvents on living matter. In 1980, during the first Solidarity movement when restrictions on such activity were lifted, she helped organise the Polish Ecological Club (PKE), the first independent ecological NGO, and worked on its national board. In June 1990 she was elected president of the Polish Ecological Club.

Fred Harrison is director of the Centre for Incentive Taxation in London. He is editor of *Land and Liberty*, a bi-monthly journal, and he writes *Economic Intelligence*, a monthly news bulletin. He has authored several books, including *The Power in the Land* (1983). In 1990 he initiated a conference in New York to provide a forum for Soviet and East European officials to meet western economists to discuss the problems of transforming the socialist system.

Sandy Irvine has been a teacher in further education for 16 years. He is an associate editor of *The Ecologist* magazine and author (with Alec Ponton) of *A Green Manifesto*, published by Optima. He also wrote *Beyond Green Consumption* for Friends of the Earth, London.

Carlo Jordan, born 1951, studied building construction and philosophy in Berlin. In the 1970s he was active in the cultural opposition to the GDR regime, and in the first ecological circles. From 1978 to 1983 he travelled extensively in the Soviet Union. From 1983 he campaigned openly on ecological issues and organized the first annual Öko-Seminar in 1984, leading to the Berlin Environment Library in 1986, the Arche network in 1988 and the founding of the GDR Green party in 1989. He was the Greens' speaker at the Round Table of December 1989-March 1990 that negotiated the revolutionary change in east Germany, and since then a deputy in the state parliament.

Petra K. Kelly was born in Günzburg/Donau, Germany, in 1947. Educated in West Germany and the USA, she worked from 1972 as a European civil servant. Founder and co-chair since 1970 of an association to support cancer research in children, she has been actively involved in the German and worldwide anti-nuclear, anti-war and feminist movements. From 1980 to 1982 she was chair and spokesperson of Die Grünen. Elected to the Bundestag in 1983, she was reelected to a second full term in 1987. She was awarded the Alternative Nobel Prize (1982), Woman of the Year (USA) and Women Strike for Peace award (1983).

Wilhelm Knabe was born in 1923, has a master's degree in forestry and a Ph.D. in agricultural sciences. He is an internationally known research scientist and consultant in the reclamation of industrial waste land and the effects of air pollution and acid deposition on terrestrial ecosystems. He presently lectures on ecology for engineers at the Technical University of Dresden. He was a co-founder of Die Grünen in 1979 , speaker of the state party of North-Rhine-Westphalia (1979-80), speaker of the federal party (1982-84), member of the German Bundestag (1987-90), and an active participant in meetings of the Canadian, US and Chilean Greens.

Jeremy Leggett was an earth scientist on the faculty at Imperial College of Science and Technology for eleven years. Winner of two major awards for his research, he was a member of several advisory committees to the UK government's Natural Environment Research Council, before becoming Greenpeace UK's director of science in May 1989. In January 1990 he became director of science in Greenpeace International's Atmosphere and Energy Campaign.

Amory B. Lovins, a 44-year-old American physicist, has been active in energy policy in some 20 countries over as many years, based in England for two-thirds of that time. He has an M.A. from Oxford and later five US honorary doctorates. He has been Regents' Lecturer at the University of California both in Energy and Resources and in Economics; Grauer Lecturer at the University of British Columbia; Henry R. Luce Visiting Professor at Dartmouth College; and Distinguished Visiting Professor at the University of Colorado. For the past decade he has worked as a team with his wife and colleague Hunter, a lawyer, sociologist, political scientist and forester, and in 1982 they co-founded Rocky Mountain Institute, an independent nonprofit foundation which fosters resource efficiency and global security. They shared a 1982 Mitchell Prize (for work on utility policy) and a 1983 Right Livelihood Award. In 1989 Amory Lovins received the Onassis Foundation's first Delphi Prize for their contribution towards finding alternative solutions to energy problems.

Jacqueline McGlade is an ecologist and currently director of the Theoretical Ecology Working Group at the national Research Centre in Julich. Her main research is in the field of marine ecology and fisheries oceanography. During the past 15 years she has worked throughout the world and developed dynamic models to study the effects of human and environmental change on natural resources. She has led a number of international programmes, such as Project Prospero, to improve our current understanding of marine ecosystems. She has also been employed as a research scientist and acted as advisor on marine affairs for the Canadian, USA, Indonesian and Thai federal governments, the World Bank, the United Nations Food and Agricultural Organisation and Environment Programme, the European Commission and various non-governmental organizations such as Greenpeace. She now lives in Germany with her two children.

Freda Meissner-Blau, born in 1927, is a journalist and long-time activist in the anti-nuclear, ecological, peace and women's movements. She was the Green candidate for the presidential elections in Austria, co-founded the Green party and was the first speaker for the Green Group in the Austrian Parliament. Since 1989 she has worked primarily in international networks like Ecoropa, Anti-Atom International, Helsinki Federation for Human Rights, etc. She has written numerous articles on ecological and societal questions.

Philippe Van Parijs teaches philosophy and economics at the Université Catholique de Louvain (Belgium) and is currently on sabbatical leave at the Istituto Universitario Europeo (Florence). He is the author of *Evolutionary Explanation in the Social Sciences* (New Jersey and London, 1981), *Le Modèle économique et ses rivaux* (Geneva and

Paris, 1990), *Qu'est-ce qu'une société juste?* (Paris, 1991) and *La Pensée écologiste* (Brussels, 1991, with Frank De Roose). He is also a founding member of ECOLO's local section in the university town of Louvain-la-Neuve, and a member of the executive committee of the Basic Income European Network.

Sara Parkin is a speaker for the Green Party and former co-secretary of the European Greens which comprises 24 Green parties from east and west Europe. She speaks and writes on a wide range of Green issues in Britain and abroad and is a regular panellist on BBC current affairs programmes such as TV's *Question Time* and Radio 4's *Any Questions*. She is author or co-author of election programes for both the Green Party and the European Greens and has written two other books: *Green Parties: An International Guide* (1989), also published by Heretic Books, and *Green Futures: An Agenda for the 21st Century* (1991), published by Collins.

Vello Pohla was born in Tallinn, Estonia. He studied law at Tartu University (graduating 1960), philosophy in Tallinn (1966), politics in Moscow (1982). He has worked as a lawyer, lecturer in philosophy, a diplomat (in Stockholm 1967-71), party functionary, editor-in-chief of an art weekly newspaper, film-maker (TV documentaries, films on folklore), farmer and parliamentarian. Between 1980 and 1988 he was politically persecuted and unable to take part in official political and cultural life. In 1988 he was one of the initiators and then one of the leaders of the Estonian Green Movement (attempts to start this movement date back to 1972). He is chair of the board of the Estonian Green Party and in 1989 was elected to the USSR's Chamber of the People's Deputies. In 1990 he became a member of the parliament of the Estonian Republic and is currently chair of its Green fraction.

Ranchor Prime is a follower of Krishna who lives in London and works as a writer and consultant on multi-faith issues and the environment.

James Robertson is a writer, speaker and consultant. His books include: *The Sane Alternative* (1978, revised 1983), *Future Work* (1985), and *Future Wealth* (1990). He was one of the founders of The Other Economic Summit (TOES) in 1984, and has been prominent in the new economics movement. With Alison Pritchard he publishes the twice-yearly newsletter *Turning Point 2000*. His work during the 1980s included assignments for WHO-Europe, and he took part in the Ottawa Conference on Health Promotion in 1986.

Nick Robins is an independent consultant, currently working on a business and environment project for the United Nations Conference on Environment and Development in 1992. He is a member of the executive of the New Economics Foundation.

Colin Tudge is author of *Last Animals at the Zoo*, published by Century Radius, 1991.

Jakob von Uexkull was born in Sweden, grew up in Germany and has both German and Swedish nationality. After graduation from Oxford University in Politics, Philosophy and Economics, he worked as a specialist in philatelics and postal history, and as a freelance journalist and translator in various countries, including the Near East and the Caribbean. Through the sale of his valuable postage stamps he endowed the Right Livelihood Awards, the first presentation of which took place in December 1980, and he is chairman of the Right Livelihood Foundation. In 1984 he was elected to the European Parliament on the list of the German Green Party (1984-86 alternate member, 1987-89 full member).

Josef Vavrousek is Czechoslovakia's Federal Minister for the Environment. An economist and former vice-chairman of the Ecological Section of the Czechoslovak Academy of Sciences, he emerged as one of the country's key figures during the revolution. In 1988, with Bedrich Moldan, currently Czech Minister of the Environment, he edited the Section's report on the state of the Czechoslovakian environment. This report became the basis for subsequent government environmental policy.

Teo Wams, born in 1959, has a degree in biology from the State University of Groningen, specializing in ecology, environmental science and policy. Since 1984 he has worked with Friends of the Earth Holland (Vereniging Milieudefensie), first as education officer, then as a specialist on waste issues, and currently as policy coordinator. He is a representative of FOE on the National Council for Environmental Hygiene (CRMH), an official advisory body to the minister of the environment, and chairperson of the CRMH's Commission on Substances. He has organized campaigns on the export of toxic waste, management of domestic waste, batteries, PVC packagings, spray cans, etc. His publications include the following themes: waste problems, product policy, strategy of environmental movement, toxic substances, agriculture, and technology.

Also from Heretic Books:

GREEN POLITICS

Sara Parkin
Green Parties: An International Guide   £7.95

Rudolf Bahro
Building the Green Movement   £6.95

Die Grünen
Programme of the German Green Party   £1.50

ANIMAL LIBERATION

William Johnson
The Rose-Tinted Menagerie   £8.95

William Johnson
The Monk Seal Conspiracy   £4.95

Marjorie Spiegel
The Dreaded Comparison   £3.95

Kath Clements
Why Vegan   £3.95

NORTH-SOUTH

Erik Dammann
Revolution in the Affluent Society   £5.95

Guy Brett
Through Our Own Eyes   £9.95

Please order where possible from your local bookshop. Prepaid mail orders to Heretic Books, P O Box 247, London N17 9QR, adding £2.00 for postage and packing.